EARNHARDT
NATION

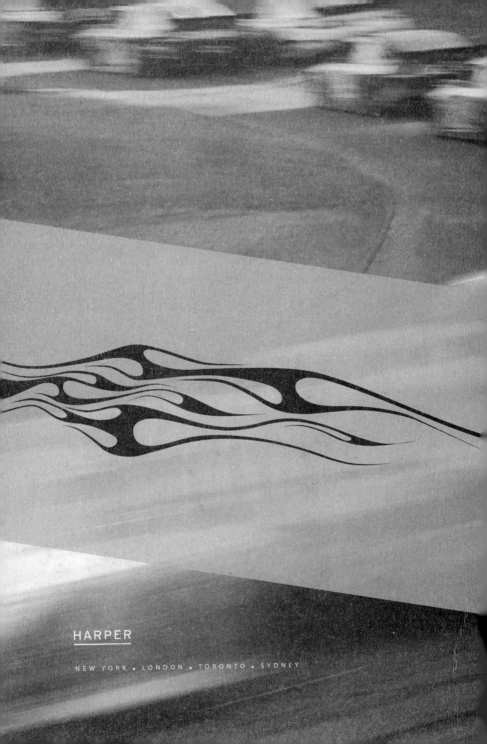

HARPER

NEW YORK · LONDON · TORONTO · SYDNEY

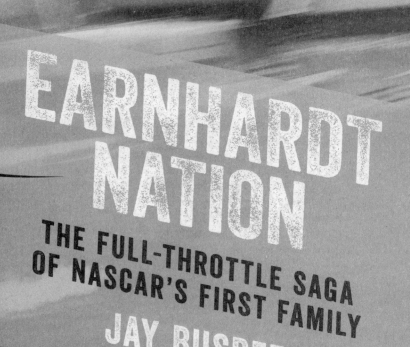

EARNHARDT NATION

THE FULL-THROTTLE SAGA OF NASCAR'S FIRST FAMILY

JAY BUSBEE

A hardcover edition of this book was published in 2016 by Harper, an imprint of HarperCollins Publishers.

HarperCollins books may be purchased for educational, business, or sales promotional use. For information, please e-mail the Special Markets Department at SPsales@harpercollins.com.

FIRST HARPER PAPERBACK EDITION PUBLISHED 2017.

Designed by Bill Ruoto

Frontispiece and chapter openers: Image from Doug James/Shutterstock, Inc.

Library of Congress Cataloging-in-Publication Data has been applied for.

ISBN 978-0-06-236772-3 (pbk.)

17 18 19 20 21   LSC   10 9 8 7 6 5 4 3 2 1

FOR MOM AND DAD,
MY FIRST READERS

AND

RILEY AND LOGAN,
MY COOLEST

CONTENTS

CONTENTS

EARNHARDT NATION

ALL THESE YEARS later, what still gets you is the kiss.

It's just minutes before quarterback-turned-broadcaster Terry Bradshaw will wave the green flag to start the 2001 Daytona 500. In the midst of the usual chaos on pit road, Teresa and Dale Earnhardt are standing together, leaning against Dale's gleaming black Chevrolet Monte Carlo. He's looking around at the pandemonium before him, seeing photographers, crew members, fellow drivers, and fans, thousands upon thousands of them, all shoehorned into one two-lane stretch of concrete that runs parallel to Daytona's looming grandstands. But Teresa's eyes are only on him.

Sharp and businesslike in a deep purple blazer, black slacks, and sunglasses, she kisses him once, her right hand curled around the back of his head. Then she kisses him again. They're not long kisses or deep, meaningful ones. They're the loving but routine kisses a wife gives her husband as he heads off to his job. They'll have more time for each other when he's finished the day's work, just a few hours from now.

Daytona is a beloved winter escape for NASCAR fans and drivers alike, and mornings like February 18, 2001, are the reason why. An impossibly clear sky stretched from horizon to horizon. The shorthand description of the Daytona 500 is "NASCAR's Super Bowl," but that's a flawed comparison on several levels. To start, the Daytona 500 is much older, dating back to 1959. It kicks off a season rather than concluding one. And every year the Daytona 500 draws up to three times the crowd of an average Super Bowl.

This particular Daytona 500 came closer to the prestige of a

Super Bowl than most. For the first time, Fox Sports was broadcasting NASCAR, and this marked Fox's very first race in a multiyear, multibillion-dollar contract. But the network was still working in its comfort zone. Fox had wrapped a successful broadcast of Super Bowl XXXV three weeks earlier, and the prerace package leading off Fox's Daytona 500 coverage featured stick-and-ball notables like the Ravens' Trent Dilfer and the Yankees' Derek Jeter. Bradshaw served as Fox royalty-in-attendance.

Fox was the first of the major networks to build its sports broadcast packages around personalities rather than scores, and in Dale Earnhardt Sr. they'd found their hook for NASCAR. Sure, he spoke with a Carolina drawl, but his charisma played well everywhere. A segment with Bradshaw the day before was a ceremonial torch-passing, a way of welcoming Earnhardt into the Fox family of superstars. It wasn't a stretch to envision Earnhardt on an "NFL on Fox" set some Sunday that fall, crowing about the Carolina Panthers or his boy's beloved Washington Redskins.

"He had the coolest mustache," Bradshaw would remember years later. "He had that shit-eating grin. He was just cool. He just had the 'it' factor."

In the pretaped segment, Earnhardt showed Bradshaw just how much precision and control Daytona demands. He introduced Bradshaw to the subtle bumps and dips of the track, the banks too steep to stand on, the unique fingerprint of Daytona. He threw the pace car into a burnout and hauled a clearly rattled Bradshaw out of the car, showing him how to climb on the roof to "celebrate."

"You gonna be here tomorrow?" Earnhardt asked Bradshaw.

"Of course I'm gonna be here," Bradshaw said, trying to relocate his stomach. "They sent the A-Team!"

Earnhardt hauled Bradshaw close in an embrace around the neck. "Good," he said. "I'm awful lucky when you're around."

Earnhardt had reason to feel lucky. Though he was forty-nine, he felt like he was at the absolute top of his game, both on the track and in life. He was racing without pain for the first time in years. He and team owner Richard Childress felt more united and determined in their championship chase than they had in several seasons. He and his son, Dale Earnhardt Jr., were closer than they'd ever been, bonding over Junior's ever-increasing on-track success. They'd just completed their first-ever father-son driving stint as part of a four-man squad at the Rolex 24 Hours of Daytona. Earnhardt's own NASCAR team—the one he'd created to diversify his racing interests—now looked promising. Junior, alongside Steve Park and new addition Michael Waltrip, formed a solid, if not domineering, 1-2-3 combination for Dale Earnhardt Inc.

Waltrip was the most questionable driver of the three. A sixteen-year veteran of NASCAR, he'd never won a race at the Cup level. Never. He was 0 for 462. But he was a friend of Earnhardt's, and Earnhardt took very good care of his friends. Throughout press sessions during the days before the race—the period known as Speedweeks—Earnhardt had stressed how close Waltrip was to breaking through. Nobody believed him, of course, but Earnhardt believed in Waltrip, and that was enough.

This day also marked a significant on-track transition in NASCAR history. Waltrip's older brother Darrell, one of the winningest drivers in the sport's history and a longtime foe of Earnhardt's, had finally hung up his steering wheel and moved upstairs to join Fox Sports. Along with lap-by-lap announcer Mike Joy and color commentator and former Earnhardt crew chief Larry McReynolds, Darrell Waltrip would be NASCAR fans' connection to the new world of Fox.

Darrell Waltrip began his Fox career with a plum assignment: interviewing Earnhardt on the eve of the race. "So tell me, Dale," Darrell asked, "when are you going to retire?"

"Why should I retire?" Earnhardt shot back, grinning. "*I'm* still competitive!"

Talk turned to safety. Three drivers had died on the track in NASCAR-related events in the last year, including Richard Petty's grandson Adam. In response, NASCAR was encouraging—though not mandating—the use of a new safety measure: the HANS device, a helmet-restraint system designed to protect the head and neck from sudden impact. For a driver like Earnhardt, one of the few still wearing an open-face helmet, switching to the new version would be like racing with a burlap sack over his head.

"The open-face helmet lets you hear better and feel more in the open than the full-face helmet does," Earnhardt said. "I also think it's safer in a head-on collision. It doesn't break your neck."

The interview ended on a hopeful note, with Earnhardt thrilled about his life and his family. What he didn't tell Darrell Waltrip was that he had a plan to win the entire race . . . or, barring that, clear the way for one of his drivers to take the checkered flag. From an outside perspective, Earnhardt's approach might appear a conflict of interest—a driver representing Childress helping drivers from DEI win a race—but this was NASCAR, and the lines between team loyalty and family loyalty often blurred into invisibility.

Daytona is a restrictor-plate track, meaning NASCAR enforces specific power limitations on the engines. Restrictor-plate racing at Daytona and Talladega, the other plate track, requires drivers to sync up with one another—to "draft"—in order to cut through the air with efficiency and speed unreachable at most other tracks. Earnhardt was just a few months removed from one of the most astonishing wins of his career—a Talladega victory where he'd jumped from eighteenth place to first in just a handful of laps—and he intended to use what he'd learned that day on this one.

"We will get together at the front," he told Michael Waltrip in strategy sessions before the race. "And when we do, we're staying there. Locked together."

Waltrip thought the plan sounded good in theory, but he wasn't sure how realistic it was. He wasn't alone. "At Daytona, you can plan who you want to run with and who you draft with," Mike Joy said later, "and then they wave the flag."

EVERY RACE BEGINS with a formal drivers' introduction ceremony—a fireworks-and-pounding-music spectacular designed to amp up the crowd and throw some extra love to the sponsors. Dale Earnhardt needed no pyrotechnics or bass drums; his presence alone was enough to get the denizens of a nursing home up on their feet. He was in one hell of a fine mood, crew chief Kevin Hamlin noted as the team prepared for introductions, bouncing around like a kid on his first visit to the big track. Hamlin knew why: Earnhardt had his plan, and if anyone could execute a plan on the track, it was him.

As the waves of boos and cheers greeted the No. 3 team, Earnhardt turned to Hamlin with his familiar, cockeyed grin. He leaned in and spoke loud enough for Hamlin to hear over the crowd: "They're really going to be booing us at the end of the day after we kick their ass."

AT 1:02, THE drivers climbed into their cars. Taped to Earnhardt's dashboard was an index card with a line of Scripture—a longtime prerace tradition of Darrell's wife, Stevie. Today's card bore a quote from Proverbs 18:10: "The name of the Lord is a strong tower; the righteous man runs into it and is safe." A few minutes later, the cars began rolling off pit road, and soon afterward, Bradshaw waved that green flag.

5

A truism, then as now: you can't win the Daytona 500 in the first 100 laps, but you can damn sure lose it. Drivers spent the early part of the race testing themselves and their machines, taking turns at the front and dropping back, pairing up and practicing for the inevitable final-lap dash. Earnhardt took the lead at lap 27, the sixth driver to do so. By lap 70, Waltrip had found his way to the lead, and he'd hold it for much of the rest of the race.

Earnhardt was in classic form right from the start. On lap 77, he took a sharp bump from rookie driver Kurt Busch. Earnhardt responded by slamming Busch nearly into the infield grass, flipping the kid the bird as he drove past. Earnhardt's crew collapsed in laughter.

With about 25 of the 200 laps remaining, the race turned serious. On the backstretch of lap 175, Robby Gordon tapped the back of Ward Burton's car. Tony Stewart's No. 20 Home Depot Pontiac couldn't dodge Burton, and Stewart's car took to the air in a heart-stopping flight. It was the kind of terrifying, out-of-control flip that proves that drivers in a wreck are only along for the ride, and that physics are in charge. Stewart flipped twice before coming to rest right-side-up. Another eighteen cars were involved in the crash, virtually halving the field.

Stewart not only escaped serious injury but walked away from the wreck to the ambulance under his own power. His helmet had hit the steering wheel head-on, minimizing the lateral trauma, a lucky break that would haunt everyone before the race was over.

Stewart may be the only driver who still watches that Daytona 500 on YouTube, including his own wreck—not for enjoyment but for appreciation of what Earnhardt did and could do. Earnhardt's deft driving skills in the midst of that wreck would form the basis for one of the great what-ifs of NASCAR history. In a photo of Stewart's car just beginning its pinwheel, his car is virtually vertical, nose pointing down, back bumper up in the air a good twenty feet off the ground, about to take out so many other cars. Right below Stewart—right where the No. 20 is about to land—Earnhardt's No. 3 is clearly visible. Earnhardt should have been caught up in that wreck, but he eluded it with a couple deft flicks of the steering wheel.

"I always see that picture and think what would have happened if I had clipped him just a little then," Stewart would say a decade later.

The Stewart wreck red-flagged the race, requiring all drivers still in the running to stop their cars along the front stretch while cleanup crews worked to clear the track. As luck would have it, the first three cars remaining mobile were Waltrip, Dale Earnhardt Sr., and Dale Earnhardt Jr. All three drivers were pleased at the way the field had sorted itself out and the way the path had opened wide before them, but all three also had the viciousness of Stewart's wreck on their minds.

"Part of your brain always thinks, someone could be hurt back there. Could be someone I'm close to. Heck, it just as easily could have been me," Waltrip would say later. "But at the same time, there is also relief. Your car's not torn up. You can race."

Junior took a moment in the silence to address his crew over the team radio. "No matter what else happens," he said, "let's be thankful. We've had a great week, a great race. We're so lucky we missed that crash."

Dale Sr., seeing the wreckage of nineteen other cars, was blunter. "Richard," he said over the radio to Childress, "if they don't do something to these cars, it's gonna kill somebody."

At 4:08, the race restarted with only twenty-two laps remaining. Earnhardt was sizing up the field and the flow of the tide behind him. He reached out on the radio to Andy Pilgrim, a friend and Rolex 24 teammate who was following the race in Earnhardt's motorcoach.

"So, you got any advice for me here coming up?" Earnhardt asked.

Advice? To Dale Earnhardt at Daytona? That would be like offering songwriting pointers to Johnny Cash. "No, man, I haven't got any advice for you," Pilgrim said, laughing. "Just keep doing what you're doing."

"Okay," Earnhardt replied. "Just wondering."

And then his radio went silent. There was driving to do.

The Earnhardts and Michael Waltrip were up front. "Mikey, that's two Earnhardts up there," Darrell Waltrip said of his younger brother from the Fox booth. "I think you're the odd man out, buddy."

But Darrell was wrong. Dale Earnhardt Sr. wasn't looking to overtake Waltrip. With thirteen laps remaining, Waltrip held the lead as Junior pushed him. Behind them, Dale Earnhardt Sr., the most aggressive driver in NASCAR history, was playing defense, trying to hold off a hard-charging field made up of some of the best drivers in NASCAR, now teaming up to take Earnhardt out of the picture. Kenny Schrader. Rusty Wallace. Sterling Marlin, driving probably the strongest car in the field. Each took a run at Earnhardt, but none could pass. Earnhardt was, as the old NASCAR saying goes, running three-wide all by himself. He was pulling off the equivalent of juggling three different sets of balls at once, running between them as they were in the air.

"What the hell is he doing?" Childress asked crew chief Hamlin. Earnhardt playing defense was like a dog reciting Shakespeare.

"Don't worry, don't worry," Hamlin said. He knew that this was all part of Earnhardt's larger plan, and he hoped like hell that it all panned out.

Ahead of that mess, Waltrip began to grow more concerned about Junior. They hadn't talked before the race, and Waltrip was wishing they had. Driving with his eyes glued to his mirror, Waltrip tried to keep Junior aligned with him. Given room, Junior could have made a move to slip around the No. 15. The two men were playing a combination high-wire act and poker game at two hundred miles an hour.

"Michael, you're in the best place you've ever been," Darrell said in the booth. "My poor momma, she's gonna be havin' a fit."

Dale Sr. was in a hell of a mess, trying to keep the ever-gathering field from making a run at his team. Darrell realized that this defensive strategy had all been part of Dale's plan to get a win; neither Junior nor his brother Michael could do what Earnhardt was now doing—holding back the wave of cars like a man trying to hold back the ocean. And succeeding.

Michael could hear his spotter in his headset: "All clear," said Chuck Joyce. "It's you and the eight, single file."

At 4:24, the white flag flew. A single lap remained in the race.

In the Fox booth, Darrell Waltrip faced a dilemma. He was supposed to be a professional journalist now, but here was his baby brother about to win the Daytona 500. He wasn't the first announcer to face this particular predicament; eight years before, at this very track, broadcaster and former driver Ned Jarrett had cheered his son Dale on to victory over Earnhardt. Waltrip also abandoned all pretense of objectivity, screaming advice to his brother: "Keep it low, Mikey. Keep it low. Don't let 'em run up on you. Come on, man. Come on, man. Block him. Block him. You got him, Mikey. You got him, man!"

The field hit the back straightaway. Two more turns left in the Daytona 500. Marlin and Schrader took one last shot at Dale, and this time they caught him, splitting wide on either side of him. But it was too late; as they did, Waltrip and Junior cruised away in the clean air. No one would catch them. Dale Earnhardt's plan had worked to perfection.

Daytona had been Earnhardt's greatest foe, the enemy that had beaten him nineteen straight times to start his career. He'd conquered it three years ago, and he was now showing that he could lead others to victory there as well. Whenever Dale Earnhardt wanted a win, he'd eventually get it.

Two more turns. Just two more turns.

AS THEY ENTERED those final two turns, Dale Sr., Marlin, Schrader, and Wallace bunched together. What happened next happened fast. Wallace's car apparently pulled air from Earnhardt's spoiler, robbing Earnhardt of control. Marlin got the nose of his car slightly lower than Earnhardt's, and their cars touched. Earnhardt's car suddenly sliced downward toward the infield, and then knifed right back up the 31-degree bank. Just before Earnhardt's car hit the turn 4 wall, Schrader's bumper plowed hard into the No. 3's right-side door, making Earnhardt's angle into the wall a much sharper one. The impact destroyed both cars' front ends, and they both slid slowly back down the banked turn, into the infield grass.

"Son of a bitch," Hamlin spat in frustration. A third-place finish, ruined.

"Big trouble!" Joy told the national television audience. "Big! Right behind them!"

"They're crashing behind you," Joyce told Waltrip.

Darrell Waltrip had seen enough wrecks to know how bad this one might be. Stewart's wreck, while more dramatic, was actually far safer; the kinetic energy in the car dispersed as Stewart flipped over and over. The kinetic energy of a car going two hundred miles per hour into an immovable wall had only one way to go: through the driver.

"I don't like that," Darrell told his national audience. "That's not the kind of crash—that's the kind of crash that hurts you."

As Waltrip cooled down for a lap after the checkered flag, he wove back through the wreckage. He didn't even notice Dale's car crumpled on the infield. He didn't stop. He had Victory Lane in his sights. Junior also drove past the wreck, not wanting to alarm fans.

The ambulances were already converging on the apron between turns 3 and 4, where smoke was thick. Some drivers had climbed from their cars. Some, but not all.

"That sudden stop," Darrell said, his eyes still on turn 4, "that's a driver's worst nightmare."

Schrader climbed from the wreckage of his car, figuring he'd just go hang with Dale. He wasn't going to be in the best mood, Schrader thought, but he couldn't be that frigging mad. After all, he'd just seen his two drivers finish 1-2 in the Daytona 500, right? Schrader walked around the back of the ruined No. 3 and approached Earnhardt's window.

When drivers are in a wreck, their standard procedure is to take down the window netting that covers their driver's-side window. This lets emergency crews know that the driver is conscious and aware of his surroundings. As Schrader approached Earnhardt's car, he could see that the window netting was still up. He reached in, unhooked the window, and saw Earnhardt.

To this day, he won't discuss what he saw. He waved frantically for the emergency crew to get there. He stepped back from the car, stunned, and didn't protest when emergency workers led him to Daytona's infield care center. Two EMTs approached the car, one from each side, and leaned in the windows.

In the No. 3 pit box, Childress keyed his headset microphone, trying to get Earnhardt on the line. "Dale, you all right?" Childress asked with rising concern. "Talk to us, Dale. Dale? Dale . . . ?"

Childress switched over to the frequency of another of his drivers, Mike Skinner. "Stop there and make sure Dale's okay," Childress instructed Skinner, who was still circling the track, cooling down his engine. Maybe Earnhardt's radio had broken in the wreck. Maybe it had come unplugged. Or maybe Dale was just so goddamned mad he didn't want to talk to anybody.

Skinner stopped his No. 31 Lowe's Chevrolet by the wreckage. He observed the demeanor of the EMTs and told Childress, "You'd better go to the infield care center. It doesn't look good."

The track's brand-new infield care center carried all the resources of a standard urgent-care facility, including an ambulance to transport more serious cases to the nearby Halifax Medical Center. The care center stood close to turn 4, well over a quarter mile from the start/finish line. Schrader had already arrived by the time the drivers who'd finished the race intact and others along pit road made their way there.

Meanwhile, back at the finish line, Dale Earnhardt Jr. encountered his PR man, Jade Gurss. "How's my daddy?" Junior asked.

"I have no idea," Gurss replied. "I haven't heard anything."

Junior asked anyone he could find; getting no good answers, he took off running toward the infield care center. He caught Schrader's eye, and understood immediately that something was very, very wrong. Junior, along with Teresa and other Earnhardt associates, immediately headed for the hospital.

Childress, the next to arrive, found Schrader.

"How is he?" Childress asked. "We going to be out for a while?"

Schrader shook his head. "We've got bigger problems."

Meanwhile, the EMTs arrived at the wreckage of the No. 3 car in the grass below turn 4 and began to work. The ambulance driver, Tommy Propst, had been a first-grade classmate of Dale at Royal Oaks Elementary back in Kannapolis. One EMT, Jason Brown, raced to the driver's side of the car, while another, Patti Dobler, leaned in from the other side.

They took one look at Earnhardt, and then their eyes met.

What happened next would be debated in courtrooms and

boardrooms for several years to come. Did Brown cut the seat belt? Was the seat belt already broken? The possibility of seat belt failure would haunt the Earnhardt family, the seat belt manufacturer, and NASCAR.

Dobler took off Earnhardt's right glove and tucked it into his pocket. She could see the steering wheel crumpled and damaged from impact. All around her, an extraction crew sawed off the roof of the car.

As the saws ripped through the sheet metal, Dobler cradled Earnhardt's head and gently closed his eyes, then briefly bowed her head in prayer.

Seventeen minutes after they arrived at the wreckage of the No. 3—it was now 4:54 p.m.—the EMTs and the ambulance departed for Halifax Medical Center. A Fox Sports camera recorded the ambulance leaving the speedway and turning right down International Speedway Boulevard. The sirens were on, but the ambulance was moving at a slow pace. There are only two reasons why an ambulance would run at a controlled speed. The first is if the patient has sustained a back injury and cannot be jostled.

The second is if there's nothing more to be done.

CHAPTER 1
UP FROM DIRT

TAKE SUNSET ROAD off Interstate 77 just north of Charlotte. Cruise past the local McDonald's, Arby's, and other classic symbols of Americana. Turn on Statesville Road, and drive past the exhibit halls of the Metrolina Tradeshow Expo, home of dusty rows of discount DVDs and decades-old Beanie Babies. Park in the open field near the rusty fence that encloses something large beyond. From this distance, you can't quite tell what.

There's a bouquet of plastic flowers jammed into the chain-link fence, a jarring splash of brilliant purple amid rust and ruin. The flowers mark the entry to the long-defunct Metrolina Speedway, a place every bit as legendary here as old Ebbets Field in Brooklyn. The chains that held the fence together lie on the ground, their locks beside them. If you like, you can walk right in.

A short, root-cracked paved road leads up to the top of the grandstands. The sign that used to arc over this walkway—Welcome to Metrol1na Speedway, the "i" a stylized number 1—is long gone, as are the red-and-white-painted ticket booth at the base of the hill and the press box atop the grandstand. All that's left now are those grandstands, giant steps of painted concrete looking out on emptiness. Graffiti-covered walls circumscribe the track's half-mile oval. Weeds and time have claimed it all.

Look a little closer, though. Use a little imagination. Once, two dozen cars wheeled through these turns, spitting red Carolina clay into the exhaust-and-oil-scented air, the sound of their engines so loud it was just one unified, bone-rumbling hum.

In these stands, families cheered on sons and brothers and fathers (and, on rare occasions, daughters) who threw themselves hard into the turns—and often hard into the walls—where something they'd labored over for days, months, even years could be reduced to scrap in moments. Imagine the desperation of crews trying to coax life out of a dead engine; imagine the exultation of drivers using wits, cunning, brains, and balls to triumph over a field of sonsabitches every bit as crafty as they were. The races often ran on Saturday night, yes, but what happened here was as holy and sanctified as anything you'd experience the next morning.

This desolate track is the place where family bonds were forged, broken, and then forged even stronger. This once-proud arena is the place where the most famous story in racing first hit redline speed.

BUT IT ALL started a few miles up the road. It all started with the mill.

Kannapolis, North Carolina, thirty miles from Charlotte, began life as a company village created to house a workforce that labored in a local mill. The tiny central Carolina town existed in the shadow of smokestacks that ran twenty-four hours a day and in the social wake of nearby Concord, the seat of Cabarrus County.

J. W. Cannon, a nineteenth-century lord and master of manufacturing, had built his fortune on cotton and self-reliance in the ragged years after the Civil War. The South in those days was an economically ravaged land, and the Cannon cotton manufacturing process was a godsend for North Carolina. Most cotton mills of the time spun cotton into yarn and sent it north to be woven into products, but Cannon kept the entire process in-house. His mills spun cotton into Cannon Cloth, a fabric that housewives around the country would cut and sew into whatever they needed around the home. Cannon had owned a number of smaller mills around the South, but the demand for Cannon Cloth allowed him to begin unifying the manufacturing process at a single location.

In 1906 Cannon created a new mill on six hundred acres of land in that rural patch north of Concord. He built rental houses and a school, creating a planned community as quintessentially American in its promise of opportunity and its understated mission of control as the one Walt Disney dreamed up in the wilds of Florida. This was Kannapolis, and this is where the Earnhardt story begins.

The city's name is a combination of the Greek words for "loom" and "city," but the actual etymology is humbler: the name derived from the Cannon Mills themselves, with the town being named first Cannon City, then Cannapolis, and finally Kannapolis. In 1928, just before the Great Depression hit, Cannon consolidated all his textile plants into the Kannapolis facility, a strength-through-unity move that allowed the business to survive the economic ravages. The mill was Kannapolis, and Kannapolis was the mill.

"Lint heads," the Concord types called the residents of Kannapolis, which lay on the far side of the tracks in the poorer sector of the county. Kannapolis bred the men and women who'd handle the scut work and hard labor, while the sons of Concord dallied through college and then slid smoothly into a position at their fathers' company. It was a system as tightly regimented as a military organization, an iron fist wrapped in a security blanket.

You worked for the company, you got the opportunity to rent a home from the company. The further you climbed up the corporate ladder, the nicer the mill-owned home you could show off. There were mill-funded schools designed with the express intent of funneling the sons and daughters of mill workers right into their parents' footsteps. The mill would see to it that your lawn was mowed, that your lights stayed on, that your house got a fresh coat of paint every year. The graduation speaker every year at the high school was a representative of the mill, always offering salvation in woven cotton.

The mill provided a fully planned life, birth to death. For a man like Ralph Earnhardt, born the very year Cannon brought all its operations to town, it was suffocating.

EARNHARDT. IT'S A name straight out of a Charles Dickens novel. The same way Scrooge implies surliness and misery, Earnhardt sounds as American as the National Anthem. *Earn* is the first syllable, *heart* the second . . . and you can't miss the *hard* tucked in there. If the name didn't already represent an American legend, some poet would have had to create it.

Most Earnhardts in America trace their lineage back to one Johannes Ehrenhart, a working-class type who emigrated from the town of Speyer, Germany, to the United States in 1744. While it's a mistake to look for common personality traits among family members living two centuries apart, Ehrenhart nonetheless undertook a hazardous, life-threatening voyage across the Atlantic at a time when such journeys were foolhardy at best. Ehrenhart, his wife, and seven children piled into the cargo hold of a ship named *Friendship*, risking everything for vague promises of better days ahead. Deaths on ships were not uncommon, and the ships themselves would occasionally sink, taking all aboard to the bottom of the ocean. Immigrants traveled in ships meant for cargo, not humans, and paid their way with terms of indentured servitude for up to seven years. German law at the time prohibited both emigration and removal of personal property from Germany, so many slipped out of the country under cover of darkness.

The Ehrenhart family eventually settled in Bucks County, Pennsylvania, where they began begetting the family line. The English bureaucrats entrusted with keeping records of immigrants had difficulty with the German spellings, and the Germans had trouble speaking English. Miscommunication led to multiple variations of the name Ehrenhart, one of which became Earnhardt.

For Johannes, crossing an ocean was enough travel for a lifetime. But his children longed for further adventure and greener fields. Two of Johannes's sons would soon travel south to Rowan County, North Carolina, and a third followed in the late 1760s. The three of them would combine to create the largest concentration of Earnharts/Earnhardts in any state in the union.

These were brutal times for German immigrants, who scratched out a life on an American frontier that was caught in the middle of the French and Indian War. You couldn't know from year to year, or even month to month, whether your cabin would be burned, your family kidnapped or murdered. The men and women who survived carried scars the rest of their lives.

One of Johannes Ehrenhart's sons, Johannes Philip, served as a soldier in the Revolutionary War. Records of the day indicate that he was good with his hands, building everything from furniture and farm implements to wagons. For Peter Earnhardt, an orphan five generations later, genealogical records would include only a single item aside from his birth and death dates: "Wagon Maker." Clearly, an affinity for wheels runs deep in the Earnhardt bloodline.

Earnhardts elsewhere on the family tree made their own small marks on history. At least four of Ralph's ancestors fought in the Revolutionary War. Henry Earnhart was a survivor of the catastrophic wreck of the *Independence* off the coast of Baja California in 1853. Ralph's grandfather Peter Earnhardt fought for the Confederates in the Civil War, serving Company A, Twentieth

EARNHARDT NATION

Regiment of the Cabarrus Guards. An Earnhardt was on the *Carpathia*, the ship that rescued the survivors of the *Titanic*.

The eighth generation of Earnhardts in America made the family name start to ring wide. The ninth would make it legendary.

LONG BEFORE INTERSTATE 85 cut a swath right through the center of town, long before US 29 was renamed NC 3, there were the roads of Kannapolis—roads whose names were designed to make you think of places other than Kannapolis. There were echoes of England (Sheffield, Windermere, Cambridge) or other states (Utah, Indiana, Kansas, and more). Then, naturally, there were the streets named after automobiles, like V-8, Bel Air, Coach, and Sedan. Follow these roads through hard angles and up sudden hills, and within moments you're on the outskirts of town, beyond the grid. Once you've passed the last of the regimented streets— once you're behind the wheel and looking out at the grand sweep of Carolina woods and the lakes and mountains that lie beyond— there's only one thing left to do: floor it.

Ralph Earnhardt was born in 1928, the second of four boys born to John and Effie Earnhardt. As with most boys of his age in Kannapolis, Ralph's life appeared set on a predictable path: birth, school, work, family. He dropped out of school in the sixth grade to work at the mill. He spent years toiling in unremarkable mill labor, punching a clock to start and end his shifts.

One night, he and a friend went to watch the local high school boys' and girls' teams play basketball at the Armory in Concord. Ralph got one look at a girl playing for the opposing team and declared, "That's the girl I'm going to marry." Six months later that basketball player— Martha King Coleman—became Ralph's bride.

Martha wore a tasteful white dress to their wedding, and not long afterward she wore that same dress to a local dirt-track race. "I'd never been to a race before," she said. "I didn't know what you were supposed to wear. I wanted to look good." Young Martha Earnhardt's white dress turned red with track dust, which seems wholly appropriate.

Ralph and Martha lived in a tidy home on the corner of Sedan and Coach Streets in Kannapolis, a home with a decent patch of land, a home amid so many similar homes. The kids came soon after the marriage, one after the other, eventually totaling five in all.

Ralph, not yet twenty-five, was already merging into the Kannapolis groove worn deep by so many ahead of him. Racing fans of a bygone era describe Ralph Earnhardt as looking like the old movie star Randolph Scott—lanky, with dark eyes and a low Carolina drawl. He sported a crew cut high on his forehead, and the seams in his face made him appear weary long before he hit middle age.

Ralph first broke out of his rut by supplementing his mill income with night shifts at a local mechanic. The garage's owner happened to race cars, and in 1949 Ralph took a liking to the idea. He sized up the old barn on his property and decided to take matters into his own hands.

Working alone, Ralph laid down a concrete floor, brought in a few tools, and presto—he had a racing garage. Soon afterward he shored it up with cinder-block walls that remain there to this day. He filled his handmade paradise with welding apparatus, engine cranes, tools upon tools—everything a man could need to transform an everyday car into a thing of sublime beauty.

AMERICAN LEGENDS ARISE through a combination of will, hard luck, and favorable circumstance. Had Elvis Presley been born in Sweden, he wouldn't have absorbed the sounds of both country music and African American gospel to create a wholly new strain of music. Had Bill Gates or Steve Jobs been born a decade earlier or later, someone else would have had to kick-start a technological revolution. Ralph Earnhardt was lucky enough to live in the one part of the world where he could use his particular talents to become one of the great drivers of his time.

There was racing in the South before NASCAR, but it wasn't organized or pretty. News of races would travel by word of mouth. Drivers would show up, race, and get paid a pittance even in victory—if they got paid at all, as race promoters often scheduled a race, filled the stands, then skipped town with the gate receipts well before the checkered flag waved.

North Carolina drivers grew up with speed as a defining characteristic in their lives. And what good was speed if you couldn't use it to get ahead of someone? Especially the local authorities. The generation of drivers before Ralph had perfected their wheelman talents by bootlegging liquor from stills in the hills to speakeasies in Charlotte, Atlanta, and other large towns.

It's impossible to overstate the importance of bootlegging to the birth of what is now NASCAR. It gave the world far more than just the "bootlegger's turn"—a 180-degree spin achieved by slamming on the brakes and twisting the wheel that's useful for evading hot pursuit but not much good on a NASCAR track. Raw speed wasn't enough to elude the law; you needed innovation as well. Car engines in the early twentieth century weren't designed for the high-speed demands of bootleggers, so mechanics resorted to souping up stock models. The cops had also learned to spot a car carrying moonshine—the payload made it ride lower in the trunk—so mechanics strengthened the shocks to keep overloaded cars from sagging. All this shade-tree knowledge filtered its way down from father to son, family to family, helping create the racing industry as it exists today. The arrogance and courage it took to climb behind the wheel, risking destruction or imprisonment every night, also helped spawn the legend of the Great American Race Car Driver, faster, tougher, and better-looking than you, a seductive image that persists to this day.

Add direction and intent to speed, and you've got the seeds of something special. Around the time Ralph Earnhardt was starting to believe that mill work wasn't for him, something was happening five hundred miles to the south that would have a profound impact on his life and that of his descendants.

Daytona Beach, Florida, had long been a hotbed of racing excellence, its flat, packed sands ideal for setting, and breaking, speed records. Races ran up Daytona Beach and back down Atlantic Avenue, much to the delight of drivers and their families. But the area's increasing popularity among tourists was starting to raise the ever-greater possibility that a catastrophic wreck could injure or kill innocent bystanders. The merchants of speed-for-speed's-sake soon decamped to the Bonneville Salt Flats and other locations in Utah for safer opportunities for wide-open driving. Racers, a surly, disorganized lot, could see the end of their days at Daytona drawing near.

Enter a driver by the name of Bill France. A tall, tough, imposing man with a silver tongue, France wasn't the best driver of his day by a long shot. But he had an entrepreneurial soul, a promoter's eye, and a dictator's will, and he soon controlled the marketing and operation of the beach races. This gave him the opportunity to set the fields as he saw fit, occasionally adding himself to the mix even when he failed to qualify.

Eventually France decided to organize racing in the region with the creation of what he optimistically termed the National Championship Stock Car Circuit. The NCSCC's inaugural season began in Daytona in January 1947 and wrapped up forty races later in Jacksonville. France organized the events, paid the drivers, attracted over-capacity crowds to view his creation, and at the end of the season presented series winner Fonty Flock with a $1,000 check.

Emboldened by the success of the NCSCC, France gathered a coterie of drivers, car owners, and mechanics at the Streamline Hotel in Daytona Beach, and on December 14, 1947, began drafting the basics of a new, sanctioned racing series. France's initial name, the National Stock Car Racing Association, had already been claimed by another group with similar grand visions, so the group went with the suggestion of legendary auto mechanic Red Vogt: National Association for Stock Car Auto Racing. NASCAR.

The first-ever NASCAR race took place at Daytona Beach on February 15, 1948, and Red Byron, a World War II tailgunner with a leg so mangled in a plane crash that it had to be bolted to the clutch, won the race. Initially NASCAR established three divisions: Roadster, Strictly Stock, and Modified. NASCAR fans had little interest in the elitist, Yankee-based Roadster racing, in which drivers drove open two-seated vehicles with more focus on appearance than performance. The Roadster series was quickly abandoned. The Strictly Stock division, named because these cars, at least theoretically, had to be "stock"—unaltered from their showroom-floor state—got a slow start because of the high demand for automobiles in the wake of World War II.

So it fell to the Modified division—so named because the vehicles were lighter, chopped, and altered versions of road cars running on dirt tracks—to carry the early days for NASCAR. The series featured a stunning fifty-two races in 1948, with racers compiling points based on how they finished each race in a formula France drew up on the back of a cocktail napkin. As racing grew in popularity, NASCAR immodestly renamed its elite Strictly Stock division "Grand National." In 1950 NASCAR also created a new touring series, the Sportsman division, focusing on smaller tracks all over the Southeast.

Bill France and NASCAR had built a glorious new highway, and all Ralph Earnhardt had to do was find an on-ramp and step on the gas.

CHAPTER 2

GO OR BLOW

IN MID-TWENTIETH-CENTURY North Carolina, short-track racing captured the imagination of an entire region. Anybody with a few dozen acres and a bulldozer could clear some property, dig a few latrines, and sell tickets. And anybody with a few dollars and a dream could field a car.

These little rings were worlds away from the behemoths that we now think of as tracks. These Carolina racetracks were bulldozed red clay ovals with a few makeshift grandstands. Fans would park or sit close to the action, close enough that waves of dust would wash over them and coat every surface.

The races were competitive beyond belief. Today, the last-place finisher in the Daytona 500 earns more than a quarter million dollars. The fourth-place finisher in a Carolina dirt-track race, and the dozens behind him, often walked away with nothing. Winners of the big races might pocket a mere $200, a tiny sum even in the 1950s. But no one was racing for money. Drivers ran for pride and speed, a few minutes spent running wide open to balance against the years crawling in first gear.

"These cars would go upward of ninety miles an hour," recalled Humpy Wheeler, a North Carolina racing promoter turned track president. "You had guys getting concussions, and they'd race two days later. How hurt you got depended on who built your car."

Roughly eighteen hundred dirt tracks dotted the country in those days. Race rules at these tracks were as varied as the promoter's imagination, but there was a general format: drivers ran in preliminary heat races, with the best finishers in each heat earning the right to compete in the day's feature event. After all heat races wrapped up, there was often a consolation race, where drivers who didn't make the feature in their heat got one last shot at racing their way into the feature.

One such track was the old Concord Speedway, just off Poplar Tent Road in Concord. On Easter Sunday 1949, twenty-one-year-old Ralph Earnhardt of Kannapolis, North Carolina, became the first Earnhardt to run a recorded race. Naturally he brought home a victory, winning his consolation race before going on to finish third in the late-model Sportsman feature.

There would be many after that. Ralph Earnhardt, still working at the mill, burned with a fever for racing that his wife, Martha, could neither understand nor extinguish. Like most men of his era, Ralph kept a tight seal on his emotions—his passion was a fire that burned underground, out of sight but spreading farther than anyone could have imagined.

He spent long nights tinkering with his race cars in the cinder-block garage behind the house. *If it's good, make it better. If it's better, make it great. If it's great, make it the best. And if it's the best, someone's still going to figure out how to beat it soon enough.*

He'd hitch the magnificent product of his labor to a tow-truck rig or load it on a low-riding platform and set off for tracks throughout the area: Concord, Metrolina, McCormick Field in Asheville, Columbia Speedway. He'd be gone four and five nights a week, piling up win after win at track after track, paying for his car and feeding his family one three-figure check at a time.

It's not quite certain where or when one of the most significant conversations in racing history took place. It's been a long time, and memories dim. What's indisputable is this: at some point, Ralph Earnhardt decided he'd had enough of mill life. Shifts ended at 7:00 a.m., 3:00 p.m., and 11:00 p.m., and every day except Sunday the streets of Kannapolis would be gridlocked at those times. Ralph had had all he could handle of working under another man's thumb, working on another man's clock, earning money for another man and getting back a fraction for himself. One day in 1953 Ralph announced to Martha, "I want to quit my job. And I want to race full-time."

Martha thought he'd lost his mind. She understood he had talent, and she knew the toll the mill took on his body and soul. Still. Racing? Really? She threatened to leave him, to take their children and go find a man more stable.

"He promised me that if he couldn't do it without taking away from the family, he would quit," Martha would remember. "He always kept me and the five kids up without me having to work, so I couldn't say too much."

Ralph lived by a simple rule: never put more than $800 cash into a race car each year. In today's dollars, that's somewhere between $6,000 and $7,000, barely enough to start the engine on a competitive local race car, so Ralph himself handled every bit of car fabrication, maintenance, and repair. His cars were always white, because that was the only shade available in the cheap, tough Sears refrigerator paint he used. He'd scare up a bit of sponsorship here and there—the first company to sponsor an Earnhardt ride was EDLEMAN'S GARAGE, CARSON BLVD, KANNAPOLIS, painted right there alongside Ralph's preferred 8—but by and large Ralph made a go of it himself.

Across the top of the windshield, he wrote GO OR BLOW in large block letters. It was a hell-bent-for-leather, rally-the-boys-in-the-stands battle cry that didn't describe Ralph Earnhardt's driving style at all. In truth, Ralph almost never wrecked. He kept the car largely clean, largely undented—a conservative trait that would skip at least one generation.

Anyone who mistook Ralph's protectiveness of his car for weakness learned the error of his ways in a hurry. Ralph had no problem mixing it up with any driver who deserved it. One of his more notable showdowns came in 1958 at McCormick Field in Asheville, once a minor-league baseball park but by Ralph's day a quarter-mile dirt track. He and a fellow named Banjo Matthews staged a remarkable fifty-miles-per-hour battle on the flat track that ended with Matthews flipped upside down and Ralph wedged in the first-base dugout.

Scraps like that were rare, however. More often disputes ended peaceably, like the one Ralph had after a race in Columbia, when he nudged Buddy Baker out of the way on the final lap to claim a victory. Furious, Baker left his car and stalked off in the direction of Victory Lane to confront Earnhardt.

"Gee, son, I don't know what happened," Ralph drawled. "My car got to bouncing up the track, and I barely touched you."

"By the time we quit talking," Baker said, laughing about it years later, "I'd apologized for being ahead of him in the first place."

Ralph ran race after grinding race nearly every night of the week, never sitting still but rarely traveling far from Kannapolis. And he kept winning at every track, in every circuit. During one of his peak years, he won track titles—in other words, won the most races at a given track throughout the year—at an astonishing *eleven* different speedways. One year, Ralph won seventeen different races at Hickory, a feat so dominating that the track promoter refused to give him the check or let him kiss the beauty queen. Hundreds of trophies—not even Ralph knew how many for sure—lined the walls of their house, covering half the living room.

The economics worked, a rarity in racing. A victory would pay, say, $200 for winning at Columbia on Saturday, then $400 for winning at Greenville/Pickens on Sunday. Deduct the $150 or so in expenses for a given race weekend, and Ralph would earn enough to pay for his annual $800 expenditures within just a handful of races.

Working almost completely alone, Ralph eventually hit on several race team techniques still in effect today. When you don't have the money to compete with the big boys, you've got to have the brains and the ingenuity. He had three to four cars ready at all times, and would roll up to each track completely ready to race. While his competitors were still fiddling with their setups, Ralph Earnhardt was already prepared and knew exactly what he needed at any track. After the race, he'd quietly reattach his car to the hauler and drive off into the night. His reticent style was part natural personality, part simple pragmatism, and part a desire to control everything and make good on his promise to Martha.

In the course of his career, Ralph would solve two major technical problems that plagued drivers of the day. First, consider a car traveling in a straight line. Both sets of tires turn the same number of times while the car moves forward. But in a turn, the inside tires—the ones closest to the turn—travel a measurably shorter distance than the outside tires. On a car making left turns dozens or hundreds of times in a race, this differential in distance can cause tire problems that go from inconvenient to catastrophic in a hurry. Ralph, one of the first drivers to observe the differential in tire and axle wear caused by this inside-outside phenomenon, introduced the practice of tire stagger—using larger tires on the outside of the car than the inside. The result was a car that handled better and tires that wore more evenly and predictably. Ralph could throw his car hard into a corner knowing his tires would hold while his competitors would slip up the track.

Working in the garage on Sedan Street, Ralph Earnhardt also labored for months to solve another problem: achieving optimum longitudinal traction, or "forward bite." On a dirt track, where the car was always slewing sideways to some degree, forward bite was the difference between holding one's line and flying into a wall. The more forward bite, the tighter drivers can corner their cars, and the lower the likelihood of catastrophe in a turn. Ralph thus moved weight forward in his car to gain more grip on the track. Not bad on-the-fly geometry for a middle-school dropout.

Once on the track, he had a cunning style. Wheeler detailed Ralph's strategy in a typical forty-lap race: "He would sit there back in second place inches away from the leader, putting intense pressure on him. He'd sit and wait until the last two laps, and suddenly the leader would make a mistake because Ralph had been playing with him all night. Ralph would pass and win the race, though usually not by more than a car length."

"On that last lap, you didn't want him nowhere around you," recalls Little Bud Moore, a fellow dirt-track driver. "You weren't going to outdrive him. You had to outrun him."

Small margins of victory were part of Ralph's strategy. He knew that NASCAR officials would take a close look at cars that won by a significant margin, checking for violations, but they tended to ignore cars that barely eked out a win. (Winners now get checked out no matter how close the finish.) Ralph could keep his learned advantages secret by keeping prying eyes away from his car.

Wheeler, who'd navigated every aspect of the North Carolina racing scene since childhood, often served as the liaison between drivers, tracks, and manufacturers. At one point Wheeler was doing some work for Firestone and hired Ralph to test some tires. Ralph's reports were typically laconic; prying an extra word out of him was like pulling a lug nut off a moving tire. "Don't know if I'd run on them again," he'd say if the tires were awful. "Might want to send down another set and let me try them again," he'd say if the tires were tolerable, but not enough to get the Ralph Earnhardt seal of approval. The finest tires earned this: "I really like those tires."

"He never would tell you no, and he never would tell you something was bad," Wheeler said. "He would camouflage it."

Wheeler and Ralph became fast friends, traveling the same circuit, hitting the same tracks and hamburger stands along the way. When Wheeler visited Ralph at home, the two would spend time out back in the garage, eating "slick meat" sandwiches (bologna, cheese, mayo, white bread) while Ralph worked on his car. Wheeler was just one of many friends who'd swing by—someone was always getting off a mill shift. Ralph would welcome the visitors, but he never, ever stopped working on those cars, looking for every possible edge. The best drivers knew that with the right preparation, you could win a race long before engines even started. Nobody prepared with more dedication—and more genteel craftiness—than Ralph Earnhardt.

"There's not a driver today who could do what he did," said David Oliver, a longtime friend of Ralph's. "Jimmie Johnson couldn't do it. Jeff Gordon couldn't do it. People don't realize that he was an engine builder, a body builder, he'd measure his own tires. He did it all."

Oliver recalled accompanying Ralph to one track. He looked around and saw all the other drivers surrounded by their pit crews. Ralph only had Oliver.

"Ralph, what are we going to do when we have to pit?"

"We ain't gonna pit."

"Well, what am I supposed to do?"

"Set up there on the truck and watch."

One season, Ford drivers kept suffering breakages of the rear axle key, a small but essential part within the axle that turns the wheel. Ralph suffered no such breakages, and eventually someone discovered that he'd devised a workaround: a particular size of Craftsman screwdriver, with its handle sawn off, fit neatly into the axle key's slot, serving as a far stronger substitute. Word spread, and drivers headed to the Sears in nearby Charlotte, the only local distributor of that particular screwdriver. A regretful Sears clerk explained that as soon as a new shipment of these particular screwdrivers came in, some fellow from up in Kannapolis would show up and buy them all.

How many dirt-track races did Ralph Earnhardt run in his career? Hundreds? Thousands? It's impossible to even guess. Over the course of a twenty-three-year career, he would run several days a week, several races a day, depending on the condition of his cars and his finances. On rare occasions he'd drive as far north as New York and as far south as Savannah, always in search of another race, another opportunity.

The dirt-track life had its allure, but the disorganization and corruption wore on Ralph. He knew that NASCAR was the way of the future, and he entered and won the NASCAR Sportsman Championship in 1956. Six years in a row, he finished in the top ten in points.

"When I was starting out," Ralph said in 1967, "a fellow heard about races coming up by the grapevine, or by a phone call from a friend or the promoter. Purses were still mighty small, and now and then a promoter took it on the lam before the payoff. No one will ever know what NASCAR has meant to racing. It made a haphazard affair into a business, and brought safety to a game where there was very little, if any."

Although he preferred the smaller tracks and lighter cars, Ralph still drove fifty-one races at NASCAR's highest Grand National (now known as Sprint Cup) level. He couldn't maneuver the heavier, more expensive cars to his satisfaction, and he didn't enjoy traveling such long distances from home. Even so, Ralph managed six top-five finishes in his Grand National career, with his best season coming in 1961. That year he ran only eight of the season's fifty-two races but still had two top-five finishes, led ninety laps, and earned $11,473. More than a half century later, his grandson would earn that much in less than two laps at the Daytona 500.

"The Grand National league is a bit rich for my blood, meaning my pocketbook," Ralph said. "It's quite different from driving a Sportsman car on short tracks, but not so great that a man can't make the switch. The major difference that I found is that on the superspeedways a man has to stay extra cool and extra wide-awake. No time for easing up, taking a little rest."

The superspeedways were Ralph's Achilles' heel—the one time he appeared mortal. While racing at what's now Atlanta Motor Speedway one year, he lost control of his car during a qualifying race and took out fellow driver Roscoe Thompson.

"There's no excuse for that," Thompson seethed. "He doesn't have the experience on these bigger tracks, and I can't see why they allow someone like that to drive. . . . Earnhardt's just got too much car under him and he can't handle it."

Ralph's short-track driving skill, on the other hand, was so pronounced that other owners would ask him to drive their cars. He'd wheel for owners such as Cotton Owens and Lee Petty, Richard's father, marking the first connection between the two most famous families in NASCAR. He'd hold his own against legends or soon-to-be-legends like Petty, Ned Jarrett, and David Pearson.

Ralph won, by some estimates, more than 250 Sportsman-level races. Along the way, his hard-driving ways and persistence earned him the moniker Ironheart. One of the first full-time racers, he kept his promise to Martha, always making enough to keep food on the table. By the end of his career he was earning $20,000 a year—more than $110,000 in today's dollars—and he carried absolutely no debt.

Martha remained the dutiful wife, though by no means a meek one. After one race Ralph kissed the beauty queen in Victory Lane, as was the custom at the time. He then turned to Martha, but she turned away.

"What's wrong, Mrs. Earnhardt?" the flagman asked.

"I don't like secondhand sugar," she replied.

Martha tried her hand at racing exactly once, participating in one track's "Powder Puff" competition. For some reason, the track promoters decided it would be a good idea to let the inexperienced wives drive their husbands' cars *before* the actual race. Martha proceeded to roll the car and bang her nose on the steering wheel, right in front of the grandstands.

"Ralph checked the car out first," Martha recalled, "and then made sure I was all right."

No matter how far he drove, Ralph would always come straight back home to Kannapolis, back to the waiting arms of his family. He wasn't much for talking, so the words he spoke carried weight. He'd rather draw schematics of cars' chassis and suspensions, demonstrating how action begets action. He'd sketch layouts of tracks, showing the best line and the way to handle each turn.

The family knew the best time of the year was the moment that a revving engine from the garage cut through the winter's chill. "We loved that sound," Ralph's daughter Cathy would say decades later. "The first time those cars started up before race season we knew it was almost race season, and that would just thrill us all to death."

Each of Ralph's children—two girls, three boys—helped him in his or her own way, from cleaning up the shop to posing for pictures beside the old No. 8. But it was oldest son who became Ralph's partner in crime—first as a little kid wheeling toy cars in the shadow of the garage, next as a gofer sorting parts and cleaning tools, and finally as a full-fledged assistant. Ralph thought enough of his son to praise him to a reporter in 1967.

"Dale is getting to be a good mechanic," Ralph said. "He is a hard worker, and he is learning fast."

CHAPTER 3

THAT EARNHARDT BOY

CONTRARY TO WHAT some of his fans may believe, Dale Earnhardt was not born sporting a mustache, sunglasses, and a smirk. He came into this world in the usual way, on April 29, 1951, after the racing bug had bit his father but before Ralph quit the mill once and for all. Photographs of a young Dale show that half-grin, the left side of his smile rising while the right side stayed put. Before he'd gotten out of grade school, he could look like he was sizing you up.

"From the day he could ride a bicycle or a tricycle," his mother recalled, "he wanted to be in front."

Young Dale enjoyed one of those classic all-American childhoods. He played cowboys-and-Indians and touch football on Sedan Street, running with friends until it was time for supper. He taught himself how to ride a bike backward, a skill he continued to show off as an adult. He looked out for his brothers and sisters, supporting—and in some cases vexing—his two overworked parents. Once, when Ralph was away at Daytona and Martha had had enough of her boys' mouthiness, she grabbed a belt and began swinging. "Boys, y'all run!" Dale told his two younger brothers, laughing. "Mom's gone crazy!"

Dale idolized Ralph in that pure, innocent way sons love their fathers: without reservation, without expectations that anything would ever change. He liked to wait up in bed for Ralph to return, listening for his trailer to roll in off Coach Street. The next morning, he'd try to deduce how his still-sleeping father had fared the previous night by inspecting the car. A clean car was good news; that meant Ralph had stayed out of trouble and had almost certainly won. A car with mud on the paint meant that Ralph had been stuck in race traffic. A car with battered front or rear bumpers meant—well, it was just better to let him sleep.

Once he was old enough to accompany his father on business trips, Dale realized he'd never care about anything but racing. He'd stand in the back of his father's truck and watch Ralph sling No. 8 around turns racing men like Ned Jarrett, a fine film of dirt coating everything. Dale would be there in victory, and he'd be there in defeat; for a boy who idolized his father, it must have been the best of all possible worlds.

Ralph was no more talkative with his oldest son than he was with anyone else; they'd work for hours in silence, punctuated only by requests for tools. "You knew he loved you," Dale said as an adult, "but he didn't say that. He didn't say he loved you all the time. I knew he loved us by the way he provided for us and the things he did for me when I was a child."

Along the way, Ralph planted in Dale's head seeds of racing wisdom that wouldn't bloom for years or even decades: *Always stay cool in a race car. The other guys will make the mistakes if you let them. Establish your territory.*

One Christmas young Dale asked for a model car with an actual motor. Santa Claus, apparently knowing potential when he saw it, left the car under the Earnhardt tree. "He put it together start to finish," Dale's sister Cathy recalled. "We were so proud and excited for him. It was quite an accomplishment. Then Dad saw it and started picking at him: 'Boy, can't you see right here . . .' "

The first racing trophy Dale Earnhardt ever won was in a toy store. He and his best friend, Gregg Dayvault, regularly raced slot cars at a store in Kannapolis's Midway, the stretch of stores that constituted downtown. Earnhardt kept that trophy in his office for decades afterward, a Rosebud-like totem of innocent days long gone.

Years go by, and boys grow into young men. Boys only a few years older than Dale were dying in Vietnamese jungles and on Mississippi back roads. Leaders were falling. Hair was getting longer. Sitting in a classroom learning about Shakespeare and the Civil War and fractions seemed more pointless than ever. It was background noise for Dale, noise that he wanted to drown out with the roar of an engine.

"I can remember sitting in school," Earnhardt later said, "counting the seconds ticking off the clock until I could get home and help him in the shop."

He lasted until the ninth grade before dropping out. His parents were enraged. Ralph didn't want his son to live the life he had, journeying from track to track, night after night, for scrappy little purses. Dale saw only the romance; Ralph and Martha knew the hard, cold reality. They refused to allow him to get a driver's license at sixteen, forcing him to wait two years. They even offered him a new car if he graduated, all to no avail.

In the end, what could they do? Ralph himself had quit school three grades before Dale, and look how he'd turned out. Plus, Dale wasn't exactly the kind of kid you could sit down and talk sense into. He had to learn everything the hardest possible way, and it usually took two or three times for the lesson to fully penetrate his thick skull. There was a reason Dale later earned the name Ironhead, an ironic counterpoint to Ralph's Ironheart.

"When Ralph started, I was only about nineteen years old, and I didn't have sense enough to worry," Martha recalled. "When Dale got into a race car, that was just altogether different from Ralph. I grew up with Ralph racing and I knew he knew what he was doing. When Dale got in, that was part of me getting in that car, and it was just a different story."

Dale wasn't just skilled behind the wheel. Thanks to his father's tutelage, Dale also achieved expertise under the hood. He was a "crew chief" at age thirteen to a family friend named Gray London. "Dale Earnhardt was a good welder," London said. "He was a good painter. He was a good mechanic. He had a whole lot of talents in a lot of ways. But I never ever, ever heard him say 'If I can't make it as a driver, I'll do this.' He was single-minded, and that's what it takes. He never gave himself another choice."

On the track, where there were defined rules, Dale had at least a vague idea of what he was supposed to be doing. Off the track, his life was a succession of pileups. In 1968 Dale, all of seventeen years old, married Latane Brown. A year later the two had a son, Kerry. Dale had wanted to name the boy Ralph Dale Earnhardt Jr., but Latane refused. A year after Kerry's birth, Dale and Latane divorced. Earnhardt spent the money he earned working a day job on car parts, not child support, and eventually Latane's second husband, Jack Key, formally adopted Kerry. Dale and Kerry would not see each other on a regular basis for another fifteen years.

TRUE STORY: the big, bad Intimidator's first car was pink.

Dale Earnhardt's first car was an old beat-up 1956 Ford Victoria owned by his neighbors. David Oliver owned the car, Ralph built the engine, and Dale's buddies—Gregg Dayvault and his cousins Wayne and Frank—tuned the car to dirt-track specs. All it needed was a fresh coat of paint. The car already had a sweet purple metalflake roof that glittered in the sunlight. Wayne tried to create an avocado color to complement it, but the paint dried pink—the ruddy pink of an undercooked steak. The "team" didn't have enough money to buy more paint, so the car stayed pink, adorned with the number K-2 and "Dayvault's Tune-Up & Brake Ser."

Dale ran that pink beast in 1970 at his very first race at Metrolina, the dirt track not far from the Charlotte Airport, and finished tenth. He earned his first professional win at the same track the next year. He spent the next couple of years racing there and at Concord Speedway, over and over again. He piled up roughly twenty-five wins during this period, doing everything he could to keep his car on the track. It was an impressive enough record if you didn't consider the legacy of the man who'd cleared a path for Dale.

According to legend, Ralph and Dale shared a track just once, at a particularly memorable 1972 Metrolina race. At the time, Dale had been running six-cylinder semi-modifieds in the Sportsman division. The field was small, so promoters invited Dale and a few other semi-modified drivers to join a race Ralph Earnhardt had already entered. Ralph took the lead in the race's closing laps, as he always did. Dale was in fourth place, nearly a full lap behind. Ralph wheeled around the red clay track and came right up on Dale's bumper. Dale yielded the lane, thinking his father was looking to pass him. Respect. But Ralph was having none of that; he moved up behind Dale, put his front bumper on his son's car, and began pushing. He shoved Dale forward, hard, right past another driver and into a third-place finish and a payday. (Wheeler questions the story's authenticity—"Ralph was not the kind of man who would push Dale into something he hadn't earned himself"— but Dale would tell it for decades afterward.)

Off the track, Dale's life had grown no more stable. In 1971 he married Brenda Gee, daughter of NASCAR car builder Robert Gee. They promised to love one another for better or worse, for richer or poorer, and there was a lot more of the latters than the formers. Earnhardt worked a succession of jobs, from welder to mechanic, trying to do all he could to make enough money to buy parts for that weekend's race. One job even involved a brief return to the mills. "I was insulating some pipe and working over at the weave room in the mill," he'd say years later. "I would look down at those people, shake my head, and say, 'Boy, there ain't no way.' I watched those people working in that mill, and I knew I could never do that."

Brenda was a racing wife—at the track every Saturday night, living the erratic, cloistered life of a racing family during the week. Though drivers race in front of hundreds, thousands, or hundreds of thousands of people, their personal circles are often very small— usually just the people working on the car and relatives. Brenda would accompany Dale to the short tracks, often keeping him awake on the drive home. She'd score races for him, keeping track of his position on the track and how he fared at every point in the race. She was Dale's first fan and, given how much he trashed cars and equipment, often his *only* fan.

"I figure I have a lot to learn," Earnhardt conceded in 1972. "I guess it took Daddy ten years to know what he was doing. I hope I progress as rapidly as he did."

It made for a tough life, rattling hard and held together with duct tape. Then everything in the world of the Earnhardt family turned upside down.

THE LEGEND GOES that Ralph Earnhardt died in his garage, working on his car—tinkering yet again for that tiniest performance edge. It's a perfect scenario: the driver who's never satisfied, the mechanic always seeking that edge, driving himself right into the hereafter. If you must go, go doing what you love, right?

The truth is more mundane, though no less painful. On September 26, 1973, Ralph Earnhardt died of a heart attack while working on a carburetor at his kitchen table. He was just forty-five years old. He'd been a smoker, he'd probably breathed more exhaust than air during his days on earth, and he had lived for years with the crushing stresses of racing for his supper every night.

Ralph's death devastated his family and blew a hole in whatever stability remained in Dale's daily life. His rock, his inspiration, was gone. What the hell was he supposed to do now?

"I was so mad at him for leaving this world," Earnhardt would say years later. "I didn't get over it for a year. I'm still not over it. There isn't a day that goes by that I don't think of my father."

All the activity in the garage at Coach and Sedan came to an immediate halt. Dale sold both of his father's dogs, unable to bear the memories they summoned. The garage stayed locked and shuttered for years, leaving the dust to settle on the cars, trophies, and tools within.

Dale drifted, wanting and needing to race but unable to break through. He had potential, but he also knew there were few curses more insidious than "potential." Potential gives you hope, but burdens you with expectation. Potential never stops reminding you what you could be doing, and where you're falling short.

"Say you're a track star, and everybody says your potential is to run the 100-yard dash in 10 seconds," Earnhardt once said. "Then one day you actually run it in 10 seconds. That's no longer your potential. Now your potential is 9.9 seconds. It never stops." Potential keeps you hoping, though, until your noble calling has become a fool's errand. Potential can block your heart from hearing the truth your life is screaming.

At age twenty-four, Dale Earnhardt had trophies. But he also had mounting debts, a wife, an ex-wife, a son he rarely saw, and a three-year-old daughter named Kelley and another son, an infant named Ralph Dale Earnhardt Jr. There was racing to be done, and only so much time to dote on his children. Dale's life became a frenetic balancing act; he'd borrow $500 at a time on ninety-day notes just to race, hoping and praying he'd make enough to pay back the bank without losing all he had. He was good enough to stay afloat, but he was one single catastrophic wreck from ruin.

"I've had it rough and I'll have it rough in years to come," Earnhardt said in 1975. "It's not over with. The tough part will always be tough."

Brenda stayed by his side as much as she could, even meeting Dale at Hickory Speedway shortly after Junior's birth. But the jobs of racing wife and mother began to diverge. Her patience wearing thin, Brenda begged Dale to stop racing. She had two kids in diapers. She needed groceries, not trophies. The Earnhardts had to look up to see the poverty line. Their friends, their family, everyone was telling Dale to quit this racing silliness—to go get a real job and stop smashing the family's money into unforgiving track walls. When Earnhardt quit his last real job, at Punchy Whitaker's Wheel Alignment, Whitaker, a local legend, asked, "What are you going to do?"

"I'm going racing," Dale told him.

"You gonna starve to death, boy," Whitaker declared.

Dale's one-page 1975 application to race in NASCAR is a country music song in Courier font. Beside "Children (Names & Ages) Earnhardt wrote "Kerry Dale, 5 / Kelly [sic] King, 2 / Dale Junor [sic], 3 months." Beside "What happened in first race," he wrote "finish 10th." And beside "Ambition (other than racing)," he wrote "None."

Dale saw a glimmer of something more in himself, and each weekend he drew just enough encouragement to keep running—sometimes literally. One night at some dirt track—it could have been any of them, really—he was running in fourth place when third paid enough for his family's food for the next week. He had one hell of a problem right ahead of him in the person of Gene Daves, a locally famous driver who went by the *nom de track* of Stick Elliott.

Stick was a man in Ralph's mold; he'd mortgaged his life in the early 1960s and gone on to win hundreds of races in his career. But where Ralph preferred the solitude of his own tools and motors, Stick had gone for the glory. Stick had served as a stunt driver for the 1968 Elvis Presley flick *Speedway* and, according to legend, even took Elvis on a terrifying ride around Charlotte Motor Speedway. In short, young Dale Earnhardt was about to toy with the man who'd intimidated the King himself.

Not that it mattered. Dale Earnhardt would have put a bumper to the devil if need be. On the final lap, Dale caught Stick, turning the veteran and scooting past his spinning car for that third-place finish and some critical grocery money. As Earnhardt was climbing out of his car, word reached him that one of Stick's crewmen was headed his way with a pistol. Earnhardt fled the track, still wearing his dirt-covered fire suit. The next weekend, Earnhardt showed up at the track only to see Stick and his crew headed Dale's way.

Oh, hell, Dale thought.

Stick walked right up to the kid, stared straight at him, and then broke into a grin. "You know, son," he said, "you might just make a driver yet."

Dale had talent. He also had that rock-hard skull, and he was convinced that racing on asphalt would suit him better. It would be more profitable in the long run, but there was a huge difference between slick dirt and merciless asphalt. A canny driver can work his way around a dirt track and vulture out a win at the last second. On asphalt, the same aggression would get you knocked into the wall. And Dale didn't have the benefit of Ralph's tutelage for asphalt driving, since the old man almost never raced on it, preferring the give-and-take of dirt.

Young and wild-haired, Dale Earnhardt did little to distinguish himself from any of a dozen other drivers' kids. He drove a '55 Chevy, same as his father, but that and the surname were the only connections between Dale and Ralph. Where Ralph was precise, Dale was ragged; where Ralph worked his car like a scalpel, Dale wielded his like a club. "That Earnhardt boy," an old driver named Red Farmer said one night, "hit everyone and everything at the track except the people in the grandstands."

At one 200-lap Sportsman race in Savannah, Dale prepared to race against a crew of luminaries that included fellow future Hall-of-Famer David Pearson.

"I got to win this race," he told Gary Hargett, his car owner and mechanic at the time.

"No way," said Hargett.

"I'm broke," Dale said. "I got to win this race."

And that's exactly what he did. For 199 of the race's 200 laps, he tailed Pearson, but on the race's final lap, Dale turned Pearson, putting him into the wall and sliding past him for the win.

Hargett was furious; turning a man was no way to win a race. "Why in the world would you do something like that?" he complained.

"Fuck him," Earnhardt shot back. "He's got money, and I'm broke." He and Hargett had to peel out of the track at full speed to avoid a pack of fans eager to discuss sportsmanship with the kid from Kannapolis.

"You didn't want to mess around at these tracks," his friend Little Bud Moore said. "Some of these places, you didn't want to get too close to the wire fence or the women would cut you."

"Racing was his mistress, whatever it cost," family friend Marshall Brooks recalled. "Soap and toothpaste were a luxury."

"Dale knew that the difference between doing well and doing poorly would determine whether he was headed back to the cotton mill," said NASCAR Hall of Fame executive director Winston Kelley. "The thing about Earnhardt is, even when he got to the point where he didn't have to be successful every race, he raced just as hard."

Earnhardt spent most of the mid-1970s driving wherever he could find a race. He ran anywhere from Myrtle Beach, South Carolina, to Coeburn, Virginia, and all points in between, just like his father had. He was driving on instinct, balls, and will. "The only thing that makes you a good race driver," he said, "is experience, knowing what to do when you get into a situation. Because you get to a situation on a race track, you got to do something. And you can't think about what to do, you got to know what to do. By the time you think about what to do, it's done happened."

Finally, he impressed enough of the right people to get a shot at the biggest of the big time: NASCAR's Grand National division. At the 1975 World 600 in Charlotte, driver/owner Ed Negre decided to put Earnhardt behind the wheel of a 1974 Dodge, numbered 8—Ralph's old number—and sponsored by "10,000 RPM Speed Equipment."

Earnhardt knew a golden opportunity when he saw one. "Who knows what a good showing might mean?" he said in anticipation. "Assurance of a future ride in some more big races at best. Putting my name in some people's memory could help later on. I'm hepped up about the chance, no sense denying that."

"It has been a long time since I've seen a youngster so determined, so hungry," Wheeler said days before the race. "If nothing happens to sour his attitude, I think he's going to be a star within a few years, and a big one."

The World 600—later the Coca-Cola 600—is still the most demanding race on the Cup schedule, a 600-miler that tests drivers and equipment in the extreme. This was an era when the gap between the haves and have-nots of NASCAR was so vast as to be unbridgeable. Richard Petty won the 1975 race, and nobody—not one other driver—was on the lead lap with him. Cale Yarborough finished second, one lap down. The third-place finisher, David Pearson, was four laps behind Petty.

From there, you've got to go a fair way down the standings—all the way down to twenty-second—to find Earnhardt, forty-five laps off the lead. He earned $2,425—about $11,000 in today's dollars—but at least he managed to outrun his boss. Incidentally, he also finished just ahead of another young driver by the name of Richard Childress.

Earnhardt's performance wasn't enough to vault him out of obscurity. He ran two races in 1976, the World 600 once again and the Dixie 500 in Atlanta. He finished thirty-first and nineteenth respectively, completing barely half of the possible laps and winning a total purse of only $3,085. No owner was moved to bring Earnhardt back for a second audition.

In October 1977 he took one more shot at racing in Charlotte at the NAPA National 500, driving the No. 19 Belden Asphalt Chevy Malibu. He was racing on behalf of Henley Gray, a notable driver in the 1960s and '70s who'd hit a concrete wall at Michigan International Speedway earlier that same year.

Dale could manage only 25 of 334 laps. His racing career was headed nowhere, and his personal life had stalled out as well. That same year Brenda left him, taking Kelley and Dale Jr. with her.

This was as dark as it ever got for Dale Earnhardt, personally or professionally. He couldn't have known—and nobody would have expected—that salvation lay just around the bend.

CHAPTER 4
GIMME BACK MY BULLETS

IF DALE EARNHARDT was headed back to a life in the mills, he was going to enjoy the hell out of his final moments of freedom. In the late 1970s he reveled in beer, women, and rock 'n' roll in equal measure, and took advantage of every benefit afforded a bad-ass local racing champion.

"Dale would be upstairs, and no telling who was up there," recalled Little Bud Moore, who lived with Dale after his marriage to Brenda dissolved. "But every morning at 6:30 a.m., his alarm would go off, and he'd play the same song to get himself going: Lynyrd Skynyrd's 'Gimme Back My Bullets.'"

Dale Earnhardt was one wild-ass talented son of a bitch, but he needed someone to help him stay on the road, and he needed someone fast. That someone turned out to be Robert Gee, his ex-father-in-law.

Tall, beefy, with a head like a cinder block and a torso like a fifty-five-gallon drum, Gee and his ever-present cigar were a NASCAR fixture in the 1970s. He was the best body fabricator in North Carolina, and teams from all over the area flocked to his shop. Wheeler sent a reluctant Earnhardt to Gee's door with the admonition that "sometimes to go forward in racing, you have to go back."

By "back," Wheeler meant back to dirt. Gee had an old dirt car under a canvas tarp, and he allowed Earnhardt to work on it during stints at Gee's shop. (During one memorable afternoon, Earnhardt and Gee managed to cover themselves in bright Clemson orange while painting a truck for Wheeler, a memory that makes Wheeler laugh to this day.)

Earnhardt and Gee powered the car with an engine made by another local named Papa Joe Hendrick, with the help of his son Rick. Behind the wheel of his latest ride, Earnhardt started winning at Metrolina, Concord, and other dirt tracks. He won an awful lot, and before long, his step backward had resulted in a leap forward.

"They were winning everywhere they were going," Wheeler recalls. "With Robert Gee's ability to make a car handle, with Hendrick's power, with Dale driving the car—they were unbelievable."

IN THE LATE 1970s the South was experiencing a full-on cultural renaissance. A Georgia peanut farmer occupied the White House. *Smokey and the Bandit* was the country's hottest movie. *The Dukes of Hazzard* inspired *yee-haw!* Rebel yells from coast to coast. Lynyrd Skynyrd owned the airwaves. Atlanta was growing exponentially. The ugliness of the civil rights struggles of the 1960s had given way to hope, optimism, and an incursion of Yankee capital across the South. Racing, a sport that combined grit and daredevil grace with a chance to make a few bucks and pose with some pretty women in Victory Lane, stood at the center of the South's rebirth.

Wheeler had worked his way up to the presidency of Charlotte Motor Speedway by the late 1970s. A man not given to half gestures, his idea for promoting the World 600 on Memorial Day Weekend 1978 struck some as genius, others as insane: Wheeler would enter Willy T. Ribbs, an African American driver, in a race in the heart of the South—a South barely a decade removed from forced integration and Freedom Riders. The Greensboro Woolworth's, where four students from North Carolina A&T staged one of the era's earliest and most influential sit-ins, was just ninety miles up the road.

Ribbs was no mere publicity gimmick; he'd won a regional championship in Europe and knew how to wheel. NASCAR hadn't seen a competitive black driver at the Cup level since the retirement of Wendell Scott in 1973, and to date it has not seen one since.

"Willy is what we promoters have been waiting for since Wendell Scott," Wheeler announced at the press conference introducing the young driver, "an African-American driver who can compete. That's like discovering oil in your ground."

Ribbs, however, had a bit of a problem with authority. Not long before the start of the World 600, Ribbs decided to take one of the track's pace cars out for a shakedown. He caught the attention of the local cops when he turned the wrong way down a one-way street. The cops were soon on his tail, and Ribbs took off. He easily eluded the cops—hell, he *was* a professional driver—and eventually abandoned the car in a high-end suburb of Charlotte known as Queens, home to Queens College. Ribbs then ran into the gym and pretended to be a humble student shooting baskets. There was just one problem, which one officer pointed out to him when they tracked him down.

"Sorry, son," the policeman reportedly said to Ribbs, "but this is an all-girls school, and it's lily-white."

It was a great story—perhaps *too* great, given Wheeler's knack for promotion—but when Ribbs also skipped two practices, Wheeler and Ribbs's car owner, Will Cronkrite, had had enough. Ribbs wouldn't race in the 1978 World 600, and wouldn't get a chance to race at the Cup level for another eight years.

Cronkrite fit into the NASCAR culture of the mid-1970s about as well as a cocktail umbrella in a jar of moonshine. A college graduate in a world of high school dropouts, the bespectacled Cronkrite brought some erudition to a world of hard knocks. An engineering graduate of the University of Cincinnati, Cronkrite began his career as a car owner underwriting a car for Ricky Rudd. He'd backed Ribbs for the 1978 World 600, but Ribbs's removal from the race meant that Cronkrite had a car but no driver. Getting wind of the opening, Dale Earnhardt talked Cronkrite into taking a chance on him.

Earnhardt replaced Ribbs in the red, white, and blue No. 96 Cardinal Tractor Co. Ford for the World 600, and proceeded to finish seventeenth—enough to persuade Cronkrite to keep him on for a few more races. A month later Earnhardt earned a seventh-place finish at Daytona, his first-ever top ten. Soon afterward he made his first trips as a NASCAR driver to Talladega and Darlington, driving the same No. 96 Ford and finishing twelfth and sixteenth, respectively.

Earnhardt could now sense that there might be bigger rewards down the line. But he was not under contract to Cronkrite, so for the last race of the 1978 season he would drive for another owner, Rod Osterlund, the first race in what would be a highly fruitful partnership.

Osterlund, who'd built his fortune on California rental property, was one of a number of 1970s entrepreneurs who decided to try their hand at racing. After decades in which a few teams dominated the sport, NASCAR was now entering a more egalitarian era, when any team with enough money could buy the same parts as the big boys. The larger, more established teams had traditionally claimed all the best equipment, but racing had come a long way since Ralph Earnhardt had to buy up all the Craftsman screwdrivers to gain an edge. Now the road was wide open.

Osterlund was one of the first team owners to develop a full self-contained shop, one of the first to begin hiring specialists for every aspect of the racing operation. He'd hired some of the best in the business, and positioned himself to be a major player in an expanding sport for years to come.

Osterlund hooked up with a driver named Roland Wlodyka, who convinced Osterlund to move from California to North Carolina, the white-hot center of stock car racing in the United States. Wlodyka had an eye for on-track talent, and the two had enjoyed some success. For the 1978 season, Wlodyka put together a group that included "Suitcase" Jake Elder, engine builder Lou LaRosa, mechanics Doug Richert and Eddie Jones, and drivers Dave Marcis and Neil Bonnett. Marcis finished the year fifth in the standings.

Wlodyka knew the team still needed a driver it could rally around, and Osterlund offered him a choice of three drivers: Cale Yarborough, David Pearson, or the new kid on the block, Dale Earnhardt. (It was like offering an NBA team a choice between LeBron James, Kobe Bryant, and Stephen Curry: two proven legends, one with all the tools to join them.)

Osterlund had traveled out to Metrolina Speedway to watch Earnhardt race, at Wheeler's urging. All Earnhardt did was charge from the back of the pack to win a 100-lap race by several laps. "Man," Osterlund said, "I've got to have that boy in a car."

Earnhardt had by now established a reputation as a serious driver of Sportsman cars, generally finishing toward the front of the pack while taking paint from half a dozen rivals in the process. Earnhardt had been buying parts from Wlodyka and knew he was in with Osterlund. Earnhardt convinced Wlodyka and Osterlund to let him audition for a spot on the 1979 team in two races: a three-hundred-mile Sportsman-level race in Charlotte and the top-level Winston Cup season finale in Atlanta.

Staking their fortunes on Earnhardt, while brilliant in retrospect, wasn't an easy decision at the time for Osterlund and Wlodyka. Earnhardt was twenty-eight years old, twice divorced, with three children and oppressive and inescapable child support payments. His remaining tenure as a devil-may-care driver could be measured in months. Something needed to happen for Earnhardt, and soon, or he'd be consigned to a life in the mills.

"We'll take him," said mechanic Jim Delaney, "but the son of a bitch will tear up a lot of equipment learning."

With a $5,000 stake from Wheeler, Osterlund decided to create a two-car team for 1979 and beyond. Dave Marcis, Osterlund's then-current driver, wasn't so keen on the idea of splitting resources, and bailed out.

Osterlund was suddenly down to one car, so he needed Earnhardt as much as Earnhardt needed him. Aware that the talented and fatherless Earnhardt was stumbling through life with little stability, Osterlund took it upon himself to serve as a surrogate parent to the young man.

He took Earnhardt on fishing and boating trips, helped him resolve his outstanding child support problems, and put him on a budget. He eventually even helped Earnhardt buy a $145,000 house on Lake Norman. In exchange, Earnhardt went out and drove the hell out of Osterlund's No. 98 Chevy, starting with a fourth-place finish at the Dixie 500 in Atlanta to end the 1978 season, his best Cup-level race finish ever.

Stability. Quality equipment. A loyal owner in Osterlund guarding his back. Everything was coming together for Earnhardt, and it was all about to get even better. Like his father before him, Dale Earnhardt was about to find himself in the right place at the exact right time: driving in the most important race in NASCAR history.

TO UNDERSTAND THE importance of Daytona to the world of NASCAR, it's necessary to grasp its importance to racing as a whole. On the beaches of Daytona in the 1930s, a weather-beaten farmer by the name of Marion MacDonald changed the course of automotive history with a length of rope and a pocketknife. Nicknamed "Mad" because he used to eat hamburgers while racing, MacDonald was one of many drivers who challenged the hard-packed sands of Daytona. And like all the other drivers of the time, MacDonald raced without a seat belt. Cars tended to flip over with some regularity on the sand, and the thinking ran that being thrown from the car was far preferable to being trapped inside it, either underwater or amid burning fuel.

The problem was that without any form of restraint, drivers tended to slew back and forth across the front seat. This made an already difficult task—driving across sand—borderline impossible. MacDonald hit upon the idea of belting himself into the car with a rope. In order to make a quick exit if necessary, he taped a pocket-knife to the steering wheel to cut himself free.

Pocketknives can be tricky to open even when you're standing still. How did MacDonald plan on fiddling with a knife while the world collapsed around him? He kept the blade out as he drove, of course. You had to be a little bit insane to drive at Daytona.

AT THE TURN of the twentieth century, conventional wisdom held that if you traveled faster than seventy-five miles per hour, the air pressure would rip you apart from the inside. Then, at Daytona Beach in 1904, a man named William K. Vanderbilt disproved the theory by driving 92.3 miles per hour and surviving with all his internal organs intact. He launched a half century of thrill-seeking and speed-chasing on the Daytona sands, where speed was cherished above safety and sanity.

In 1927 Major Sir Henry O'Neil de Hane Segrave visited Daytona Beach. Segrave was one of those dashing late-colonial-period

Englishmen who specialized in throwing themselves into extreme situations. He walked the beach and judged it car-worthy. As *Boys' Life* magazine later described the moment, Segrave found "a beach smooth as a billiard table, hard as marble, 100 feet wide and 27 miles long, straight as an African spear." And this at a time when there were fewer than two hundred miles of paved roads in the entire country.

On March 29, 1927, Segrave launched a three-ton, 1,000-horsepower beast called the Mystery S across the sand at a speed of 203.79 miles per hour. "He had gone faster on land than any other man in this world," *Boys' Life* breathlessly recounted. "He had ventured into a new world of speed where on every side instant death poked its skinny fingers at him. It beckoned to him to make just a wee error and be blotted from the universe."

What makes speed even sweeter is someone in your rearview mirror. As news of Segrave's accomplishment trickled out across the globe, daredevils of all stripes journeyed to Daytona to test themselves against the record. One way or another, something almost always broke—the record, the car, or the man.

In 1928 Frank Lockhart tried to break Segrave's record but ended up establishing a far more dubious mark. Attempting to crack the 200-mile-per-hour barrier, Lockhart sent his Stutz Blackhawk pinwheeling into the waves. He survived that crash and immediately set about planning a second attempt. Six weeks later, he wasn't so fortunate. Lockhart's tire blew, throwing him violently from the vehicle and killing him instantly, the first recorded racing-related fatality at Daytona.

The specter of death was a cost of doing business, but that didn't faze the drivers and investors who sought to challenge Segrave's record. Later in 1928 a driver named Ray Keech actually pulled it off, driving a "car" that was essentially a chassis powered by three aircraft engines. The "Triplex" rocketed down the beach at a speed of 207.55 miles per hour. When Segrave managed to reclaim the record by ticking off a speed of 231.44 miles per hour, Keech folded, declaring that "there is not enough money in the world to get me back in that hot seat." A local by the name of Lee Bible didn't hesitate to strap himself into the Triplex, all smiles and good cheer. He hit 202 miles per hour before losing control of the car, flipping into the sand dunes at the far end of the beach track and killing himself and a nearby photographer.

A dead driver was one thing, a dead spectator quite another. Given the vast crowds that now gathered along the beach to watch, the Land Speed Trials organizers knew they were one malfunction away from a major catastrophe, and took their vehicles west to Utah's empty Bonneville Salt Flats. The final speed record at Daytona, set in 1935 by Sir Malcolm Campbell, stands at 276.82 miles per hour.

Back in Daytona, city leaders hit upon another way to keep local racing fires stoked: a race course running a mile and a half up the beach and the same distance back down a parallel paved road. Spectators weren't any more protected, but at least the cars weren't traveling at record-breaking speeds.

The first race, held in 1936, was scheduled to run 250 miles. Within seventy-five laps the cars had carved the sand in the turns to a dusty, almost impassable mess, and the race ended right there. The fifth-place finisher was one Bill France, but he wasn't yet the force he'd become.

One of NASCAR's earliest hell-raisers was a driver named "Reckless" Roy Hall, who had honed his automotive technique running illegal moonshine through the hills of North Georgia. Race strategy for the beach-and-road course held that you drove all-out in the straightaways and eased off the gas in the softer transition sand at the turns. Hall ditched that strategy in favor of keeping the hammer down in the turns; the move would lift his right-side tires off the sand in the turn but, if executed properly, made him all but unbeatable when he ran on the beach. You can draw a direct line from Hall and his compatriots to Earnhardt: drivers who wrung performance out of their cars that others couldn't imagine, much less emulate. Savvy drivers would run at the very edge of the surf where the sand was firmest, but the spray was also greatest, coating their windshields so much that they'd have to lean their heads out of the window to see where they were going.

The antics of Hall and others drew race fans to the beach, but common sense wasn't exactly in high supply. Fans would still stand just a few feet from the speeding cars, and local newspapers would beg fans to keep away from the track, as "a fatal accident might be caused by a foolhardy decision." Many drivers would dump their cars into the ocean rather than take out a fan who had edged too close to the action. Cars still rumbled into crowds with terrifying regularity, but whatever force protects drunks, fools, and little children kept the Daytona Beach fans safe and mostly unharmed. Rare was the driver who didn't have to call on spectators to help him right his overturned vehicle by hand, dodging cars on both sides.

World War II put a halt to most racing activity at Daytona— and everywhere else in America—but the postwar boom meant renewed interest in speed . . . and in the beachfront property where racers ran at Daytona. Hotels were rising along what had been empty stretches of sand, and by the 1950s, the end of Daytona Beach as a racing hub was near.

Bill France, who'd established NASCAR in the heady days after World War II, saw opportunity in the looming crisis. France looked with envy at a major new track that had been built in Darlington, South Carolina, and decided to craft a marquee track of his own, one he hoped would equal Indianapolis Motor Speedway.

France organized a coalition of local government and business leaders into the Daytona Beach Motor Speedway Corporation, and on October 16, 1955, he signed a ninety-nine-year lease for 446 acres of swampy property adjacent to sleepy Daytona Beach Airport. Groundbreaking of the new Daytona International Speedway took place on November 25, 1957, and the speedway opened for its first race in February 1959. That race, France promised in a press release, would be "a NASCAR-sanctioned 500-mile late model stock car race on George Washington's birthday, February 22."

With 31-degree banking in the turns, a seating capacity of a quarter million fans, and a footprint large enough to hold a lake in its infield, Daytona was a monstrous two-and-a-half-mile marvel— so large it could be raining on one section of the track while the sun shone on another. Architects used railroad engineering techniques to construct the high banks on swampy land, and France built concrete pads large enough to accommodate grandstands that wouldn't be installed for years. Built in just fifteen months, start to finish, Daytona International Speedway transformed a tiny beachfront town into one of the most significant destinations in American sports.

The track had been open only a few days when Marshall Teague, a beach-racing veteran, started testing an open-wheel car. The car caught air and flipped five times. Teague, thrown from the car while still in his seat, died instantly.

The first Daytona 500 was still eleven days away.

BY 1979 DAYTONA was a regional institution, but not yet a national one. That was about to change. For the first time, CBS would be broadcasting the entire Daytona 500, start to finish, green to checkers. Up until that point, most networks had either started their broadcasts with the race halfway over or settled for showing highlights that evening or the next day. Not only would

CBS broadcast everything, but the network introduced two elements that would become standard for every future NASCAR telecast: the in-car camera and the low-angle "speed" camera, giving viewers a better behind-the-wheel look than they'd ever had before.

NASCAR and CBS could not have timed the 1979 race any better. Football had been over for nearly a month; in Super Bowl XIII, held just a few hours down the coast in Miami, Terry Bradshaw's Pittsburgh Steelers had defeated Roger Staubach's Dallas Cowboys 35–31. Magic Johnson and Larry Bird were still in college, their landmark NCAA championship meeting still a few weeks away. Between the lack of alternatives for American sports fans and a heavy snowfall that kept most of the East Coast indoors, NASCAR suddenly had a captive audience.

Earnhardt, driving a '78 Buick squareback, was a minnow in a pool of sharks. He made no waves for the majority of the day. He did manage to take the lead for a spell and eventually finished eighth, a stunning achievement for a rookie. His accomplishment that day didn't warrant a mention in what would turn out to be one of the most famous moments in American sports.

Two members of NASCAR's "Alabama Gang," Donnie and Bobby Allison, were racing hard against tougher-than-cheap-steak Cale Yarborough. On the backstretch of the final lap, Donnie Allison was leading the race, with Yarborough on his rear bumper. With two turns left to go, Yarborough dove low to try to catch Allison on the inside. Allison saw the move and went for the block, forcing Yarborough's left tires into the infield grass. Yarborough spun, collecting Donnie Allison with him. The cars pirouetted up toward the turn 3 wall and then slid down into the infield grass, miraculously not getting clipped along the way. Richard Petty, who'd been running third, suddenly found himself in front, and held off Darrell Waltrip to get the victory. Petty's triumph ended a personal forty-five-race losing streak, but even *that* wasn't the story of the day.

Bobby Allison, driving one lap down, drove over to check on his brother and Yarborough. That turned out to be a mistake. Bobby had pulled his car alongside Donnie when he heard Yarborough shout that Bobby had been blocking him. Yarborough then showed his displeasure by walking over and hitting Bobby in the face with his helmet through Allison's car window.

"It cut my nose and my lip," Bobby Allison said years later. "It stunned me. I looked down, saw some blood dripping in my lap, and I said to myself, I gotta get out of this car, handle this right now, or I'm going to be running from him the rest of my life."

And from there, the brothers Allison and Yarborough descended into a graceless melee of kicks, punches, and curses. "I got out of the car," said Bobby Allison, who still can't resist jabbing Yarborough to this day, "and he went to work beating on my fist with his nose."

In an instant, NASCAR had gone from regional curiosity to nationwide phenomenon.

BUOYED BY HIS eighth-place finish in the season's marquee race, Earnhardt raced with overflowing confidence. "There might be a trick or two that Richard Petty and Bobby Allison haven't shown me yet," he exulted early in the season, "but I know I'm as good as they are."

He wasn't. But he was pointed in the right direction. To help keep Earnhardt in line, Osterlund had recruited Jake Elder, a crew chief nicknamed Suitcase because of his tendency to pack up and leave teams when the mood suited him. With his drooping mustache, reflective sunglasses, and cigar, Suitcase was an iconic presence, the kind that no longer exists in the NASCAR garage. Though he had no more than a third-grade education,

Elder was nonetheless one of the most widely respected wrench jockeys in the sport. He was impolitic, hard-edged, and absolutely brilliant.

"Jake Elder has forgotten more about racing than most crew chiefs have ever learned," broadcaster Mike Joy would say. "Every time he packs up his suitcase and moves, he makes a contender out of somebody."

Elder's protégés all frustrated him. He had worked in some capacity for every major driver in NASCAR, including Richard Petty, David Pearson, Darrell Waltrip, and Benny Parsons, but no one could keep up with him.

"I have a problem getting people to understand how I want things done," he once carped. "Usually, I can get it done myself quicker than I can explain to them how I want it done."

He was exactly the kind of demanding, irascible surrogate father that Earnhardt needed. The two often sparred like father and son, with Earnhardt assuming he knew what was wrong with his car, and Elder certain he knew what was wrong with the driver.

"Goddamn," Earnhardt would say, "I'm driving this son of a bitch, and it won't go at all."

"You're driving it too hard," Elder would reply. "That's the trouble. Let the car carry you, and save the brakes. Don't get the car upset."

Their partnership paid almost immediate dividends; in the season's seventh race, at Bristol, Earnhardt brought home his first Cup-level victory. It inspired Elder to utter one of the most memorable lines in all modern sports: "Stick with me, kid, and we'll have diamonds as big as horse turds!"

"If Jake hadn't taken Dale under his wing," LaRosa told writer Peter Golenbock for the book *The Last Lap*, "if Jake hadn't been that capable father-like figure, Dale might not have made it, or he might have floundered a few more years."

"If he don't get hurt," Elder said after Earnhardt's Bristol win, "I think he's got at least twelve good years ahead of him."

"He was a smartass, which is great," LaRosa said of Earnhardt at this stage. "I compare good drivers to Navy fighter pilots coming off aircraft carriers. If you ever meet a Navy fighter pilot off a carrier, they are young, cocky, and aggressive. You've got to be aggressive."

Earnhardt was indeed throwing himself around the racetrack, making foolhardy passes on the outside, the trickiest maneuver in the game. He'd try to squeeze his car where it wouldn't fit, and more often than not he'd take a few cars with him into the wall. He also learned how fragile a racing career could be.

At Pocono, a tire failed and he lost control of his car, spun backward, and hit the retaining wall on the driver's side. A similar wreck had killed Joe Weatherly in 1964 at Riverside, but Earnhardt got off easy, relatively speaking. The impact only snapped his collarbone and broke his sternum, knocking him out.

Earnhardt regained consciousness while being airlifted; he later said that all he could see upon awakening was clouds, and he assumed he'd died and gone to heaven. Pearson subbed in for four races, even notching a victory at Darlington, reminding Earnhardt that there was always someone right behind you to fill your seat.

Earnhardt conducted a press conference by telephone so reporters wouldn't see the extent of his injuries. "They said I bruised my heart," Earnhardt told the media. "Heck, I've had a broken heart before. I'll get over it."

Out of the public eye, Earnhardt seethed. He didn't wish another driver ill, but he'd be damned if another man was going to succeed in his ride. Although he was in agony, he came back to run at Richmond, and in his very first race back put the car on the pole. Even with the injury-induced layoff, Earnhardt finished seventh in points, ahead of such notables as Terry Labonte and Harry Gant.

He closed 1979 by winning Rookie of the Year, the very same year Richard Petty won the last of his seven championships.

At last Earnhardt felt he was standing on his own, and he had enough perspective to understand the power and temptation of a famous name. "I am Ralph Earnhardt's boy, but I couldn't ride my daddy's reputation forever," he said. "My daddy's name opened a lot of doors for me along the way, and sometimes I was ashamed I had to use his name. It seemed I was taking advantage, and it wasn't fair to do things that way."

Right after the season wrapped, Earnhardt and Osterlund worked out a long-term agreement: a five-year deal with three option years at $30,000 a year and 50 percent of his winnings. The move raised eyebrows in the garage; some big names at more established teams were growing older, and Earnhardt could have moved into one of their rides. But Earnhardt wasn't in a speculative frame of mind. He was in this to win *now*.

"I couldn't be more tickled," Earnhardt said. "Talk about job security, I've got it. It frees me to concentrate on winning races and going for the driving championship, and believe me, that's a tremendous plus."

CHAPTER 5

KEEP YOUR DAMN COMPOSURE

EARNHARDT HAD SPENT the 1970s looking no farther ahead than next Sunday, knowing he was always one bad race away from ending up under cars with a wrench in his hand instead of inside them. For the first time in his life, he had some measure of security. And it showed in his wide-open driving.

He finished second in the 1980 season-opener at Riverside, then reeled off five more top-five finishes, including wins at Atlanta and Bristol. The Atlanta race marked both Earnhardt's first win at a large track—the same one that had bedeviled his father two decades before—and the Cup debut of a driver named Rusty Wallace.

Earnhardt's overnight success simply did not happen in NASCAR. Never before had a second-year driver challenged for a title, never mind a driver from a new, untested team. Certainly the team would fall apart over the course of the full thirty-one-race season.

Sure enough, the first cracks showed up shortly after the World 600 in Charlotte on Memorial Day weekend. Suitcase Jake Elder lived up to his name, bailing on the Osterlund team (or perhaps getting fired, depending on who's telling the story.) Elder claimed that Earnhardt's attitude was worsening as his finishes improved. Elder also clashed with Wlodyka, who didn't exactly fight Elder's departure and insisted that twenty-year-old Doug Richert could sub in effectively using the notes and charts Elder had prepared.

LaRosa was furious. "You stupid son of a bitch," he told Wlodyka. "It ain't what's on paper. It's how Jake arrived at the conclusion."

"He was so meticulous about his cars that he didn't trust anyone else to work on them," Darrell Waltrip would say of Elder decades later. "After everyone else was done working on the car, he would go back and put the finishing touches on it. Every bolt had to be Jake-tight. Every part and piece on that race car had to be checked off by Jake. . . . Let's be honest, he was cantankerous and hard to get along with a lot of the time. Before you knew it, you would have your guys coming to you saying, 'You gotta do something about this, or we are walking.'"

Jake did the walking—again—but he left his lessons behind. Earnhardt still had a checkers-or-wreckers mentality, but he also followed every poor finish with an exceptional one. Finish twenty-ninth at Darlington one week, come back and finish sixth at North Wilkesboro the next. Finish thirty-fifth at Michigan one week, come in second at Bristol the next. Earnhardt finished out of the top ten seven times in 1980, and every time—*every single time*—he rebounded with a finish of ninth or better. And that—combined with five wins—is how you won championships.

Earnhardt's fellow drivers weren't quite as enamored. "I guess NASCAR thinks that overaggressive driving sells tickets," Waltrip said after one incident in which Earnhardt punted him en route to Victory Lane. When asked to be more specific, Waltrip simply pointed at Earnhardt's car. "Y'all know who to watch if that's what you want to see."

Richard Petty tried his damnedest to reel in the young driver. Petty had built a career on having better equipment than most of the scrubs he raced against in his early days, but he found himself betrayed by his own engines as the 1980 season wore on. Cale Yarborough gave Earnhardt much more of a scare, winning two of the season's last three races. He came into the season finale, the Los Angeles Times 500 in Ontario, California, just 29 points behind Earnhardt. Earnhardt needed to finish no lower than fifth to ensure a championship.

The Los Angeles Times 500 would be held on November 15 at Ontario Motor Speedway, a gargantuan track that presaged NASCAR's twenty-first-century ambitions and woes in that it tried to be all things to all people. The track was built in the mid-1960s as a replica of Indianapolis Motor Speedway, and pioneered such elements of racing as skyboxes and high-tech timing systems. Celebrities like Paul Newman, James Garner, and John Wayne flocked to IndyCar races there, and festival concerts starring the Eagles, Aerosmith, and others drew 400,000 fans to the track. But by 1980 the track was in serious financial trouble. The Los Angeles Times 500 would mark the final race at the facility, which would be demolished in 1981 and subdivided into a typical suburban sprawl of residential and commercial development.

The race had been switched from Sunday to Saturday to avoid conflict with the NFL. The schedule change gave the entire country a look at Earnhardt, the sport's newest icon. If Earnhardt was worried about the exposure or about Yarborough, more than a decade his senior, he didn't show it.

In the days leading up to the race, Earnhardt was the very picture of cool, slouching low behind the wheel of his Monte Carlo as he prowled the garage and the track, once even catching a nap on the garage floor before qualifying. While Earnhardt didn't quite match Yarborough's qualifying speed, he came closer than anyone else on the track, and the two rivals lined up 1-2 on the front row.

How could this be? How was this crew of castoffs and rookies outrunning legends of the sport? It wasn't proper, it wasn't correct. No one could possibly know it then, but the upstart upending

NASCAR's natural order would come to embody its traditions. Earnhardt respected history, but he wasn't going to bend a knee to anyone. He knew that he could run with the best, no matter how green he might be.

"There are no deep, dark secrets," Earnhardt said just before the race. "That's part of the old philosophy my daddy taught me: you prepare that race car the best you can, and you work hard and run hard and keep your damn composure about you, and it'll all work out."

While Earnhardt was keeping his composure, he tried to make those around him lose theirs. Just before the race, Yarborough approached Earnhardt.

"Use your head," the three-time champion said.

"The both of us," Earnhardt shot back.

On the pace lap, just before the green flag flew to start the race, Yarborough gave Earnhardt the good-luck thumbs-up. Earnhardt did not reciprocate.

Early on, it looked like Yarborough had little to fear. Wind gusted as high as forty miles per hour across the track, and Earnhardt's car lacked the horsepower to overcome it—he really could have used a genius like Elder at a time like this. He slipped back in the pack, eventually going a lap down.

Earnhardt needed that fifth-place finish, and so he drew on some of his old dirt-track mentality. He made the most daring move of his young career on a restart, diving low past five cars, including Yarborough, to put himself back on the lead lap. A caution flag soon afterward allowed him to rejoin Yarborough at the front of the pack. All he needed to do was remain on Yarborough's bumper, and the championship would be his.

It wouldn't be that easy. On the final pit stop, Earnhardt skidded into his stall, smacking the wall and sending his own crew flying to avoid being crushed. Then he rolled out while the car was still on the jack, and had to come back in to change that nearly blown tire. Thanks to the spread-out field, he remained in fifth place. And there he would stay—a finish good enough to give him a 19-point margin of victory for the Winston Cup championship. In Victory Lane, Earnhardt held up a mockup of the *Los Angeles Times* with the headline "Earnhardt 1980 NASCAR Champ" and his signature smirk already on his face.

Earnhardt and his crew decided to celebrate the win that night in Vegas, a short plane flight away, and brought reporters from the *Charlotte Observer* and *Sports Illustrated* along for the ride. When Dale and his brothers Randy and Danny wandered into their suite at the Circus Circus Las Vegas hotel and casino, the Kannapolis boys' eyes just about bugged out of their heads at the floor-to-ceiling mirrors, spiral staircase, piano, and bar that was—for the moment, anyway—fully stocked. "Golleee!" Earnhardt drawled in imitation of Jim Nabors's then-popular TV character Gomer Pyle. "This is as big as most houses back home!"

Down on the floor, Earnhardt's hot streak continued: he won $500 in blackjack and $100 on a single pull of the slot machine. Later, at that year's Winston Cup banquet, Earnhardt posed with the trophy wearing khaki pants and a navy blue blazer with gold buttons, which made him look more like a ten-year-old on his way to church than a NASCAR champion. He had the first wisps of the Mustache as well as the characteristic chunky sideburns of the era, and he looked like he'd just as soon throw that trophy in the back seat and motor on out of there. It was a scene, and a facial expression, the rest of the sports world would see repeated often.

Osterlund didn't show up for the season-ending banquet. That set off alarms in Earnhardt's head, but he pressed onward, emboldened by a new deal with Wrangler Jeans. The company wanted to make Earnhardt the centerpiece of its "One Tough Customer" campaign, and would be paying Osterlund a reported $400,000 a year to sponsor Earnhardt's ride. Meanwhile, Earnhardt had set up shop in his father's old garage, hoping and praying that Osterlund would live up to his end of the five-year bargain.

Dale's presence electrified the neighborhood. Old friends who'd once worked on Ralph's car and dined on slick-meat sandwiches happily stopped by to watch Ralph's boy working under a hood. "It has been like old times, having Dale back around," said his sister Cathy. "We worship him, just like we did Dad all those years he raced out of that old cinder-block shop."

His most important ally was nowhere to be found. Osterlund's real estate development partners and investors demanded he focus on his California endeavors. "I had to choose between the racing and the development business. I couldn't go back there," Osterlund said of his NASCAR world. "I knew that if I ever was in a room with all those people I never could go through with [selling the team]."

The end of the Earnhardt-Osterlund partnership came with surprising swiftness. On June 26, 1981, Osterlund signed papers transferring ownership of his team to J. D. Stacy, a man whose cigar and cowboy hat earned him the nickname Boss Hogg, after the villain in *The Dukes of Hazzard*. The sale caught both Earnhardt and Wrangler by surprise and taught Earnhardt a hard lesson in racing economics.

Earnhardt and Osterlund had never formally signed that long-term contract, meaning Stacy didn't have to recognize it. Stacy, who'd made his fortune in coal mining, was in the process of buying up NASCAR teams up and down the starting grid, seeking to flood the market in search of a championship. Stacy didn't have much of a rep in the garage—he'd clashed with various drivers and crew for years, and slung lawsuits like rice at a wedding. But he had cash, and in NASCAR, cash can drown out caution. Like many others before and after him, Stacy assumed that with enough money, he could simply buy checkered flags and championships.

Stacy already had Joe Ruttman driving for him and apparently told Earnhardt that "drivers are a dime a dozen," a line reminiscent of the music executive who once rejected the Beatles by saying, "Guitar groups are on the way out."

Earnhardt lasted five weeks—through the summer Talladega race—before pulling the plug on his tenure with Stacy. He took the high road in the press, issuing a statement that read, "Jim, you're a nice fellow and I haven't got a thing against you. But I've got to do something I should have done when the team changed ownership. I'm going to quit. I wish you well." Privately, Wheeler said, Earnhardt simply didn't trust Stacy.

The coal baron would eventually leave NASCAR in 1983. Despite having drivers such as Mark Martin, Tim Richmond, Neil Bonnett, Sterling Marlin, and Earnhardt on his teams, Stacy could manage only 4 wins in 126 races, and never got that championship.

The defending champion had no car, but he did have a sponsor. Wrangler, which was sponsoring Earnhardt's car to the tune of $400,000 a year, decided to pack its jeans and join Earnhardt in leaping off into the great unknown. For a guy who'd spent most of his adult life wondering where his next week's grocery money would come from, this was like playing with house money. Now all he needed was an owner to gamble on him.

CHAPTER 6

WIN SOME, LOSE SOME, WRECK SOME

FROM THE MOMENT he founded NASCAR in 1948, Bill France ruled his empire autocratically, changing rules at whim and ensuring NASCAR would benefit no matter which way the money flowed or who won on the track. His dominion over the sport was apparent at the opening of Talladega Superspeedway in 1969.

France's new gem, built in the hinterlands of east Alabama, was a terrifying tri-oval beast—2.66 miles in length, the largest oval on the NASCAR circuit. When it opened, its asphalt surface was so rough that tires lasted as few as twenty laps. Richard Petty and other prominent drivers of the day, fearful of a catastrophic wreck, petitioned France to delay the opening until there were improvements. France denied the request, and thirty-seven drivers pulled out of the race. A nascent drivers' union headed by Petty hoped the strike would force France to reconsider. No such luck; France rounded up replacements and ran the race anyway, breaking the union with no more trouble than it would have taken him to snap a pencil. NASCAR would not face an organized drivers' movement for nearly another half century.

A NASCAR footnote named Richard Brickhouse won that Talladega race, but the driver who finished twenty-third, an unknown by the name of Richard Childress, would shape the sport's history. Childress was a race-by-race grinder, a kid from Winston-Salem,

North Carolina, who lost his father when he was only five. "From then on," he once told writer Ed Hinton, "I considered myself a man. Had to. There was nobody to go home to and whine, 'Johnny whipped my ass today.' I had to fight my own battles."

He also had to make his own money, and he did so in the classic American way: by busting his butt. He worked custodial duties to pay for his lunch in elementary school; he sold peanuts and Cokes at Bowman-Gray Stadium while races ran below him.

Childress soon found a more lucrative part-time gig: running moonshine from the gas station where he worked to the illegal speakeasies in Winston-Salem. The job of middleman was one of the riskiest and most exposed in the bootlegging business. Childress quit soon after he saw one man blow another to pieces with a shotgun.

Stock car racing seemed positively benign by comparison. Beginning in the mid-1960s, Childress drove across the country looking for races, driving first with No. 96, and later with No. 3. He was never a champion—never even a contender—which forced him to learn a humility sorely lacking in other racers of his day.

"Never forget where you come from," he once said, "and never forget you may end up having to go back there someday."

Midway through the 1981 season, while Earnhardt marked time on J. D. Stacy's team, Childress saw opportunity: he offered Earnhardt a seat in his own No. 3 Chevy. Earnhardt accepted, and Wrangler accompanied him. In one weekend, Childress went from driver to owner with full sponsorship, a remarkable transformation.

One of NASCAR's greatest owner-driver partnerships didn't last long in its first incarnation; Earnhardt was far from fastidious about taking care of his equipment, and even in a shortened season wrecked so many cars that Childress was left $150,000 in the red. Wrangler pitched in $75,000, but Childress had to leverage every asset he owned just to keep his nose above water. He made a tough decision, kicking his talented but destructive driver out of the nest.

"We're not ready for a championship driver like you," Childress told Earnhardt. That forced Earnhardt to connect with his fourth owner in a year: the legendary Bud Moore—no relation to Little Bud Moore, Ralph Earnhardt's old dirt-track rival and Dale's one-time housemate. This Moore embodied exactly what Earnhardt needed at the time—hands-on ownership and deep pockets.

At long last, Earnhardt was pointing the right direction on the track. Against all odds, he was starting to get his life together off it, too.

TERESA HOUSTON WAS one of many young women in the 1970s whose lives were circumscribed by the racetracks at which their fathers, brothers, grandfathers, and uncles drove. Teresa's father, Hal, was an owner, and her uncle Tommy remains one of the winningest drivers in what's now known as NASCAR's Xfinity Series.

It's hard to grow up in central North Carolina without getting racing in your veins. Maybe Teresa Houston was just doing what came naturally in 1978 when she met the bullheaded young man who drove one of Hal's cars at Martinsville. Earnhardt didn't win the race, but he caught the eye of the owner's daughter, a slim, shy woman with long brown hair and a twang-edged southern accent. She wasn't the type of woman Earnhardt generally ran with, but that likely made her all the more attractive to him.

They were both ambitious, but in different ways. At the time they met, he still wasn't far removed—emotionally or financially—from his ill-fated decision to drop out of high school in the ninth grade. Teresa had blazed her way through Bunker Hill High School in Claremont, North Carolina, in just three years, finding the time to become a varsity cheerleader, before earning her real estate license and starting classes in interior design. The two of them connected, bonded, and eventually formed a partnership that would change the face of NASCAR.

But that would be years in the future. In the early 1980s, Earnhardt was a guy with family obligations from every direction. Back in Kannapolis, his second ex-wife Brenda and their two young children, eight-year-old Kelley and six-year-old Dale Jr., were living in a dilapidated old mill house. Faulty wiring at the house sparked a fire in May 1981 that consumed it all, leaving the three of them unharmed but without a home. Brenda had family in Virginia, but they lived as close to the bone as she'd been.

Brenda agonized over the decision she had to make, and would wonder for years afterward if she'd made the right one. She summoned up her courage and asked her ex-husband, the onetime dirt-racing bum turned champion, if he'd take custody of their two children. He had the money, he had the stability; he offered the best chance for Kelley and Dale Jr. to have the best in life.

Earnhardt became a father in truth as well as name—a role that would prove far more of a challenge than racing. Teresa, and a succession of nannies, would raise the children—Earnhardt later acknowledged that he didn't have much to do with their upbringing. "Teresa raised them," he once said. "I didn't do much." The family dynamic forged in those early days—Dale absent, Teresa in charge, Kelley watching out for Junior—would prove significant to NASCAR a quarter century down the line.

Earnhardt now had more people under his roof, but the drive to race hadn't slowed. Bud Moore knew he was getting a tough dog in Earnhardt. Just how tough became clear during the season, when Earnhardt had another dramatic wreck at Pocono. Driving the blue-and-yellow Wrangler No. 15, Earnhardt collided with Tim Richmond, flipped just outside turn 1, and nearly flew right over the low red-and-white concrete wall that lined the track. The back half of his car was sheared off, and he almost took out a radio booth overlooking the track.

In those days, when an accident occurred, drivers would "race back to the flag"—in other words, race back to the start/finish line to determine their position when the race restarted. It was a dangerous practice for many reasons; it left the wrecked driver vulnerable to getting hit from behind as cars came around again, and it delayed the response time to a wreck, since rescue vehicles couldn't enter a track with cars flying at five times their speed. (NASCAR didn't change this lunatic rule until 2003.) Earnhardt had to scramble out of an inverted car while being doused with hot oil from a ruptured line. Richmond and a photographer helped Earnhardt clamber from the wreck and limp to the waiting ambulance.

He raced the next week at Talladega and wrecked again, hyperextending his left leg and chipping off a small chunk of bone on his kneecap. This time, he couldn't elude the hospital. Earnhardt didn't believe the injury was serious, but surgeons advised him to have the fractured bone repaired with tiny plastic screws to minimize the possibility of a future limp. Doctors declined the sponsor-minded Earnhardt's request to make the incision in the shape of a W—for Wrangler, of course.

Earnhardt decided to take the plunge into marriage for the third time while still in the hospital. He popped the question to Teresa from his hospital bed, and she said yes. Teresa's father Hal, familiar with drivers and their temperaments, put Earnhardt through a full marriage-material shakedown. He took his future son-in-law hunting and fishing, knowing that a walk in the woods with him and his loaded gun would send Earnhardt the right message.

And he was happy with the reply. "There was never a doubt in my mind that he was devoted to her," Hal said in 2001. "She was what he lived for. She was everything he wanted in a mate, in a wife. And she was the same way he was."

Dale and Teresa Earnhardt married on November 14, 1982. Earnhardt, not to mention NASCAR, would never be the same.

"Teresa won the race," Osterlund would say years later in Leigh Montville's book *At the Altar of Speed*. "She was always around, but she was part of a group [of ladies clamoring for Earnhardt's attention]. Dale had a lot of women. He had women, I think, at every track during that 1980 season. Teresa did a smart thing. She became involved with his kids. Whenever they were around, she was taking care of them."

"He won the [first] championship and he didn't know what to do with it," Wheeler said. "It came too fast. He knew he didn't know how to dress right, talk right. He was not comfortable with executive people. He was doing a lot of things he should not have been doing. Drinking too much, running around with a lot of girls, doing things that a lot of single race drivers still do."

Teresa changed all that. "She cleaned him up, taught him to drink wine, taught him to soften himself," Wheeler continued. "She definitely calmed him down, and she was good for him."

Over the course of the 1982 and 1983 seasons, the newly married Earnhardt won three times under Bud Moore, including his first-ever wins at Darlington and Talladega. On the other hand, he was still tearing the crap out of his equipment, and he didn't even finish half of the races he ran for Moore, completing only 29 of 60. He managed to place twelfth and eighth in the 1982 and 1983 seasons despite all the carnage. Earnhardt's talent was climbing off the charts, but so were the expenses.

As the 1984 season approached, Richard Childress wanted Earnhardt back, and badly. Bud Moore knew it. He told Childress, "Boy, he'll break you."

Break his heart? Break his spirit? Break his wallet? Childress didn't care. He believed in Earnhardt, and Moore stepped aside to allow Childress and Earnhardt to do whatever they could manage together.

A NASCAR SEASON proceeds through dozens of different tracks, virtually none of which are exactly alike. The skills necessary to compete at a mixing bowl like Bristol are useless at a road course like Sonoma; the fearlessness needed to go four-wide at Talladega doesn't match up with the endurance necessary to survive six hundred miles at Charlotte. This isn't, say, football, where the cities change but the dimensions of the field are the same. Ironically, the closest comparison might be golf, where courses vary from week to week . . . although, of course, golf proceeds at a glacial pace relative to racing, and competitors don't have forty-two challengers teeing off right next to them.

Earnhardt and Childress, seizing on their second chance together, decided to race both hard *and* smart. Richard Childress Racing operated out of a tiny shop on Gum Tree Road in Winston-Salem, North Carolina. Childress began plowing money into the operation, building a self-contained engine shop for LaRosa, who'd also come on board.

Before their first full season together, Earnhardt, Childress, and new crew chief Kirk Shelmerdine devised a long-term plan for sustained success. They divided the season into segments by track and set out to conquer each of those in turn: short tracks, superspeedways, and intermediates.

The Earnhardt-Childress team first focused its efforts on the short tracks that comprise about a third of the season. The team designed and built its own cars with the express purpose of handling the tight, give-no-quarter short tracks like Bristol and Martinsville. The strategy paid off—the Wrangler No. 3 team followed two go-or-blow victories in 1984 at the large tracks of Talladega and Atlanta with four victories in 1985 alone on the short tracks.

These were good days for the Childress operation, days when no divide existed between boss and workingman. The team would bond over shared pranks, like the evening at Daytona when the entire gang—Childress, Earnhardt, everyone—was out to dinner. Childress excused himself to go to the men's room, leaving his suit jacket on his chair. LaRosa proceeded to fill an inside pocket with anchovies. The next night, when LaRosa left his jacket unattended at a restaurant, the crew filled his pockets with utensils, telling the manager he'd been trying to steal silverware. This was the camaraderie of Ralph Earnhardt's garage writ large, men working together in search of speed and getting paid ever-larger sums of money to do so.

Despite the victories, 1985 proved to be a rough year. "Everything in a motor that could break, did," LaRosa said. "It wasn't because Richard didn't spend the money on the parts. He did. A cloud hung over us like we were jinxed." Earnhardt's hard-driving style was a factor in engine wear, but here's a curious aspect about the mechanical side of race cars: sometimes they just don't work right. Preparation, expectation, testing . . . sometimes engines are just plain cursed. The team finished eighth, and nerves began to fray.

Childress doubled down, knowing he had a special team. He built a new shop in Welcome, North Carolina, and the group spent the winter prepping the new headquarters. The pit crew bonded, dubbing themselves first the Junkyard Dogs and later the Flying Aces, with gas man Chocolate Myers as their unofficial leader. Wrangler was on board for a third season—cause for optimism—but Earnhardt needed to win another championship, and soon.

Then came 1986. The season began as several had before, and so many would afterward—with a great Daytona 500 run spoiled at the last instant. The culprit this time was a gas tank that came up empty with only three laps remaining while Earnhardt was in the lead, allowing Geoff Bodine to skirt past Earnhardt for the win.

After the disappointment of Daytona, Earnhardt began to grind down his rivals, race by race, one by one. At the season's second race, in Richmond, he and Darrell Waltrip tangled hard. With three laps left in the race, Waltrip tried to sneak past Earnhardt, who retaliated by spinning out Waltrip, along with three other cars. Earnhardt would be fined $5,000 for reckless driving, put on probation, and ordered to post a $10,000 bond to race again. Earnhardt played his usual role of guileless innocent. ("Win some, lose some, wreck some," he liked to say.) He protested the fine, and on appeal the bond and probation were dropped and the fine cut to $3,000. It would be the last time Waltrip left a mark on Earnhardt that season.

Waltrip fought back with his mouth, saying after a victory at North Wilkesboro that he'd considered "putting some psychological stuff in the papers, but it wouldn't do any good because Dale and his boys can't read."

"I can read," Earnhardt replied. "Just like in a kid's early reader. See Darrell run his mouth. See Darrell fall."

Waltrip never got close enough to scare Earnhardt in the points standings. Earnhardt won at Darlington and North Wilkesboro in April, finished second in the season's ninth race, the Winston 500, and that was enough to give him the points lead for the rest of the 1986 season.

"He really matured. He mellowed from being a smartass to being a mature person who used his head driving," LaRosa said. "When he was driving for Osterlund, Dale was winning on aggressiveness. Now he was winning on intelligence, maturity, and thinking."

Earnhardt's second championship wasn't the story of the year, however. That honor belonged to a younger driver even cockier than Earnhardt, Tim Richmond, who courted celebrity and speed in equal measure—a driver who could have been the great rival Earnhardt needed all throughout the 1980s and 1990s. Richmond was the kind of ridiculously talented athlete who succeeded instantly at any event he attempted. He won the Indy 500 Rookie of the Year in 1980, the same year Earnhardt won his first championship, and made the jump to NASCAR shortly afterward.

Richmond and Earnhardt could not have been more different. Richmond came from enough money that his parents bought him his own private plane at age sixteen, while Earnhardt spent his teenage days watching those planes fly far overhead. Richmond showed up at tracks in Armani suits and Rolexes; Earnhardt wore the same jeans he'd use while working his newly purchased Mooresville farm.

They bonded in their love of NASCAR's hell-raising past, and they did their best to re-create it in the 1980s. Their antics were the kind that kept sponsors and team owners sweating, like the time they whipped up some "cherry bounce"—cherries soaked in moonshine—and decided to get stupid.

"Dale and I took a jug of that stuff out on his boat to do some water skiing," Richmond remembered. "The deal was that the guy in the boat would fish the cherries out of the jug and throw them back for the skier to catch in his mouth. Dale is a pretty good thrower. I caught enough that I got a little woozy from eating so many cherries and, well, I fell off the skis and nearly drowned myself." It is entirely possible that neither man left the boat, or even the dock, but the rest of the story is likely gospel truth.

Richmond had talent, but he wasted it like a drunk spilling whiskey. Around the time of every Coca-Cola 600, Earnhardt would rent out an entire bar for drivers to unwind, and Richmond would always get into a fight and get thrown out on his ass within minutes of his arrival. He'd bottomed out in 1985, getting into fights and showing up at races disoriented enough to arouse suspicions of alcoholism or drug abuse.

Richmond had cleaned up and dried out in the weeks before the 1986 season started, though, and his work paid off. Driving for still-new Hendrick Motorsports, he won seven races that year, very nearly catching Waltrip for second place. He and Earnhardt shared Driver of the Year honors.

Richmond lived a life as grandiose and undisciplined as Earnhardt's was determined. He would make sure every restaurant knew he'd be arriving soon, and he'd hang banners out the windows of his hotels to alert his fans of his exact room. His fiery relationship with his crew chief formed the basis of the Tom Cruise–Robert Duvall dynamic in *Days of Thunder*. Stories abounded of a turnstile set up beside Richmond's bed. His extracurricular activities didn't sit well with NASCAR, but they made him a household name, however briefly.

"I'm trying to prove that I was put on this earth to have fun," Richmond said at the time. "To succeed at the fun department."

RICHMOND WAS AN erratic driver, but at his best an insanely talented one. At Pocono during that summer of 1986, Richmond was leading Earnhardt. Richmond keyed his radio and called out to his team owner, Rick Hendrick. "Watch this," Richmond said, and he took his car deep into Pocono's turn 3. Earnhardt skirted past Richmond for the lead, but on the front stretch, Richmond slid behind Earnhardt, then passed him for the victory.

"Did you like that?" Richmond asked Hendrick.

"Yeah, that was cool," Hendrick allowed.

Tim Richmond was not the least intimidated by Earnhardt.

His true nemesis, it turned out, wasn't on four wheels. Late in 1986, Richmond began suffering from a persistent sore throat and pneumonia, and an examination brought the most dire news possible: he had contracted AIDS.

He decided to keep the diagnosis secret; this was years before Arthur Ashe and Magic Johnson would change the nation's perception of HIV and AIDS. Richmond would try to race in 1987, but the disease and his lifestyle ran him into the ground. Competitors complained about Richmond's diminished ability on the track, and gossip followed in his wake.

NASCAR tried to test him for drugs, and he refused, fearing that the test would reveal his disease. Richmond suffered in silence until he died in a West Palm Beach hospital in August 1989. With him died the last of NASCAR's naïveté. Richmond would be the last driver to live his life so publicly without regard for perception or consequences. The only secret he kept was the one that would define and ultimately destroy him.

Had Richmond lived, he might well have claimed some of the seven championship trophies that went to Earnhardt. "I think probably one of the biggest rivalries that there ever, ever, ever could have been, had Tim not gotten sick . . . would probably have been Tim Richmond and Dale Earnhardt," said Larry McReynolds, who would briefly serve as Earnhardt's crew chief before commentating for Fox Sports. "There are a lot of races that other drivers won, and there are probably several championships that drivers won, that they would not have won had Tim Richmond still been driving a race car and not have gotten sick."

THESE WERE BY far the best days Earnhardt the driver had ever known. He was rolling in money—1986 marked the first year his on-track earnings cracked seven figures, with a total take of

$1,768,880—and he had the attention, if not always the respect or admiration, of everyone in the garage and the grandstands.

Back home, Kelley and Dale Jr. went several days at a time every week without seeing their father. "Dad was always busy," Kelley once recalled on her *Fast Lane Family* podcast. "When we were kids, he wasn't home much. He'd work on the farm until dark . . . I just wish there had been more time to have a dad and do dad things."

They got used to being raised by Teresa and nannies. "That was weird, because a nanny is a stranger," Junior said in 2001. "They weren't bad, but they were strict. Nannies want to make a good impression on their employers, so they're tough on the kids."

Kelley and Junior rarely saw their mother in those early years— only twice a year at times—and Kelley looked out for her beloved younger brother in every way possible. The rules around the Earnhardt household were strict: no warnings, you screwed up and you were grounded, no TV, toys, or electronics.

"Dale was annoying when he was a kid," she recalled. "I was organized. I was the one that did what Dad said. What made me so mad is, I constantly got him out of trouble. He didn't care. He could get in trouble a zillion times and he wouldn't care. He always left cereal bowls under the bed, and I would clean up after him so he wouldn't get in trouble."

Earnhardt tried to bring his children into his world, though he didn't have the lightest touch. He showed Kelley how to ride a motorcycle, then groused when she popped an unintentional wheelie on her Yamaha 125 as he was sitting on the back. He taught Junior the techniques of sizing up a racing line by taking the boy to a go-karting track, standing in the middle of the track and forcing Junior to go around him. Earnhardt would take a step closer to the wall with every lap. During one of these teaching sessions, Junior wrecked, and Earnhardt raced over to check on his boy. "By the time he'd stopped I'd run across the track and was standing next to him," Earnhardt said. "He said, 'Where's my go-kart?' That was the only thing he was concerned about. It was pretty awesome."

Earnhardt also imparted Ralph-style wisdom, like the time he ordered eight-year-old Dale Jr. to haul a heavy five-gallon paint bucket across a garage floor. Junior didn't do it, and Earnhardt had an assistant haul the bucket, right in front of Junior, to its proper place.

"The lesson was to try," Junior said years later. "Instead of being a quitter and not even attempting it, you should have tried. That was Daddy telling me that. If I can't pick it up, drag the son of a bitch across the floor. But I didn't even go over there to try, and he'd get so disappointed in me for being such a cop-out. Daddy would've been the kind of kid who walked over there and tried to pick it up, without a word. I should've been more like that."

Junior chafed hard against the reins held by Dale, Teresa, and the others. Eventually Dale and Teresa had had enough, sending Junior to Oak Ridge Military Academy in North Carolina for his seventh- and eighth-grade years. Kelley, ever the protector, joined her undersize brother there just to keep an eye on him.

ESPN's Ed Hinton recalled driving with Earnhardt, Teresa, and Kelley to Oak Ridge Military Academy in 1987. On the parade grounds, Junior spotted his father, broke formation, and threw his arms around Earnhardt for a hug. "Dale Sr. stood there with his arms hung beside him, seeming not to know, really, how to respond," Hinton wrote later. "It was gut-wrenching."

As his children grew older, Senior didn't much care for the thought of Kelley dating. "Dad wouldn't allow me to date without him meeting people," she recalled. "I didn't have a boyfriend Dad knew about until I was eighteen or nineteen. You had to prepare yourself for what he might call out." Driver Ron Hornaday Jr. recalls riding with Earnhardt from the airport back toward the farm when Earnhardt spotted another truck. He drove right up and rammed its rear bumper, hard. Hornaday's eyes widened, but Earnhardt had an easy explanation: "That boy's dating my daughter. I don't like him."

Family intimacy was a constant challenge for Earnhardt, and he found himself tested more often. Around this time, Earnhardt's first son reentered the picture. Kerry Key, Earnhardt's son with Latane Brown Key and adopted son of Jack Key, got his driver's license, drove over to his grandmother's house, and walked out to the garage to talk to the father he hardly knew. Earnhardt brought the boy into the fold—Kerry Key now goes by the name Kerry Dale Earnhardt—and, day by day, inch by inch, built a relationship where none had existed.

Earnhardt felt far more comfortable driving two hundred miles per hour at Talladega than conversing about the mundane aspects of a kid's life. He wasn't all that different from his own father in that respect. But Dale Earnhardt got an opportunity to bridge generational gaps in a way Ralph Earnhardt never did. Although it would take Earnhardt more than a decade to realize it, Kerry's decision to reconnect with his father set in motion events that would allow him to win a victory far more important than a hundred Daytonas.

CHAPTER 7

IF THERE AIN'T A HOLE, MAKE ONE

COMING OFF THE 1986 championship, Richard Childress was experiencing something he'd never known in his life: success, and the prosperity that went along with it. He had more than enough money to do whatever he pleased, both personally and with his race team. Some people bag some success and settle; others—Childress and Earnhardt fit into this camp—start hunting for even bigger game. Childress followed the approach that had served him well as a mid-pack driver: take what you need to feed your family and reinvest what's left in your race team. There was an awful lot left.

The Earnhardt team entered 1987 knowing it was almost certainly their last year with Wrangler as a title sponsor; Wrangler's corporate parent was in the process of redirecting sponsorship dollars away from racing. A sponsorship change would upend a nascent tradition; Earnhardt's yellow-and-blue Wrangler paint scheme was an essential element of NASCAR lore in the mid-1980s—although considering the way Earnhardt drove, black and blue would have been more appropriate.

While Childress and Earnhardt enjoyed the security that came from a long-term sponsorship, they understood economic reality— and they also understood their value in the marketplace. There would be no shortage of suitors to underwrite the No. 3 Chevy, and Earnhardt had already signed an associate deal—basically, a sponsorship that puts smaller stickers on the car—with GM Good-wrench, General Motors' parts and service division.

Earnhardt had won championships before, but 1987 was the year he began to dominate, green to checkers. After falling short at Daytona, he went on to win six of the next seven races. He used his car as a wedge, a ram, a crowbar. If there was a hole, he'd shoot through it, and if there wasn't a hole, he'd make it. Earnhardt's fans loved the all-out style. Others loathed it, condemning Earnhardt and accusing NASCAR of preferential treatment. Earnhardt's close relationship with NASCAR, and in particular Bill France Jr., would raise eyebrows throughout the rest of Earnhardt's career.

"I would like to take Earnhardt out behind the barn and beat the hell out of him," said Coo Coo Marlin, a former racer and father of Sterling, who Earnhardt spun that season at Bristol. "Earnhardt is bullying his way through racing. He has set Winston Cup racing back twenty years."

When the series arrived at Martinsville, a dummy labeled "Dirty Dale" dangled from a twenty-foot pole just past turn 3, right between the American and Confederate flags. At Charlotte, disenchanted fans wore T-shirts smeared with blue and yellow paint, reading "Guess who ran into me at Charlotte Motor Speedway."

Undeterred, Earnhardt used the 1987 Charlotte All-Star race to define exactly how far he would go to win a race. If the difference between victory and failure meant knocking the living crap out of the next guy, so be it.

NASCAR's All-Star events are a bit different from other sports' by design. In football, baseball, basketball, and the like, you only get to see stars from more than two teams sharing the field or the court once a year. But every weekend in NASCAR is the equivalent of an All-Star event. So what do you see at an actual NASCAR All-Star race? The racing equivalent of zero-defense. With no points on the line and no real reward for finishing second, drivers go all out, bringing home—as the old saying goes—either the checkered flag or the steering wheel.

The All-Star race freed Earnhardt to unleash the last bits of bastard in himself. If his rival drivers failed to catch him, hell, it was their fault for not trying hard enough.

Coming into the 1987 race, Earnhardt's chief rival was a teddy bear of a driver named Bill Elliott. Immensely talented and immensely popular, Elliott was Earnhardt's polar opposite—a genuinely nice guy in a garage full of bastards, his gentle southern accent honey to Earnhardt's whiskey growl. Elliott was the kind of boy a young lady brought home to meet her parents; Earnhardt was the kind who would be idling his motor beneath the streetlight, waiting for her to sneak out and climb down the trellis. Elliott drove Fords; Earnhardt was a Chevrolet man. The two happened to be 1-2 in points coming into the early-season break. The stage was set for a brawl between good and, well, not-so-good.

At that time, the All-Star race was divided into three segments, with pit stops between: a 75-lap run, a 50-lap run, and a final 10-lap shootout in which every driver within sight of the lead would get up on the wheel and do all he could to bring home the checkered flag. Second place, as the saying goes, is the first loser.

For the first 125 laps, Elliott, driving a No. 9 Coors Ford, was in total control, leading 121 of them. Earnhardt stalked him all the way, close but unable to narrow the gap. The final 10-lap shootout segment began with Elliott and Geoff Bodine, driving the No. 5 Hendrick Motorsports Chevrolet, knocking sides; the pace car had been slow to exit the track, causing Elliott to pull up slightly. He and Bodine collided, and Bodine got the worst of it, spinning out and losing his own chance for victory.

In the ensuing mess, Earnhardt took the lead and spent the next few laps using pure driving skill to hold off Elliott, who had a stronger car courtesy of the engine-building wizardry of his brother Ernie.

Meanwhile, Bodine was on the hunt. "When I pitted, I pushed my radio button and asked who ran into me," Bodine said. "Rick Hendrick came on the radio and said, 'Earnhardt.' I was seeing blue and yellow. I was on a mission."

With eight laps remaining, Elliott was up on Earnhardt, and a little tap sent Earnhardt sliding toward the infield . . . a little tap that resulted in one of the most famous moments in NASCAR history.

Earnhardt turned nearly sideways and shot through the grass. This would be the point where any other driver would spin out, or skid to a stop, or stomp hard on the brakes, or possibly even flip. Earnhardt, of course, was not like any other driver.

He kept his foot on the gas and kept pace with Elliott. Earnhardt wrenched his car back up from the grass onto the track, remaining ahead of Elliott the whole time. It's possible that someone else could have pulled off such a maneuver without pinwheeling, but legends accrue legendary feats. Here began the tale of "The Pass in the Grass." Even though Earnhardt didn't technically pass Elliott, it was far too good a label not to stick.

From Elliott's perspective, Earnhardt's astonishing feat was merely a case of recovering from his own mistake. "I was already up to his left-rear wheel when he turned left to try to cut me off," Elliott would say years later. "Instead, it turned him into the grass. I tried to give him the benefit of the doubt, but from then on, he was ticked off because it looked like I was trying to spin him, which I wasn't."

Two laps later, the drivers were running parallel to one another. "When we came off turn 2, he went to the inside and let me go to the outside and I knew what was going to happen when I got to turn 3," Elliott recalled. "I tried to stay square with him instead of giving him the opportunity to get into my left rear. I knew he was going to spin me when I got to turn 3. He didn't pull over and let you by for any good reason."

Earnhardt ran Elliott up high into the wall, and Elliott blew a tire, effectively ending his shot at a win. Earnhardt would contend that he never hit Elliott, but Awesome Bill had a much less charitable view of the action. Both Elliott and Bodine were livid, each ramming Earnhardt's car after the race during cool-down laps. Since Earnhardt traded paint on the track as easily as he shook hands off it, the other drivers' maneuvers didn't exactly rattle him. Elliott even tried to block Earnhardt's entrance to pit road, but Earnhardt slid around him.

During the on-track melee, Hendrick told Bodine it was actually Elliott, not Earnhardt, who'd spun him, but at this point that didn't matter. Bodine tried to convince NASCAR that he was just trying to congratulate Earnhardt, but NASCAR was having none of it.

Meanwhile, all hell was breaking loose on pit road. Elliott screamed to Winston Cup director Dick Beaty that Earnhardt had just stolen $200,000 from his race team. "You better get him calmed down before next week," Bill France Jr. told Beaty as the men met in the NASCAR hauler after the race.

Elliott's brother Ernie stormed up to Childress, calling Earnhardt's move "chickenshit." Childress replied that if Ernie didn't want his face rearranged, he'd better get the hell out of the 3's pit box. (Childress wasn't blowing smoke; a quarter-century later, in his sixties, he headlocked and punched Kyle Busch after growing enraged at how Busch was racing his drivers.)

Elliott rushed to the press box, looking to present his case. "I'm sick and tired of it," he said. "If it takes that type of driving to be the Winston Cup champion, I don't want to be the champion.

"If a man has to run over you to beat you, it's time for this stuff to stop," Elliott continued, his demeanor a relic from a more gentlemanly era. "What he did wasn't right. When a man pulls over and lets you by and then tries to run you into the wall, I'd say that was done deliberately."

"This whole deal is between me and Bill, and it has nothing to do with our teams," Earnhardt said. "We knocked each other around, but it's all over now as far as I am concerned. But if Bill still wants to do something about it, then I'll stand flat-footed with him any day."

"He discredits his sponsor and himself," Elliott fumed. "I have nothing to say to him. If that is the way he wants to win races, then I hope he wins a thousand of them. He'll be doing it all on Saturday nights"—back in the minor leagues, in other words.

NASCAR recognized an opportunity for some good publicity and fined both drivers $2,500, a sum that may or may not have ever been collected. NASCAR also stoked the carnival atmosphere by overnighting a swatch of denim and a crushed Coors beer can to members of the media. Wrangler was Earnhardt's sponsor; Coors was Elliott's.

Earnhardt and Bodine kept up with their end of the feud, resulting in both men being summoned to Daytona Beach. "Dale and I both got our butts chewed out," Bodine said. "Bill France said if we didn't do it his way, he would find a way to make us do it his way. That stopped Dale from doing all of that bumping for quite a while. It slowed him down and kept peace on the track for a couple of years. Then it started again. That was just his style— bump-and-run."

"We can't all be good guys," Earnhardt would say later. "Some of us have to wear black hats . . . it's what makes the world go around."

Earnhardt simply could not stand Bodine. The hatred ran so deep that Earnhardt used a Bodine standup as a bow-hunting target. Junior used to play with a remote-controlled car decorated like Bodine's No. 5 Levi Garrett Chevy, and one time he made the mistake of driving that car too close to his father . . . who happened to be doing some target practice with a pistol. Earnhardt began firing away at the little toy as Junior tried to run it as fast as possible to safety. Earnhardt never did hit the car, and Junior quickly repainted it.

The Pass in the Grass would become one of NASCAR's signature memories, and ranks high anytime a "greatest moments in NASCAR history" list pops up. The incident had infuriated more than just Earnhardt's fellow drivers. Ten days after the race, NASCAR's offices in Daytona Beach received a letter, printed on a dot-matrix printer, with no return address. The postmark was Elmira, New York, and the letter was addressed to NASCAR President Bill France Jr. Its grasp of grammar was questionable, its intent unmistakable:

Dear Mr. France:

When NASCAR comes north to Poccono, Watkins Glen, and Dover I suggest you leave Dale Ernhart home. If he comes to race I advise him to 1) have some bodyguards, or 2) wear a bulletproof vest. I will be at one track, probably all three with my 30.06. When I get a clear shot. . . .

You fucking people won't do anything about his dirty driving, so someone else will have to. He has pushed his way around NASCAR tracks for too long. If that fucking son of a bitch wants to drive like that, then let him drive a super modified on the dirt tracks. Then he would get pushed back, probably right off the track and into the field where he belongs. You keep talking about the integrity of the sport, and let him get away with all his shit.

It's too bad Elliot didn't take him out. You assholes had better get your shit together or you're going to be short one driver. Tell Dale to watch his ass WHEREEVER he goes.

NASCAR sent the letter to the FBI, which alerted its regional offices in Buffalo, Philadelphia, and Charlotte. "In view of threat, suspect should be considered armed and dangerous," the FBI's Jacksonville office wrote. While the FBI could identify the make and model of printer, that was all; there were no usable fingerprints on either the envelope or the letter itself.

Agents blanketed the track at Dover, the next race, keeping an eye on the stands, the infield, and Earnhardt himself. Earnhardt would go on to finish fourth, and the FBI interviewed him while at the track. From the FBI's notes:

"Dale Earnhardt related that if the letter writer were to attempt to carry out such a threat, Earnhardt would be more concerned about the tracks at Pocono and Watkins Glen, due to the layout of the two tracks that allows infield fans closer to the track. He advised this is particularly true at Watkins Glen where fans are able to sit in the grass among trees in the infield close to the track."

It wasn't a minor concern. Watkins Glen is only a half hour's drive from Elmira, where the letter originated. The .30-06 rifle was a military design specifically engineered for long-range sniping. Thankfully, both races held at Pocono that summer passed without incident. By July 30 the Philadelphia FBI office was ready to call it a day, reporting, "Inasmuch as all logical investigation has been conducted at Philadelphia; and the fact that both NASCAR races at Pocono Raceway in which Earnhardt was scheduled to appear have transpired without incident, no further investigation is being conducted."

The Watkins Glen race on August 10 also proceeded with no significant events outside the race, and the matter was closed quietly.

AFTER HIS VICTORY at Richmond in August, his eleventh win of the season, Earnhardt held a lead of 608 points over Elliott—a lead so vast that he could have skipped the next three races, or finished dead last in every one of the season's remaining seven, and still won the championship. Earnhardt did no such thing. He hammered ahead with three second-place finishes in the next five races and clinched the 1987 championship at Rockingham with two races to spare.

It was Earnhardt's greatest season ever, and one of the greatest in the sport's history. He was the first driver in the modern era to win four races in a row, and his show-no-mercy approach to driving had earned him the nickname "The Intimidator." Earnhardt and the No. 3 team were officially unstoppable. From here on it was—to paraphrase Neil Young—out of the blue-and-yellow and into the black.

Two championships in a row, both won in dominating fashion—this was the stuff of sponsors' dreams, nationwide exposure for all the right reasons. But corporate merger politics far above the racetrack level forced Wrangler off the car by removing those sponsorship dollars. GM and its Goodwrench parts division stepped into the breach. They would align with Earnhardt and Childress to form, hands down, the most popular sponsor-driver partnership in history. And it all began with a simple color change.

NASCAR has a host of strange traditions and superstitions: no peanut shells or $50 bills anywhere near the track; nobody runs the number 13. But the prohibition against black cars was motivated less by superstition than by the persistent assumption that the car would fade visually into the black asphalt around it.

Earnhardt was hardly the type to get lost against any background. Black was starting to show up in more and more uniform color schemes, inspired in part by Darth Vader and the Oakland Raiders' success in the mid-1980s wearing silver and black. Black was the bad guy. Black was the outlaw. Black was perfect for the man NASCAR fans loved to hate. In 1988, Dale Earnhardt claimed the color black as his own.

"When he rolled that car onto the track at Daytona for the Busch Clash in '88, people gasped," Wheeler said. "Now he didn't just drive mean, he *looked* mean."

The change provided Earnhardt with an opportunity to kick his off-track merchandising efforts into a higher gear. He'd already enjoyed considerable souvenir revenue, but with the arrival of the black 3, Earnhardt was about to become the centerpiece of one of the most popular sports branding efforts of all time. He had one person to thank: the quiet woman by his side, the woman who would become the most divisive figure in NASCAR history.

Most drivers' wives assumed a customary role: smile big, pop out a couple kids, don't raise a stink when Miss Winston lays one on your husband in Victory Lane, and finally slide off to a life of alimony and privilege when your man decides to trade in on a younger model.

Teresa had no patience for any of that. She maintained a regal image on the track, always dressing better than anyone there—granted, not a high bar to clear—and ensuring that she looked camera-ready at all times, primping and prepping before every appearance. She rode with Dale in the backs of prerace pickup trucks and posed with him in Victory Lane, and it wasn't long before other NASCAR wives followed her lead.

She recognized what a priceless brand her husband had become, and in the mid-1980s she began coordinating his business interests and fine-tuning his image into the tightly focused Intimidator package fans know today.

"What are you afraid of?" Waltrip would ask Earnhardt many years later in an interview.

"Oh, my wife," Earnhardt replied, laughing before elaborating. "I'm not really afraid of her. I just don't want to disappoint her."

Fiercely reclusive, even more fiercely protective of Dale Earn-hardt's name, Teresa inspired opinions ranging from admiration to frustration. There are only a few facts all can agree on when it comes to Teresa Earnhardt: she turned Dale Earnhardt into an international brand, she has had an immense and perpetual burden to bear, and damn, did Dale Earnhardt love her.

"She felt like she needed to be the bad guy to protect him," said Andy Petree, one of Earnhardt's former crew chiefs. "She wanted to make sure he was taken care of. She was such a great balance for him."

Teresa began by consolidating all of Earnhardt's sponsorship and endorsement contracts, then picking the most favorable ele-ments of each to create a bulletproof boilerplate deal. Any sponsors who didn't like the terms were welcome to pursue any of the other drivers, none of whom could equal Earnhardt's throw-weight in the marketplace. Earnhardt backed her play at every turn, staring down anyone who would question the contractual demands.

"Being the Intimidator, he would put people in situations, and they would not know if he was joking or not, just to see if they could take it," Teresa once said. "Dale could look at someone, and just by looking at them, make them doubt themselves."

"Earnhardt was as intimidating in a room as he was on the race-track," recalls Brian Z. France, grandson of Bill France and now NASCAR CEO. "He was a master at making you feel off balance."

"When fans meet me in person, they are surprised I'm not ten feet tall and bulletproof," Earnhardt used to joke. "Well, I've got bad news for everybody out there. I'm not. I'm about nine-foot-six."

Teresa also copyrighted all things Earnhardt, including his name, his signature, the Intimidator nickname, and the stylized 3 that adorned his car. Contrary to the perception of NASCAR as an indiscriminate branding entity, Teresa exercised some control over the products that bore Earnhardt's name or image, outlawing, for instance, officially licensed "Intimidator" bikinis or halter tops.

Teresa laid down several rules for marketing the Intimidator: don't sell Dale everywhere; strive to keep the demand greater than the supply; always have the ability to say no; and say no often. Her mania for control paid off. Earnhardt often joked that when he met Teresa, he owed the bank money, and by the time she'd done her work, the bank owed *him*.

Recognizing both the collectible nature of NASCAR and the intense brand loyalty of its fans, Teresa and Dale began investing in the souvenir market. After first granting Sports Image Inc. the rights to handle all Intimidator merchandise, they bought the entire company for $6 million in 1995, then flipped it to Action Performance for $30 million, while still retaining rights to the Intimidator brand. Along with future Dale Earnhardt Inc. president Don Hawk, Teresa and Dale laid the groundwork for a commercial empire in which Earnhardt's image and market penetration rivaled the most popular athletes of the era—Michael Jordan and Tiger Woods.

"It really is awesome for me sometimes when I look at the TV and there's my son in a commercial," Martha Earnhardt once said. "Everywhere you look, there he is. I go into a grocery store and there he is on a cereal box. It's hard to comprehend sometimes how far he really has come."

THE SHIFTING FOCUS from racing to business didn't fit everyone's style. The increasingly corporate environment of Richard Childress Racing finally got to master builder Lou LaRosa, who'd been with Earnhardt since his first days on a Cup team.

"In '88 it had changed from being a big family to a business, and it was bullshit," LaRosa said. "Now if you tried to see Richard

Childress in his office, you were told, 'You can't go in that office. He's busy.' That's bullshit. If I'm the chief engine builder or the crew chief, I should be able to see him at any time."

Racing's stars were outgrowing the bounds of the sport. Earnhardt was on his way to becoming an icon. Childress was diversifying his interests into everything from medical foundations to vineyards. The days of pranks around the table with the crew were long gone, and the days of men like LaRosa—men whose first and only goal was racing—were numbered.

CHAPTER 8

I DON'T LOOK LIKE NO ELEVEN-MILLIONAIRE

WHILE THEIR DAD was off winning championships, Junior and Kelley were working their way through school, first at Oak Ridge and, later, at Mooresville High School. Junior headed off to trade school at Mitchell Community College, while Kelley enrolled at the University of North Carolina at Wilmington. By completing ninth grade, Junior had already outdistanced his father and grandfather, but he kept at it, posting an undistinguished—but complete—high school career.

"In high school, I was far from Mr. Popular," said the guy who would go on to win more than ten straight NASCAR Most Popular Driver awards. "I wasn't one of the jocks. I wasn't one of the preppy kids. I fell right in the middle and got lost."

Senior had always preached the value of an education, and often told the press that his biggest regret was not finishing high school. But when Kelley's prom came around in the late 1980s, her father wasn't there to terrify her date with a threat disguised as a good-bye. When Dale Jr. walked across the stage to pick up his diploma in the early 1990s, Earnhardt was nowhere to be seen. There was always another race to run. Families understood that, right?

Five days before Christmas 1988, the Earnhardt family grew by one, as Dale and Teresa welcomed the birth of their first child, daughter Taylor Nicole. Dale now had children ranging in age from infancy to nineteen. Life at home was growing exponentially more complicated.

On the track, the 1989 season was a near-miss. Earnhardt lost the race for the championship to Rusty Wallace on the season's final day at Atlanta, winning the race but unable to close the points gap. Driver Grant Adcox died during the race, a victim of massive head and chest injuries from a head-on collision with the wall. Adcox was the fifth Cup-level driver to die in the 1980s. Death continued to stalk NASCAR as the 1990s dawned. And it wasn't just drivers at risk.

One year almost to the day after Adcox died, race leader Bill Elliott came in for his final pit stop at the Atlanta race running at nearly full throttle, as drivers had been doing for most of racing's history. Pit road was an extension of the track. When you needed tires, fuel, or other on-the-fly adjustments, you ripped down pit lane as fast as you could, looking for a guy standing in the middle of pit road holding up your number. Then you hauled ass out of there even faster. The sheer insanity of dozens of unprotected crew members frenetically rushing around moving race cars qualified as "tradition."

Elliott's crew leaped over the wall and began the crazy ballet of jacking, refilling, and adjusting the car. Ricky Rudd was trying to pull into his own space right behind Elliott, but he spun out, plowing backward into Elliott's car and the three crewmen working there. Two of the crewmen suffered only minor injuries, but Mike Rich, who had been changing the right rear tire, was crushed by Rudd's car and pinned beneath it. Rich was airlifted to Georgia Baptist Hospital, asking about Elliott's car during the ride. He had sustained what a trauma surgeon deemed an "unsurvivable injury," and died of a heart attack while in surgery.

Rich's death illuminated the utter recklessness of 3,500-pound cars flying at top speed near men carrying 65-pound tires and

70-pound fuel cells. "Seldom is a NASCAR race completed without at least one serious incident on pit road," veteran motorsports journalist Al Pearce wrote.

NASCAR implemented two important changes in response. Pit crews would no longer stand in the middle of pit road holding signs; now a sign with the driver's number would dangle over pit road. NASCAR also mandated pit road speeds well below those of actual race speeds. It wasn't the first time tragedy would force NASCAR to take belated action in the name of safety, nor would it be the last.

"Part of the popularity of motorsports is that the drivers are risking their lives," said Dale Jarrett. "You knew that, you lived in the moment, and you never looked past it, knowing it could all be taken away at any time."

THE 1990 DAYTONA 500 marked many non-NASCAR fans' only exposure to NASCAR—it was one of the set pieces for the Tom Cruise movie *Days of Thunder*. The movie's producers actually entered two cars in the Daytona field with NASCAR's blessing. NASCAR officials announced at the prerace driver's meeting that the cars would take a few laps to get some needed shots, then pull off into the garage and park for the day. Earnhardt, seething at the idea that a Hollywood production would interfere with his racing, stood up.

"If one of those motherfuckers gets in my way," he said, "I'm wrecking them." It's not surprising, then, that Earnhardt's car isn't anywhere near Tom Cruise's in the movie's version of Daytona.

Hollywood manufactures happy endings. Earnhardt wouldn't have one on this day. He absolutely owned the race once the Hollywood types left the track, leading 155 of 200 laps. With twenty laps remaining, Earnhardt had a half-lap lead. Everything seemed lined up for him to win the Daytona 500 at last, but the racing gods once again had it in for him.

On the second turn of the race's final lap, Earnhardt hit a scrap of metal—it would turn out to be a bell housing, a part of somebody's transmission—and bang, his right rear tire was gone. He rode it as long as he could, and then skidded to a stop less than a mile from the finish line. Virtual unknown Derrike Cope slid by Earnhardt to take the victory, and television cameras caught little Taylor sobbing as Teresa hung her head.

"Not in my wildest dreams did I think I could come here and win this race," Cope said, and the rest of NASCAR agreed.

"Win" the race? Earnhardt sat in his car for more than a minute after Cope's victory, composing himself. "Derrike won the race," he later seethed, "but I outran everyone all day. He didn't beat us. He lucked into it."

"I caught a lot of flak for that win," Cope said many years later. "People said I was a fluke and didn't deserve to win it. I felt bad for Dale, truly. But he and I talked after the fact and said, 'Hey, it wasn't the Daytona 499.' "

Earnhardt would get his revenge on Cope and the rest of the field. He began by hanging the shredded tire on the wall of the Childress Racing shop in Welcome, an ever-present reminder not to take anything for granted. He followed that with nine victories across the season's twenty-nine races. By the end of the year, he was running the show, with only one last competitor to outdistance—Mark Martin.

If you saw Martin outside his fire suit, you'd think "jockey," not "race car driver." Short of stature, elfin in appearance, genial in disposition, with a buzz-saw whine of an Arkansas accent, Martin seemed to have no business banging fenders with the burly, rawboned types that dominated NASCAR tracks in the 1980s and '90s. Martin embodied the old line of how it's not the size of the dog in the fight, it's the size of the fight in the dog. Often dubbed "the racer's racer," Martin earned the respect of other drivers, who appreciated someone who could pass them without driving *through* them.

Martin began driving in NASCAR's Cup series in 1981, and by 1990 he was firmly ensconced with car owner Jack Roush of what would become Roush Fenway Racing. Martin had given up many of the bad habits that had dogged him through the 1980s; he had renounced alcohol altogether and pursued a rugged fitness regimen that he would follow the rest of his career. Driving the No. 6 Folgers Coffee Ford, he was at the peak of his abilities, and about to go head-to-head with Earnhardt for the 1990 points lead.

It was almost a morality play. Martin remains one of NASCAR's all-time great good guys. The Intimidator couldn't resist the temptation to dent the smaller man's halo. In the season's penultimate race at Phoenix, Earnhardt and Martin were in the media center for a promotional champion-to-be press conference. As the press conference began, Earnhardt leaned into the microphone and challenged Martin to a little throwdown: head to Atlanta, race for fifty laps, do a shot of whiskey, race another fifty laps, do another shot, and so on, with the championship going to the last man standing.

The jab hit home. Aside from the usual worries of whether he'd ever be in position to challenge for a championship again—a fear Earnhardt could smell a mile away—Martin was the son of an alcoholic. Martin had enjoyed the hard-drinking life of NASCAR in the 1980s, a world where, as Darrell Waltrip often said, they might forget the toolbox, but they'd never forget the beer cooler. Martin wouldn't drink before or during races, but he'd crack open a beer as soon as he'd gotten out of the car, and follow that up with several more at the closest bar. Some people can handle alcohol— even significant amounts—without drastic negative effects. Mark Martin was not one of them.

"Any negative that flowed from Mark's personality, either in business matters or otherwise, flowed from his drinking," Roush once told ESPN's David Newton. "When he was sober, in all ways he was a fair, even-mannered and reasonable person to deal with. Mark certainly wasn't the Mark he wanted to be and certainly wasn't the Mark I wanted to be around when he drank to excess."

Roush had hired Martin on the condition that he stop drinking. Martin redirected the energy he'd spent drinking into a fierce dedication to fitness, highly unusual for drivers of the time. The result was a revitalized man.

Earnhardt was likely aware of Martin's drinking problem. There are few secrets in the garage. To use Martin's weakness as the impetus for a joking challenge—well, it wasn't very sporting. But effective? Probably.

Earnhardt thoroughly dominated the Phoenix race, leading 262 of 312 laps, winning easily, and snagging the points lead with just one race to go. Martin would now be racing from behind.

Earnhardt entered the season's final race having officially amassed more money than anyone in the history of NASCAR. In 1990 he'd won the International Race of Champions (IROC), the Winston, and nine points-paying races, giving him $1.5 million for the year and career earnings of more than $11 million. He loved his money, but he did his damnedest to keep it from softening him.

"You should see me at home on the farm," Earnhardt said in the days before the finale. "I guarantee you I don't look like no eleven-millionaire. I got a '72 dump truck, rusty ol' claptrap thing, I drive it, setting way up there with a big old gearshift sticking up by my ear. I come tearing around a turn over a hill, it's blowing smoke, I'm sideways, sticks and limbs are hanging out the side and branches are flying out the back, and you better get out of the way because that'll be me, and I don't back off for no one."

Once again, Earnhardt had run the table of public opinion. His fans almost surely weren't eleven-millionaires, but they drove rusty trucks and they liked to believe they didn't back off for no one either. Earnhardt was as far removed from his daddy's tax bracket as Daytona was from New Zealand, but Earnhardt still seemed like the son of a grinding auto man. That went a long way in the eyes of workingmen everywhere.

Earnhardt didn't just talk a good everyman game, he lived it. He worked his farm early, and he would be in the office by 7:00 a.m., calling the morning hours "absolutely the most important hours of the day." He'd often show up even earlier, signing autographs for hours and hours. His favorite line was "Gotta go," as in, keep moving, keep going, never ever ever stop. Teresa had him eating better—grilled chicken and salad rather than steak and potatoes for every meal—but his drive remained relentless.

"He could be bush hogging in the afternoon, then grab a shower, put on a tuxedo, and totally win over the room," Fox Sports reporter Matt Yocum said. "He had his eye on the ball in so many different areas."

Coming into the 1990 season finale in Atlanta, Earnhardt owned the technological and psychological high ground. He'd won two of the last three races at the track; Martin had only a fifth-place finish and two finishes in the thirties over that same period. Moreover, Martin had spent the week testing half a dozen Fords, finally borrowing one from Davey Allison, repainting it burgundy, and entering it in the race. Throughout the week Martin's garage had attracted rivals from different teams, all of them pulling for Martin to deliver Ford its first manufacturer's championship since 1969.

Earnhardt was amused. "They've got a lot of irons in the fire, don't they?" he said one afternoon, looking over at the chaos in Martin's corner of the garage. "It seems pretty late in the season to me to be engineering. Sure, we've noticed all the Ford people up there, but it doesn't bother us."

Earnhardt never stopped with the mind games. He'd poke and jab during the meals the teams shared in the garage. During one practice session, he kicked back and grabbed a nap in full view of the Ford team. "I looked at him sleeping there," said Robin Pemberton, then Martin's crew chief, "and I thought to myself, *we're screwed.*"

The 3 team packed up a day early, heading back to North Carolina on Wednesday night. Earnhardt added, loud enough for everyone in the garage to hear, that he would be going to Alabama to hunt deer. Whether he really hunted deer hardly mattered; the psychological damage was done. "We knew the Ford people would notice," Earnhardt said, "and that by leaving after only one day we would drive them crazy."

Martin's team managed to coax enough speed out of the car to post practice times second only to Earnhardt's. In the actual race Martin could never truly get going. His team wrestled with different setups on the unfamiliar Ford throughout the course of the race. The car stalled twice on pit road, and Martin could never mount enough speed to challenge Earnhardt or the leaders. Earnhardt was running so well that Martin needed to win the race to beat him, and that wasn't going to happen. Martin would finish sixth, losing the championship by 26 points.

For Martin, it was the first of many painful second-place finishes. His timeless driving style kept him competitive for decades, but he had the dubious honor of finishing second in championship standings to Dale Earnhardt (twice), Jimmie Johnson, Jeff Gordon, and Tony Stewart. He's one of the few drivers to have raced competitively against both the legendary Richard Petty and NASCAR newcomer Kyle Larson, who was born just weeks before Petty's final race.

Earnhardt took home another million dollars for the Cup championship, plus $300,000 in other bonuses, increasing his year's earnings to over $3 million. With a fourth title capping a three-year stretch in which Earnhardt had racked up eighteen wins, Richard Petty's remarkable record of seven championships didn't seem quite so far away. Could Earnhardt one day run down that mark, the most cherished in NASCAR?

"Three more is a long way off, way out there," Earnhardt said diplomatically. "I feel at age thirty-eight I've got ten more years of competitive driving left, so I might get that many. But even if I do, Richard Petty is way away from anything I could be. He's The King, and it'd make me proud to do something only he has done." Earnhardt had come a long way from the rookie who declared that Petty had little to teach him . . . at the very least, he'd learned to hide his true motivations a little better.

AROUND THE END of the twentieth century, golf courses tried to hold off the charge of Tiger Woods by "Tiger-proofing" their courses: lengthening the holes, tightening the fairways, and generally trying to make life a little more difficult for the world's best golfer.

NASCAR didn't bother to try to "Dale-proof" anything. No matter what obstacles stood in his way, Earnhardt would go over, around, or through them. Case in point: the 1991 Busch Clash at Daytona, the preseason race that now featured a new "inverted field" format. The driver who won the first ten-lap segment would start at the back of the fourteen-car field for the second, and vice versa. The idea, of course, was to ratchet up the difficulty for the best cars.

Earnhardt wouldn't have cared if they'd made him start the race on the beach six miles away. He won the first segment, then took the lead in the second segment in just over a single lap. Nobody could stop him.

The Daytona 500 again eluded Earnhardt; this time it was Ernie Irvan who managed to snag the sport's greatest prize. Earnhardt, Shelmerdine, Childress, and the rest of the 3 team won the very next race at Richmond, then spent the rest of the season reminding everyone that there was no answer—none at all—for the Man in Black. Earnhardt took over the points lead after Talladega in the first week of May, and wouldn't surrender it the rest of the year. "If it was up for a vote, Dale would probably vote to race at Talladega every week," Childress said. "He and the track are a perfectly matched pair."

November 17, 1991, marked one of the easiest days of Earnhardt's professional life. He needed only to start the Hardees 500 at Atlanta Motor Speedway to clinch the championship. He fired his engine, and that was that. As Earnhardt came around to the green flag, Chocolate Myers, Richard Childress, and the rest of the Flying Aces stood in Earnhardt's pit, holding the Winston Cup trophy high. When the green flag flew to start the race and officially grant Earnhardt the 1991 championship, the team held up all five fingers.

Richard Petty's once-unthinkable mark of seven career championships had just come a little closer. Earnhardt had won four of the last six championships, and placed second and third in the seasons he'd fallen short. The only thing that would possibly stop him was a rival of his caliber, and there weren't any of those on the track.

Yet.

CHAPTER 9

WONDER BOY

NASCAR DRIVERS GENERALLY find their way to the big time running on either concrete, asphalt, or dirt. Leave it to Jeff Gordon to find another route: via water.

By the time he was twelve years old, Gordon was already a weary veteran of the racing scene. He'd gotten his first BMX bike at age four. At five he was racing quarter-midgets, tiny cars that can hit thirty miles per hour. Within a year, he'd won thirty-five main events in and around his Vallejo, California, home, and six years after that, his win total was up over two hundred. He owned anyone and everyone who raced against him, so he tried his hand at water skiing, and aced that too.

The lure of driving—not just being pulled—drew him back. Gordon fell in love with 700-horsepower sprint cars. Unfortunately, nobody was running the cars in California, so Gordon and his stepfather, John Bickford, drove across the country, stopping in places like Indiana and Florida, anywhere they could get a race and maybe, just maybe, draw a sponsor's eye.

The early 1980s were a nerve-fraying time for Gordon and his family, even as Earnhardt was starting to pile up championships. Gordon had more than enough talent to win at any level; he knew it, and so did everyone who saw him behind a wheel. He needed money, however, and lots of it. The family went all in on Jeff's career, moving to Pittsboro, Indiana, a town about twenty miles up Interstate 74 from Indianapolis Motor Speedway. Any driver who wanted to create a name for himself behind the wheel of a sprint car needed to pass through the cauldron of central Indiana. (As Gordon was starting to carve out his own legend, a kid by the name of Tony Stewart was winning go-kart races less than an hour away in Columbus, Indiana.)

Every Memorial Day, Gordon would wait and watch for IndyCar legends like A. J. Foyt and Al Unser during the week-long run-up to the Indy 500. He imagined a day when he'd be running alongside them, but his dreams collided with financial reality. He and Bickford couldn't run a race team and make ends meet in a way that made any financial sense. Open-wheel racing was too competitive, too expensive.

NASCAR, though . . . NASCAR might just work. Late in the 1990 season, Gordon connected with future crew chief Ray Evernham, and the two formed a partnership driving in the second-tier Busch (later Nationwide, now Xfinity) Series. In his very first NASCAR race—the 1990 AC Delco 200 at Rockingham, driving the No. 67 Outback Steakhouse Pontiac—Gordon started on the outside of the front row courtesy of a spectacular qualifying time. An early wreck took him out and he finished thirty-ninth, for which he received exactly $400. (The second-place finisher at that race: Dale Earnhardt.)

Two years later, Gordon made his Cup debut in one of the most significant races in NASCAR history: the 1992 season finale at Atlanta. Though it bore the farcical name of the Hooters 500, the race represented the confluence of NASCAR's past and future.

The Hooters 500 marked the final race for legend Richard Petty, who took a long prerace walk through the garage handing out money clips to each of the forty competing drivers. The race would also feature one of the sport's most tightly fought championship battles, with Bill Elliott racing against Davey Allison—the latest scion of the Alabama Gang—and Alan Kulwicki, the last of the great one-car owner-operators. The race also featured luminaries such as Earnhardt, Darrell Waltrip, Terry Labonte, Rusty Wallace, Harry Gant, and Mark Martin.

The twenty-one-year-old Gordon, sporting a dead-caterpillar mustache, strode into this pantheon. This would mark his first race in a Chevy, his first race in the No. 24 for Hendrick Motorsports.

"I pretty much felt out of place and not real comfortable," Gordon said. "I was looking around, looking at these great drivers and celebrities, wondering what I was doing there." Gordon's crew was as untested as he was; during one pit stop, someone left a roll of duct tape on Gordon's hood; the tape flew off and hit Allison's car.

Petty's final race ended ugly; he wrecked out on lap 94, his car ending up in flaming shards. "I went out in a blaze of glory, but it wasn't what I had in mind," Petty said. "Make that just a blaze. There wasn't any glory." Petty's crew would patch together the car for one final ceremonial lap to conclude his career.

Gordon also wrecked out early, finishing thirty-first. The battle for the championship would come down to Kulwicki and Elliott, with the former winning based on some on-track gambling and on-the-fly math. Kulwicki led exactly one more lap than Elliott, 103 laps to 102, and that provided enough points to give Kulwicki the championship even though Elliott won the race.

More than twenty years later, Kulwicki's name has faded in the memory of NASCAR fans. Elliott's current contribution to the sport is his son Chase, who took over Gordon's No. 24 in 2016. Gordon continued to win races right up to his final season of 2015, and the experiences he would have battling Earnhardt for nearly a decade after that Hooters 500 would help shape him into a championship driver. The 1992 Hooters 500 marked the first and last time anyone would ever take Jeff Gordon for granted.

A few weeks after the Hooters 500, Kulwicki sat up at the dais at the 1992 NASCAR awards ceremony in New York City, reveling in the championship he'd just swiped from the hands of Elliott. Earnhardt sat in the audience brooding. He had finished twelfth overall in 1992, his lowest final position in a decade. Something had to change, and fast.

Earnhardt's team spent the entire offseason preparing a full-scale marketing campaign. The concept of branding was still in its infancy, but "Black Is Back" would remind everyone just who the top dog in the room was. Black would be back, but Shelmerdine wouldn't. The stresses of a high-profile crew chief on NASCAR's most prominent team had become too much, and he finally called it quits after winning four championships with Earnhardt and Childress.

"There's always so much going on that's in the back of your head all of the time that you don't really have time off for recreation, or to spend with your family like you should," he lamented. "Friends kind of go by the wayside because you don't pay enough attention to them." Childress would replace Shelmerdine with Andy Petree, and the 3 rolled on.

At the start of the 1993 season, Earnhardt found himself in unfamiliar territory: outshone by the kid with the eyebrow-pencil mustache. Jeff Gordon had won one of the Daytona 500 qualifying races, becoming the youngest driver ever to do so.

"His age doesn't really have anything to do with it," Earnhardt would say later that year. "That Gordon boy is a very good driver. I have no problem racing with him anywhere on any track. He's probably going to win a lot of races and some championships."

Gordon had won the first of those races to set the starting positions of the 1993 Daytona 500 field. Earnhardt had taken the other—the first verse of an epic rivalry that would last the rest of the decade. This marked the first Daytona since Petty's retirement, and the King himself would wave the green flag to start the race.

Gordon led the initial lap of his first Daytona 500—another impressive achievement and a sign that new days were upon NASCAR.

The old guard wasn't done just yet, though. Earnhardt, as usual, ran up front, and his 0-for-Daytona streak looked like it might end as realistic challengers for the title began dropping out. Bill Elliott surrendered after his car overheated on lap 99. Ernie Irvan hit the wall in turn 2. Earnhardt bumped IndyCar legend Al Unser Jr., driving in his only NASCAR start, rumbling him into Kyle Petty. Michael Waltrip sent Rusty Wallace rolling through the grass. Inside of thirty laps, the race was setting up perfectly for Earnhardt. He still had challengers, but he had the strongest car in the field in the one race he'd wanted so badly for his whole career.

Only one man stood in his way: Dale Jarrett. The son of legendary driver (and Ralph Earnhardt rival) Ned Jarrett, who happened to be calling the race, Jarrett was at the leading edge of what would become a Hall of Fame career. He was five years younger than Earnhardt, but the two had run in the same circles. The two Dales (in an added quirk of fate, both had mothers named Martha) first began competing against one another in the Busch series in 1982, and first met in the Cup series during Jarrett's first start in 1984 at Martinsville.

"We were battling for fourteenth position," Jarrett recalled of that first 1984 meeting. "I remember he would pass me and I'd pass him. We weren't holding positions at all. I looked over at him, and you could see the whole face in those days because of those open-face helmets, and he was just grinning."

Neither was laughing now. Jarrett knew he was in the race of his life against the toughest driver on the planet. Jarrett was in his second year of driving for new NASCAR owner Joe Gibbs, the former Redskins coach, and Jarrett's green Interstate Batteries No. 18 looked downright cheery against the menacing black of Earnhardt's 3. When Jarrett saw Gordon ahead of him on the penultimate lap, he pulled a bait-and-switch to pass the rookie, a move that wouldn't have worked on a savvier driver.

It was Jarrett and Earnhardt now. Jarrett had four fresh tires, Earnhardt had two. Jarrett had strategy, while Earnhardt had four decades' worth of desire and drive and meanness. It was going to be a hell of a fight down to the wire.

Ned Jarrett, watching from behind a microphone, was torn. He was a broadcaster, supposed to show no bias, but this was his son in a strong bid to win his first Daytona 500. How could he suppress his paternal pride? He wondered if he should back off the microphone. As the cars exited turn 2 for the final time, CBS producer Bob Stenner took the decision out of Jarrett's hands, telling play-by-play man Ken Squier to let Ned have the leeway to call this race as a father. The result was one of the most remarkable moments in sports broadcast history.

The joy in Ned Jarrett's voice increased as the tension rose. "Come on, Dale!" he exhorted. "Take her to the inside! Don't let him get on the inside of you coming around this turn!" He knew Earnhardt's style; the Intimidator would try diving low to get around Jarrett. Father and son had discussed how to handle the final laps in so much detail that it looked like Jarrett was following each of his father's instructions. "The Dale and Dale Show," as Ned Jarrett called it, roared out of turn 4 and headed down the front stretch.

"I knew who it was there, and I knew what this meant to him," the younger Jarrett said later, "but I wasn't focused on any of that. I had to figure out how to draft and side-draft him without getting crashed. I knew what he could do."

"Bring her to the inside, Dale!" Ned Jarrett begged. "Don't let him get there!" And then: "He's gonna make it! Dale Jarrett's gonna win the Daytona 500!"

CBS cameras found Dale's mother Martha Jarrett weeping and praying as her son's car wheeled toward the finish line. "Look at Martha!" Ned called. "Can you believe it?"

Ralph Earnhardt alongside one of his hand-tooled No. 8 Chevrolets in 1971. Young Dale would check out Ralph's cars the morning after a race; a spotless bumper was good news.
(SMYLE MEDIA)

Ralph Earnhardt's gravesite, Kannapolis, North Carolina. The names of his three sons, including Dale, are inscribed just behind the front wheel.
(COURTESY OF THE AUTHOR)

A twenty-three-year-old Dale Earnhart at Charlotte Motor Speedway, October 1974. Earnhardt was already on his second marriage, and was racing just to keep his family above the poverty line.
(SMYLE MEDIA)

Dale Earnhardt tore up plenty of cars in his early days, like this wrecked No. 2 from a 1979 Rockingham race. Once he learned how to drive around other cars, not just through them, he became a champion.
(SMYLE MEDIA)

Generations collide: Richard Petty, in his trademark cowboy hat and sunglasses, sits alongside then-reigning rookie of the year, Dale Earnhardt, at Nashville in 1980. Petty had just won his seventh NASCAR championship, a mark Earnhardt would eventually match.
(SMYLE MEDIA)

Dale Earnhardt celebrates, following a victory at the Busch Nashville 420 in July 1980. This was Earnhardt's fourth career Cup-level win; later that year, he'd claim his first championship.
(SMYLE MEDIA)

Dale Earnhardt poses with daughter, Kelley, and son Dale Earnhardt Jr. for a Wrangler promotional session in 1981. Dale didn't always have the closest relationship with his children, but they always craved his approval.

(SMYLE MEDIA)

Many of Dale Earnhardt's fiercest rivals gathered in advance of the first Winston All-Star Race in 1985. *Top row, left to right*: Tim Richmond, Darrell Waltrip, Richard Petty, Earnhardt, Bill Elliott. *Bottom row*: Geoff Bodine, Cale Yarborough, Harry Gant, Ricky Rudd, and Terry Labonte.

(SMYLE MEDIA)

Dale and Teresa in 1995. Teresa was the power behind the throne, crafting the contracts and cementing the business deals that made the Intimidator a national icon.

(SMYLE MEDIA)

One of Dale Sr.'s most vocal competitors was Rusty Wallace, seen here running alongside the Intimidator in Atlanta. Wallace and Earnhardt were rivals on the track, occasionally nearly coming to blows, but were close friends off it.
(ATLANTA MOTOR SPEEDWAY)

Generations collide again: Jeff Gordon, then just twenty-five years old, with Earnhardt at North Wilkesboro in 1996. The two had almost nothing in common, save for championship talent and mutual respect.
(SMYLE MEDIA)

Of all the third generation of Earnhardt drivers, Kelley may well have been the most talented. Here she is at Myrtle Beach Speedway in 1996 in what would be one of her final races before hanging up the wheel.
(SMYLE MEDIA)

Dale and Teresa Earnhardt, along with their daughter, Nicole, await the start of an Atlanta race. In his later years, Earnhardt spent more time with his family, as nagging injuries mounted up and wins declined.
(ATLANTA MOTOR SPEEDWAY)

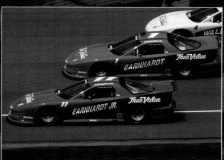

The International Race Of Champions (IROC) series pitted drivers from all over the world against one another in identical cars, and was intended as a test of pure driving skill. Naturally, Dale Earnhardt Sr. flourished there, winning four championships. Dale Jr. has the edge in this photo, taken at Michigan in 1999, but Senior would go on to win the race.
(SMYLE MEDIA)

Dale Earnhardt Jr. arrived on the scene in NASCAR with a brashness—and an ill-advised hairstyle—that belied his trepidation about following in his father's very large footsteps.
(ATLANTA MOTOR SPEEDWAY)

Dale Earnhardt Sr. raced against his son at the Cup level for only one full season, in 2000, but Junior's two victories that year ranked among Senior's proudest moments.
(NIGEL KINRADE)

Dale Earnhardt died on the final lap of the 2001 Daytona 500. The shock from Kenny Schraeder's car (36) turned Earnhardt into the wall at a sharper angle, magnifying the force of the fatal impact.
(AP)

Kerry Earnhardt, seen here in Daytona one year after his father's death, is the spitting image of Dale Earnhardt Sr. Kerry didn't have the same success as his father or brother, and in 2009 retired from racing for good.
(SMYLE MEDIA)

A nine-foot-tall, 900-pound statue of the Intimidator stands in Kannapolis, not far from the site of the cotton mills where his father worked more than half a century before.
(COURTESY OF THE AUTHOR)

Junior's 2014 victory at Daytona set off a celebration unlike any NASCAR had seen in many years. The race marked Junior's second win at Daytona, one more than his father at the track that has played such a pivotal role in the Earnhardt family dynasty.

(NIGEL KINRADE)

It was a lapse in journalistic impartiality, but given NASCAR's family leanings, a forgivable one. When Ned Jarrett later apologized to Earnhardt for having rooted against him, Earnhardt replied, "I understand. I'm a father too." Earnhardt's own father was twenty years gone—and the Intimidator's dream of winning a Daytona seemed further away than ever.

"Big damn deal, I lost another Daytona 500," he said after the race. "We've lost this race about every way you can lose it. We've been out-gassed, out-tired, out-run, and out-everythinged. We've come close. There's nothing left to do but come back and try again next year."

(Earnhardt's friend Hank Jones had a joke about that day. He prayed, he said, and asked the Almighty, "Lord, Dale has done so well at Daytona, won everything but the Daytona 500. Lord, he's a really good man. If you could let him win it'd make him very happy." Jones later laughed, saying that he'd forgotten to tell the Lord which Dale.)

After the heartbreak of the opening race, Earnhardt came close to inflicting far worse on a fellow driver at Talladega in the spring. Earnhardt was leading the race when Ernie Irvan and Mark Martin went low and shuffled him back. Fighting for position, Earnhardt tapped Rusty Wallace as they were crossing the start/finish line, and Wallace began flipping. And kept flipping, six times in all. By the time Wallace's car came to rest, it was completely stripped of any sheet metal, and sat in the Talladega grass like a skeleton. Wallace was thankfully inside, moving, and Earnhardt was one of the first to check on him.

He survived. Others did not. NASCAR had always flirted with tragedy—it was the dark, unspoken element of the sport's exhilaration—but 1993 was an especially cruel year. On Thursday, April 1, Kulwicki was flying to the Bristol race from an appearance at a Knoxville Hooters when his small plane crashed on its approach to the Tri-Cities Regional Airport in Tennessee, killing the thirty-eight-year-old Kulwicki and four others. Earnhardt's plane had landed just before Kulwicki's, and as they were taxiing in, everyone on Earnhardt's plane could hear the cries across the radio as Kulwicki's plane went down.

The next day, Kulwicki's hauler exited Bristol after driving a single solemn lap. The National Transportation Safety Board later blamed the pilot for failing to properly clear ice from the plane's engine.

The drivers were in mourning, trying to decide whether racing that weekend would be right or appropriate. On a rainy Friday afternoon, Lori Worley, a writer with Bristol's local newspaper, approached Earnhardt's trailer looking for a quote from the Man himself.

J. R. Rhodes, Earnhardt's PR man, stood at the door. "He's asleep," Rhodes said. "If you want to wake him, go ahead, but don't tell him I let you in."

Worley tiptoed inside. "Dale," she whispered, then repeated his name.

Earnhardt jumped up in shock. "What the hell are you doing?" he shouted.

Worley apologized and explained her assignment. Should they race in the wake of Kulwicki's death?

Earnhardt composed himself. "Listen," he said, "we're gonna race. It's what he'd want. It's what I'd want them to do if it happened to me."

After Kulwicki died, Davey Allison said he believed his own problems in the Hooters 500 were part of a larger design—to get Kulwicki a championship before his death. "Now I understand why I didn't win a championship," Davey said. "I'm glad he got his. I'll get mine."

He would never get the chance. Three months later, on July 12, Allison crashed while attempting to land his newly acquired helicopter in the Talladega infield. He died the next day of his head injuries at the age of thirty-two.

"What you don't know when you lose somebody like that is the butterfly effect," NASCAR president Mike Helton said. "I know Davey would have been a contender, and I think Alan would have been too. Davey would have been competing for championships, and Alan would have been redefining the sport."

EARNHARDT WON THE first race at Pocono after Allison's death. At the finish line, he prayed silently with the Flying Aces. "I've never seen Earnhardt cry until today," gas man Chocolate Myers said. Earnhardt took a flag with Allison's number 28 and drove a "Polish victory lap"—a lap in the reverse direction, Kulwicki's signature move—in honor of the two fallen drivers.

Earnhardt ran exceptionally well during the summer, winning five of eight races from May to July. With his huge lead, his sixth championship looked assured even before autumn arrived. Then Martin and Wallace got going and put a scare into Earnhardt. Over the season's final twelve races, each won five (Ernie Irvan won the other two). Wallace would win an astonishing ten of the thirty races that year and still not win the championship—something that burned him the rest of his career.

"I'm not saying that [Talladega] wreck cost me the championship, but it didn't help me," Wallace would say years later. "But I'm not going to point fingers at all, because I was driving that car.... I wanted that title bad, so I could have at least two championships, but it didn't happen and at least I can say that, damn it, I was close, I was right there."

IN MOST SPORTS, the players of both the winning and losing teams hang around in the locker rooms, then sign a few autographs before boarding a team bus or driving home. Not so in NASCAR, where every weekend is a road game. The moment the checkered flag flies, the race after the race begins. Drivers rip away from the track back into the garage, and from there to their rental cars and golf carts. The goal is to get to the nearby airstrip and get their private planes into the air before their competitors. A delay of only a few minutes can mean the difference between getting home before the winner has stopped popping champagne and a two-hour wait in the snarl of departing fan traffic.

Drivers who wanted to hitch flights with Earnhardt knew they had zero margin for error. Pit reporter Matt Yocum recalls seeing one young driver still in his fire suit after a Rockingham race, running at a dead sprint through the garage carrying his street clothes, trying to get to Earnhardt's plane before takeoff. The driver knew the rule: Earnhardt waited for no one.

When he didn't win a race, Earnhardt had a precisely choreographed exit strategy in place. He would run the car right up to the back of his hauler, leap out, head straight into the hauler, and change out of his fire suit. His rental car would be waiting for him. Reporter Monte Dutton once timed Earnhardt's sprint from his work car to his rental car at two minutes, forty-five seconds.

"After the race, if he wins he'll give everybody as much as they want for as long as they want," former DEI president Don Hawk once said. "If he finishes second, you'll get fewer sound bites and not as much time. Third place, you'll get a smile but not much in the way of talking. From fourth place on back, we're heading for the airplane right away. We're out of there."

When Earnhardt was ready to come out of his hauler, his PR man J. R. Rhodes would give The Signal to whatever media had managed to speed their way over to Earnhardt's trailer. The Signal meant it was time to get the cameras rolling, and if you didn't have your questions ready, well, that was your problem. Earnhardt would walk in a straight line from the back of his hauler straight to his rental car, and if you couldn't get an answer from him in that short time, you didn't get one. "Nobody got out of a track faster than Earnhardt," Yocum said. "And nobody got word about a rain-out before Earnhardt."

Earnhardt's relationship with the media was a dicey one. Early on in his career, he would speak openly, his accent raw, his heart on display. "When Daddy was driving," he told writer Kim Chapin in 1975, "I was always scared that he was going to get hurt. But it's never crossed my mind, especially when I'm racing. If I wreck and get hurt, I wreck and get hurt. But I can't remember ever thinking about [getting hurt] from the time I started."

Success brought with it a distrust of those who'd mock or take advantage of him, and Joe Whitlock, Earnhardt's first PR man, encouraged Earnhardt to keep lines of communication with the media open. Rhodes, who came on board following Whitlock's death, took the opposite tack, protecting Earnhardt like a bulldog on the porch and keeping him largely confined to press conferences under controlled circumstances.

Earnhardt grew more at ease in front of a microphone, but he could still be indifferent, unreceptive, or a flat-out bastard when the mood suited him. He was combative, and woe to the reporter who ventured a callow, pointless, or open-ended question, like the ones that begin "Can you talk about . . . ?" Earnhardt wouldn't do your work for you, and he expected you to meet him head-on if you were going to seek his wisdom.

That's not to say that he disliked the media categorically. He knew the media's role in promoting the sport, but he also knew he could push around reporters, and they'd have to accept the abuse or feel the wrath of their editors and readers. In that way, Earnhardt wasn't unlike Tiger Woods, pushing the boundaries of respect while delivering the necessary quotes. He would, on occa-sion, take to certain media members—these were often reporters of the female persuasion, their competitors grumbled—and trust them with confidences or supply more than the usual pablum.

"He was utterly consistent, whether it was with someone who tried to interview him or someone who tried to race him," Dutton said. "He didn't respect anyone who didn't stand up to him. For everyone on the assembly line who wanted to tell off their boss, they saw in Earnhardt something they aspired to."

Earnhardt would vent his media frustrations to a few trusted friends. Once he and Steve Byrnes were roaming the farm, riding in one of Earnhardt's trucks, and Earnhardt was livid about ESPN's coverage of him. "I can't believe the shit they're saying about me," he seethed. "They're saying I'm reckless. I race hard, but I'm not out to ruin anybody else's day."

"He didn't care if you liked him as a person, as a man," Byrnes would say later. "But if you respected him, that was a central theme in his life."

Then there were times when his actions could make you doubt his reputation as the Intimidator. In February of 1999 a young NASCAR production assistant named Ryan McGee lost his mother unexpectedly. After missing several races, he returned to the track at Darlington, where he heard a familiar rumble of a voice in the media center.

"Hey, Ryan."

McGee turned.

"I heard about your mom," Earnhardt said. "You okay?"

McGee felt himself start to well up, and it took all he had not to start crying in front of the Intimidator. He hadn't realized Earnhardt even knew his name, much less about his tragedy.

"Look at me," Earnhardt said. "Look at me. You need to know. You will never get over this. I lost my dad twenty-five years ago, and I think about him every day. But you *will* learn to live with it."

CHAPTER 10

HELL-RAISERS

THEY WERE AN odd couple, Earnhardt and Neil Bonnett—the Intimidator and, hands down, the nicest guy in NASCAR. Yet they were the best of friends, raising hell together and needling each other in equal measure. "You would get to the track each Friday morning and breathe a sigh of relief when they both came walking into the garage," Childress said. "Somehow they had survived another week without killing each other."

Bonnett and Earnhardt found in each other a soulmate who'd fight to the death for you—and perhaps, on occasion, against you. They raced against each other 296 times. Dale won 189 times, Neil 107.

"Everybody else thought we were nuts," Earnhardt said, "but once I realized that someone in the garage actually thought I was normal, I wanted to get to know that guy."

Bonnett, from the tiny hamlet of Hueytown, Alabama, had worked his way in with the famous Alabama Gang, a loosely related collection of hypertalented Alabama drivers, but never forgot his friends or his sponsors. He became one of the sport's best-known drivers, if not exactly its winningest; he had a knack for ending up on the wrong team at the wrong time, and financial and sponsor problems dogged his teams throughout his career. Writer Ed Hinton told the story of the day in 1978 when Bonnett answered the phone in his kitchen, listened for a moment, then told the caller never to bother him again. A bill collector? An overexuberant fan? "No, that was the pipe fitters' union," Bonnett told Hinton. "They're paying $50 an hour now, and if my wife knew that, she'd make me quit racin' and go back to work."

Bonnett and Earnhardt brought out the best, or the worst, in each other, no matter the hour or the day. Once, when Bonnett bought a new ATV, Earnhardt needed one right then—"right then" being three in the morning—and they woke up the local four-wheeler dealer to open up and sell him one. On their first ride together, Earnhardt knocked Bonnett into some bushes so he wouldn't have to worry about when he'd get the first scratch on his pretty new machine.

During Speedweeks, Daytona International Speedway would host a fishing tournament at Lake Lloyd, the lake in the track's infield, and both Earnhardt and Bonnett would go at each other, and the lake, in search of a winning fish. One year, Earnhardt spotted a large bass in the lake but couldn't get it to bite. He made the mistake of telling Bonnett about the fish, but made him promise not to try to catch it while Earnhardt ran a Busch Series practice session.

Bonnett, naturally, went straight out to the lake. As fate would have it, Earnhardt wrecked hard back by the lake, pieces of his car flying everywhere. Bonnett walked over to the edge of the track and persuaded the cleanup crew to hand him Earnhardt's hood. Later, he told Earnhardt he'd figured out how to catch the bass, and the two men set out on the water. Once they got close to the home turf of the bass, Earnhardt's eyes widened in surprise.

There was the bass, circling lazily right over Earnhardt's hood, which Bonnett had dumped in the lake.

THE 1980s BROUGHT Bonnett a solid eighteen Cup-level victories. In 1990 he slid so hard driver's side—first into water barrels in front of pit road at Darlington that he suffered a brief bout of amnesia. He remained connected to NASCAR through television broadcasting, but there's a world of difference between talking and driving. Bonnett needed to be behind the wheel, not just commenting on those who were.

Everyone said Bonnett should stay away from the track for his own health, but Bonnett wanted back in worse than anything. Earnhardt found a way to get his wingman back into a car: as Earnhardt's personal tester. Bonnett became Earnhardt's right-hand man, testing and picking over every element of Earnhardt's Monte Carlo. Testing went so well that Earnhardt and Childress helped get Bonnett cleared to race in 1993 and set him up with a car at Talladega.

Days before that July race, Bonnett had pulled Davey Allison and his passenger, fellow driver Red Farmer, from the burning helicopter, saving Farmer's life. Once race day came around, Bonnett ran reasonably well until lap 131. Ted Musgrave got into the back of his No. 31 Mom n' Pops Chevy and sent Bonnett flying through the air and into a catch fence. Bonnett wasn't injured, and even provided in-race commentary after he got out of the infield care center. If this was any kind of sign, Bonnett ignored it.

Bonnett got another start at Atlanta, the final race of the year, a strategic move designed to help Earnhardt. The Intimidator needed to earn just three points in that race to win the 1993 championship. Three laps into the race, Bonnett parked his car, claiming a "blown engine." Conveniently enough, Bonnett's last-place "finish" guaranteed Earnhardt would amass enough points that race to claim the championship.

In 1994 Bonnett worked a deal with another owner, James Finch of Phoenix Racing, to run at least six races, including the season-opening Daytona 500. The entire Childress team headed to Daytona to start the season once again, the fatalism of years past always brightened with optimism of a new year. Earnhardt had been here before—fifteen times now, matter of fact—but every Daytona brought the promise of a new victory. "We're bound and determined to defeat that race and be a Daytona 500 winner," Earnhardt said at the time. "The fact that I haven't won it drives me. I want to win it because it's our Super Bowl, but also because it's a race and I want to win every race I run."

On the morning of February 11, Bonnett climbed into his car for some on-track testing. For reasons still unknown, his car veered straight up into the retaining wall in turn 4 of Daytona, hitting it nearly head-on and killing Bonnett instantly. Darrell Waltrip would say later that the particular model of Hoosier tires Bonnett was running could have been tough for a less experienced driver to control. NASCAR tried to write off the accident as "driver error," but Earnhardt fought that designation so fiercely that NASCAR ultimately removed that line from its findings.

"Neil's death, in particular, had a major impact on him," said Danny Lawrence, an RCR assistant engine builder at the time. "Dale had a lot of friends, but he had only a handful of really close friends, and Neil was one of them. I know he told Neil that he probably should think more about that [new driving] deal. But Neil wanted to drive. I think Dale might have thought he should have pushed him a little harder [to reconsider]."

Tragedy struck again three days later. Rodney Orr, who would be making his first Cup-level start at that Daytona 500, lost control of his car during another practice. He hit the turn 2 wall and catch fence so hard that a caution light was embedded in the roof of the car. Orr died instantly of chest and head injuries. An investigation found that a mounting bracket had broken in the car, removing all control.

The pall of the two deaths hung over Daytona, and Earnhardt confessed to a deep well of sadness.

"You lose your best friend . . . ," he said, leaving the sentence unfinished. "There's a big void there losing Neil."

And then came the determination. "I guess it's all part of the game. But I'm not tired of the game. I'm not Michael Jordan," he added, referring to Jordan's recent retirement from the Bulls. (At that moment Jordan was pursuing a baseball career with the Chicago White Sox in spring training, across Florida from Daytona.)

Despite Earnhardt's resolution, he and the team were shaken. "We were all really close to him and the shock of it, I think it did have an effect on us during the Busch Clash," Childress said of the invitation-only exhibition event held at the speedway the week before the Daytona 500 itself. "Dale didn't know what lap he was on, and I know he says it didn't have anything to do with Neil, but we should have been telling him where he was. I think all of us were in a trance. Racing wasn't in our minds."

Earnhardt remained on the track, and stayed competitive throughout 1994. This year, his chief competition came from old friend and protégé Ernie Irvan. Like so many other teenagers in the 1970s, Irvan had dreamed of racing, but he was living in California. He knew he could go only so far in racing without heading east. In 1982 Irvan took his life savings—$700—and headed to Charlotte, where he worked odd jobs, welding the seats in the grandstands at Charlotte Motor Speedway and the like. He caught the attention of Earnhardt, who gave him work as a gofer. Eventually Irvan and his friend Marc Reno gathered up their courage and sought sponsorship from their local Dale Earnhardt Chevy dealership. Ken Schrader, a fellow driver and friend of Earnhardt's, took their offer to the Big Man and told them he'd have an answer the next day. They waited nervously for Earnhardt's reply.

Yes on the sponsorship. No on any money.

"Wait a minute, what?" Irvan said. "How are we supposed to run without money?"

"You've got the name," Schrader said. "It's up to you to turn it into money."

Irvan realized having the Earnhardt name on his car would draw attention, and his driving skill could hold that attention. Irvan worked his way up through the ranks of NASCAR to become a legitimate Cup-level competitor, earning the name "Swervin' Irvan" for the way he tended to cover all lanes of a racetrack with his side-to-side style of driving.

Irvan won nine races in his first five seasons, and by the time 1994 rolled around, he was one of his mentor's fiercest adversaries. He and Earnhardt had gone toe-to-toe and wheel-to-wheel, each notching three wins through the season's first twenty races. Irvan led in top-five finishes, while Earnhardt led by 27 points overall.

Irvan was testing on the Friday before the GM Goodwrench Dealer 400 at Michigan in August when his right front tire gave way. He hit the turn 2 wall at more than 170 miles per hour. After being flown to St. Joseph's Hospital in Ann Arbor, he was given only a 10 percent chance of surviving the night.

Irvan fought hard, and within a few weeks he was removed from ventilator support. He was well enough to greet fans at the October Charlotte race. Two months later, at the NASCAR post-season banquet in December, Irvan walked onstage at the Waldorf-Astoria to the cheers of his friends and rivals. Chief among them was Earnhardt, who had driven to an "easy" seventh championship in Irvan's absence. The nearest competitor besides Irvan, Mark Martin, trailed Earnhardt by more than 400 points. With two full races still to go, Earnhardt had locked up the championship at Rockingham with a victory in the AC Delco 500. Earnhardt's team appeased longtime Richard Petty fans by creating a line of "7 & 7" souvenir merchandise honoring both drivers' championships, and Petty himself gave his blessing to his new equal.

Irvan eventually returned to the track late in 1995, and would win three more races in 1996 and 1997. But in 1999, five years almost to the day after his catastrophic wreck, Irvan again crashed at Michigan in practice. That was enough, and he retired once and for all from driving.

As 1994 wound down and that seventh championship was all but in the bag, Earnhardt added a special member to the Flying Aces, a former major league backup catcher by the name of Ned Yost. A few years before, the Chicago Cubs' Jody Davis, a hunting buddy of Yost's, had brought Earnhardt along on one of their expeditions, and a friendship blossomed immediately. "A phenomenal shot," Yost said of Earnhardt. "I've seen him shoot things at 800 yards. Lost $200."

Yost, a Braves coach in the early 1990s, had managed to convert most of the team into Earnhardt fans. Working in the bullpen on Sunday afternoons, Yost could keep an ear on the race while his eyes were on the game, and he'd relay updates to manager Bobby Cox and others via the bullpen phone. The Braves and Richard Childress Racing sent caps and jackets to one another, and Earnhardt often wore his Atlanta cap and jacket around the garage. When Atlanta shortstop Jeff Blauser—another hunting buddy— won a playoff game for the Braves, he did his postgame interview wearing a No. 3 cap. Blauser, Yost and Cox took fellow Braves Ron Gant and Terry Pendleton to Atlanta Motor Speedway later that year to cheer on Earnhardt.

It was a perfect alliance of the sporting South; after decades of ineptitude, the Braves were suddenly one of the most dominant teams in baseball, and Earnhardt was leading NASCAR's charge into the national consciousness. Yost was the spiritual liaison between the two sports, and when baseball's players went on strike in 1994, he became a true link. Yost served as a garage gofer for Earnhardt, hauling gas cans or tires, wiping windshields, and doing anything he could to stay connected to his buddy. Yost was right there when Earnhardt won his seventh championship at Rockingham, grinning for the photos as if he was meant for this job and this moment alone.

Yost would often sit with Earnhardt as the driver prepared for the day's race. "Who are your friends on the track?" Yost once asked.

"I don't have any," Earnhardt replied.

"You don't have any friends on the track?"

"No. I don't have a friend out here."

"Why?"

"Because I don't ever want anybody looking in the rearview mirror and seeing the black number three come up behind them, and think I'm their friend."

Earnhardt's lesson in competitiveness stuck with Yost—he would go on to manage the Milwaukee Brewers and the Kansas City Royals. Yost led the Royals to the World Series berths in 2014 and 2015: a seventh-game loss to the San Franciso Giants that the snake-bit-at-Daytona Earnhardt could surely appreciate, and then a leave-no-doubt emotional victory over the New York Mets. Through it all, Yost wore the number 3.

NOT EVERYONE NEEDED to wear the 3 to understand the power of the Earnhardt name. When he was sixteen, Junior had a black-and-silver 1988 Chevy S10 4x4 with the latest in audio technology: a seek button on the radio. It was a sweet ride, by all accounts, and Junior drove it everywhere he could at top speed.

Speed among civilians had consequences. One night Junior was leaving his father's farm after an argument, flooring it back toward Mooresville. He passed a state trooper and immediately pulled over, knowing he was busted. As Junior sat in the truck waiting for the cop to write the ticket, Senior himself came rolling by, slowly and deliberately.

Ticket received, Junior drove on to find Senior waiting at a gas station a few miles down the road.

"Did he write you a ticket?" Senior asked.

Junior nodded.

"Looks like you need to get a job to pay for it," Senior said, and that's how Dale Earnhardt Jr. began pumping gas.

Junior loved that S10, and even tried to track it down via the VIN number years after selling it. Sadly, the truck's final owner had junked it just a year before Junior tracked him down. But it was a hell of a seductive truck, and when Junior graduated high school, Earnhardt forced on him another model—a ghastly two-tone brown beast with no carpet.

"I thought it was a bit of a hint that life is getting ready to get harder once you get out of school," Junior said years later, "and this here is your work truck. So I didn't like that truck too much, and I didn't treat it too well." He would eventually trade in that truck on a 1991 Chevy S10, red with an extended cab, financed for five years at $100 a month.

He had the S10 for about three months before totaling it on Christmas morning, headed from Mooresville to Kannapolis for a family reunion. Junior was driving while messing with his gift from Kelley: a brand-new Walkman CD player with a tape-deck adapter. He drove off the road, hit a culvert, and flipped, by his estimation, "six or seven times."

The prospect of calling his father was even more terrifying than the wreck. Junior borrowed the cell phone of a motorist who'd stopped to aid him. Earnhardt showed up with a rollback, loaded up the wreckage of the truck, and that was that.

A state patrolman who'd arrived on the scene didn't investigate any further. "If y'all are good," he told the two Earnhardts, "I'm good."

That's how things got done in Cabarrus County when it came to the Earnhardts.

AFTER GRADUATING FROM high school, Junior took a job in the service department at his father's auto dealership in Newton, where Kelley was a receptionist and Kerry was a service writer. Junior changed oil, did body work, and handled whatever scut work was necessary—as he would later put it, "I can take comfort in the fact that if this driving thing doesn't work out, I can always go back to being the fastest oil-change man in Newton." Right from the start, though, he also got behind the wheel of a street stock car.

Junior had always wanted to race, "but there was always this idea that you had to sweep the floor for a year before you ever got a chance to touch a wrench," he said. "I didn't want to sweep the floor."

Or do much else. Kerry was a diligent worker, up at 6:00 a.m. to head over to the dealership, while Junior would sleep until noon after wee-hours hangouts and drum sessions at the double-wide they shared near the Earnhardt estate.

In 1994 Kerry and Junior decided to see how many of their father's and grandfather's automotive genes had worked their way down the bloodline. Junior sold his go-kart and headed over to Wayne's Automotive to buy an old Monte Carlo that was in surprisingly good shape. (The year of the car varies—some remember it as a '78, others a '79. Some say they paid $200 for it, others $500. Either way, a deal.) They made a key tactical mistake in bringing the car back to the shop. Their father walked in. "And that," Kerry recalled, "is what we were trying to avoid."

"What is this?" Earnhardt said.

The boys tried to explain that they'd bought the car, and they'd be tuning it up to race.

"Don't y'all mess with this," Earnhardt said, excusing himself to take a phone call. "I'll be right back."

Earnhardt didn't believe in short cuts; there was a reason he hadn't provided the brothers with track-ready cars. Such prizes had to be earned, not merely bought. The boys reasoned that Earnhardt thought the car was too nice for them. So they went to work on it, busting out windows and breaking headlights.

"It was the worst thing we could have done," Kerry later said, laughing. The Earnhardt boys had to do double duty, first cleaning up their own mistakes, then honing the Monte Carlo to a fine racing edge, just as their grandfather had nearly half a century before.

You'd expect two children of privilege—Earnhardt's wealth was beyond staggering at this point—to have the best equipment money could buy, to run with sleek cars and fully outfitted trailers and bleeding-edge technologies. The boys' father didn't see it that way; he wanted to see just how badly his children wanted to drive. Beyond concerns of safety, he offered plenty of advice, but no financial assistance whatever.

Kerry and Junior passed the car back and forth, Kerry driving it one weekend, Junior the next. It never occurred to them that someone else in the family wanted in on the action.

CHAPTER 11

MILK TOAST

ASK AROUND WHO was the most talented driver of the next generation of Earnhardts, and the answer wouldn't be Junior. Or Kerry. The popular consensus is that the best driver of the third generation may very well have been Kelley.

Racing had touched Kelley since before her birth. Her mother, Brenda, went into labor during a Saturday-night race when Dale got into a fight with another driver. "My blood pressure went up," said Brenda years later, laughing, and next thing she knew, she was on the way to the hospital.

Twenty-one years later Kelley was studying at the University of North Carolina–Wilmington. In the fall of 1993, Dale called her back home. He sent her a bouquet of flowers with a card that read, "It's been so long I have almost forgotten what you look like." He offered to pay for an apartment for her if she'd come home and keep racing, and that was all it took.

Kelley, Kerry, and Junior formed a late-model stock car racing trio that boasted more enthusiasm than talent. Kerry, already a young father like his father had been, often stayed behind while Kelley and Junior trekked out to tracks unknown. Junior managed three wins. While Kelley didn't win any, she earned bragging rights by beating Junior on multiple occasions. Kelley was no dilettante; she would hook up and haul her own car, and she was as tough on the track as her old man. She took over that first Monte Carlo—by now "mutilated, mangled on every corner except the roof," she recalled—and threw herself into racing with a verve that surprised her more chauvinistic rivals.

At one race, she and another driver became entangled, and Kelley got the better end of the deal. Kelley was standing in the drivers' postrace payout line when the wrecked driver's girlfriend sucker-punched Kelley, knocking her to the ground.

"I wanted to get up and hit her back," Kelley recalled, "but a lot of people were holding me back. It was probably over twenty dollars."

The Earnhardt kids had their father's racing spirit, but they didn't always want his name. Brenda would recommend that they not identify themselves in order to avoid problems, so it was often "Kelley and Dale Smith" who traveled the North Carolina countryside.

Anyone with the name Earnhardt was a target, and Kelley didn't get any breaks because of her gender. She'd hold the line against male drivers at Tri-County Racetrack in Brasstown, North Carolina; Hickory Motor Speedway; and Myrtle Beach Speedway. She had an aggressive streak uncommon in racers of either gender.

"That old saying is, you can't push a rope, you can't tell somebody to drive into the corner deeper, but you can tell a driver if they need to back off if they're overdriving . . . that was her," Junior said. "She was one of them that started overdriving the car from day one, and that was good."

How good was Kelley in her father's eyes? Good enough that he hired Junior to work on *her* car. Junior went to Senior and asked for a job after he got fired from his father's dealership for requesting too much overtime, among other sins. Earnhardt put the boy to work on his sister's cars, and Dale and Kelley built a car from scratch.

"We took it to the track and somebody wrecked her and we both were about to beat the shit out of this dude with jack handles and whatever," Junior later recalled, laughing. "She was tough. She was mentally tough. It was frustrating because you could see where she could have been a good race car driver and you just wanted to see her progress and get better."

For Kelley, the dream collided with hard reality in 1996, when the last of her sponsorship money ran out and she couldn't find anyone willing to serve on her pit crew. She had just graduated from the University of North Carolina at Charlotte and was working for Action Performance, the souvenir company. She had to bail every Friday afternoon at two to get to the track in time.

"She could have had a lot of opportunities had it been a different environment and a different culture and a different climate," Junior told ESPN.com. "She was hardheaded and tough and drove hard. She would eventually have polished her abilities to where she would have been a pretty good race car driver at the higher level."

Certainly her father could have bankrolled her for years on end, but the obstacles were too high, the sexism and old ways too entrenched. The obligations were significant, the opportunities few, and Kelley decided to focus on the business of racing rather than the racing business. Her father never saw a single one of her races.

Given her history, it's no small irony that Kelley would be most responsible for bringing the most famous woman in racing, Danica Patrick, into NASCAR in 2010. The IndyCar celebrity better known for her attractiveness (and swimsuit layouts) than her on-track prowess, Patrick performed a one-year apprenticeship at JR Motorsports, the race team that Junior would form in the mid-2000s. On the day that Kelley and Dale Jr. announced Danica's arrival in NASCAR, it was impossible not to look at Kelley and think that this could have been her, perhaps even *should* have been her. But the NASCAR of the mid-1990s was an inhospitable place for anyone who wasn't a good ol' boy, with the emphasis on *boy*.

EARNHARDT NATION

AS FOR WONDER Boy—Jeff Gordon—by 1995 he had matured quickly from a poorly mustachioed up-and-comer to an actual threat. One theory held that as long as Earnhardt paid attention to you, you were doing something right. By that standard, Gordon was doing just fine.

Gordon and Earnhardt weren't particularly close off the track. Their drastically different personalities clashed in the public eye and in reality, but the respect between the two could not have been greater. "I get along with Jeff, but we don't travel in the same circles," Earnhardt said in 1995. "He plays video games, I go big-game hunting. He wears athletic shoes, I wear boots. What we have in common is that we love to race."

They also shared a love of needling one another. In one notable interview, Gordon, wearing a horrific denim jacket, walked into the middle of Earnhardt's shot.

"Here comes Wonder Boy," Earnhardt said.

"I hear you talking about me," Gordon shot back.

"You talk like a little girl."

"Sorry, man, I'm not as big as you," Gordon said, shoving Earnhardt's shoulder, "not as big a man as you." Both men were grinning ear-to-ear as Earnhardt threw a friendly arm around Gordon's shoulders.

"As intimidating as he was," Gordon would say years later, "I was at times able to intimidate him. Not from saying anything or pushing him around, just from passing him and winning."

Gordon's arrival coincided with the expansion of NASCAR's fan base. A new demographic without ancestral ties to Earnhardt and the traditional southern NASCAR constituency aligned itself with Gordon. That set off miniature Civil Wars in every infield throughout the 1990s, with Gordon fans and Earnhardt fans jabbing one another verbally and, in some alcohol-fueled moments, physically. To this day Earnhardt-focused tailgates still feature profanely decorated Jeff Gordon posters. The hatred for Gordon waned over time as he ascended to veteran status, but back in 1995 he was still the punk from Indiana trying to horn in on a southern sport. Earnhardt and his legions led the charge to remind him of his place.

Flush with cash, NASCAR decided that same year to build out an attraction at its signature speedway. Daytona USA, a multimillion-dollar museum attraction, broke ground in June courtesy of "the world's most famous construction crew": Earnhardt, Gordon, and Rusty Wallace, as well as Orlando Magic forward Horace Grant.

A simple photo op of the men posing with shovels and hard hats simply would not do for spectacle's sake. No, the plan was to put the drivers on a bulldozer and let them break the ground in gargantuan chunks, not tiny spadefuls. As the drivers gathered around the bulldozer, a Daytona PR rep asked who would be driving the tractor.

"It was a pretty easy answer," Gordon would say years later. "We knew who was going to drive the tractor, and it was going to be Dale."

A photograph from the day shows Gordon and Wallace standing on the bulldozer's treads, 1990s-era stonewashed jeans cinched painfully high around their waists. Earnhardt is seated in the shade behind the wheel of the tractor, sunglasses in place, looking as comfortable as if he were behind the wheel of his own No. 3. The entire group is wearing matching red-and-white golf shirts and white hard hats, but only Earnhardt looks good doing so.

Earnhardt wheeled the bulldozer into action, working the bucket as the others watched in admiration. "I didn't realize Dale's skills on a tractor until that day," Gordon said. "I mean, this is a big piece of machinery. This is not just some little tractor.

I mean, it was big. And we got on that thing, and . . . he had the bucket going. It's like he had one at home or something. It was so impressive."

In the coming years, the Daytona museum would host some of the most impressive and important cars of NASCAR's recent history, several of which were driven by Earnhardt with only slightly more grace than that bulldozer.

THE ONLY TRACK in the United States that equals Daytona for prestige is Indianapolis Motor Speedway. Home of the Indy 500, IMS is a virtually flat squared-off oval that runs nearly two and a half miles. A quarter of a million people can fill the stands on race day, and another 150,000 cram into the infield. A race at Indy is the largest spectator sport on the planet.

The rivalry between NASCAR and open-wheel racing has existed since the days of Bill France, and the Indy 500 was a marquee event every bit the equal of the Daytona 500. When NASCAR turned its eyes to Indianapolis Motor Speedway in the early 1990s, its drivers salivated at the prospect of sticking it to the elitist open-wheel types who'd criticized their cars as "taxicabs" or worse. IndyCar aficionados had always cast a disdainful eye at NASCAR; according to legend, Bill France Sr. was kicked out of the 1954 Indy 500 for "lack of proper credentials." France used the insult as motivation to create his own version of an iconic track: Daytona International Speedway.

When NASCAR first tested at Indy in 1992, Earnhardt made sure he was the first driver on the track. "Dale was a guy who wanted to be first to arrive at the track, first at the end of the race, first out of the racetrack, first to get to the airport—first at everything," Chocolate Myers later told NASCAR.com. "Well, we unloaded and Dale went out and actually raced Rusty Wallace—and beat him—to the finish line on the very first practice lap NASCAR had ever run at Indianapolis. Dale was proud of that, too. He wanted to be the guy who led NASCAR's very first lap at Indy."

He also wanted to win both the pole and the checkered flag for the first NASCAR Sprint Cup race there in August 1994, but missed on both. Rick Mast won the pole, and Jeff Gordon, no stranger to Indy, won that inaugural race. When Indy came back around on the 1995 schedule, Earnhardt had Gordon in his sights. Gordon was first in points, Earnhardt third. Gordon had five wins, Earnhardt two.

Decades before, Ralph Earnhardt had established himself as the best driver at every major short track in North Carolina. Earnhardt now wanted to establish himself as the best at every NASCAR Cup track. The 1995 Brickyard 400 didn't begin auspiciously for him, however, or for any of racing's old guard. Gordon won the pole, and what was left of Hurricane Erin rained out the second qualifying round. That meant Indy legend A. J. Foyt would be unable to qualify, missing a race at Indy for the first time since 1958.

The day of the race dawned ugly and stayed that way. A steady morning rain pelted the grandstands, the track, the world-famous pagoda. Forecasts indicated that the nasty weather would continue through the day and on into the next.

Races can't run with even a tiny bit of rain on the track because the slick tires on race cars don't slough off water like everyday street tires. The cars would slide into the wall at the first turn of the first lap. At the same time, it's a dicey business, postponing a race. Sticking around for an extra day isn't always an option for fans. Logistics get tricky for teams and media, so NASCAR does everything it can to run the race on the day it's scheduled. The heavens cooperated, but not in time to prevent a fair amount of chaos. Word had spread through the crowd that the race was canceled, and half the crowd left the track.

The skies cleared at 3:30, and NASCAR began its track-drying procedures. NASCAR uses everything from jet dryers to handheld leaf blowers to push the water off the track and give tires enough chance to grip the slick surface. By 4:25, officials deemed the Brickyard dry enough to race, and the green flag dropped as fans were still trying to find their seats.

The race ran flat-out nonstop, with only four laps of caution. Gordon took the lead and held it for the first thirty-one laps. Bill Elliott and Rusty Wallace took turns at the front, too; in all, eleven drivers would lead at least one lap. Wallace had trouble of every sort on pit road; he had to dodge two cars colliding ahead of him, then had to weave around a rolling tire. Earnhardt took advantage, and held off Wallace by more than half a second for the win.

Gordon finished sixth, and would go on to win the championship that season, but Earnhardt had captured his win at Indy, and he wasn't going to let it pass without a shot at Gordon. "Look at it this way," Earnhardt said on several occasions. "I'm the first *man* to win the Brickyard 400."

At one point during the 1995 season Earnhardt had joked that if Gordon did win the championship, he'd have to toast with milk rather than champagne. Later that year, at the Waldorf-Astoria's famed Starlight Roof, Gordon—who had become the youngest driver ever to win a championship—took the stage and found Earnhardt in the crowd. He acknowledged Earnhardt, who had finished second that year, and lifted a champagne glass of milk in a toast. Earnhardt grinned and raised his own glass in return.

"Someday when I retire and I'm gone from racing," Earnhardt would say years later of his Indy win, "people will look back and say, 'Earnhardt, he was a seven-time champion, but he was a winner here. There's no other seven-time champion that's ever won here.'"

"I knew it meant a lot to him when he did eventually win [at Indy] because he knew, I think, that he was on the backside of his career," Junior said in 2012. "He certainly wasn't staring at fifteen more years, and knew the opportunities would be limited coming [to Indy] once a year."

EARLIER THAT SEASON at Bristol, Tennessee, you hardly would have known that Earnhardt was on the backside of his career. Bristol Motor Speedway is one of NASCAR's iconic tracks. Shaped like a coliseum, it's every bit the bloody proving ground that word implies. The Bristol night race in August was one of sports' toughest tickets for decades. Even though the track seats 160,000, no one ever sits down at Bristol, certainly not while Earnhardt was driving.

It's tight in Bristol—a half-mile-long, high-banked track so compact that driving it has been compared to flying a fighter jet in a gymnasium. The only way to avoid contact in Bristol is to skip the race altogether. Dale Earnhardt wouldn't dream of missing a race, and he didn't mind a little contact, either. In 1995, just a couple dozen laps into the race, he spun Rusty Wallace in an incident that sure didn't seem an innocent mistake. NASCAR sent Earnhardt to the back of the field, which was roughly akin to turning a hungry dog loose in a steakhouse. Earnhardt banged his way up through the field like a man chopping firewood, spinning Lake Speed and Derrike Cope en route to the front.

Finally, only Terry Labonte remained ahead. Labonte, who'd already won one Cup championship in 1984 and would win another in 1996, was as tough a bastard as Dale but, like most of the rest of the field, didn't quite have Dale's crazed determination to win at all costs.

"We were running tires that were a lot older than Dale's, so he was coming in a hurry," Labonte recalled. "So the team was warning me over the radio that Dale was coming, and I was like, 'Um, yeah, I noticed that.'"

Earnhardt caught up to Labonte on the final lap of the night. The front end of Earnhardt's car looked like it had been chewed on, and Labonte's rearview mirror had the best view of it in the house. Laps at Bristol take about fifteen seconds, and those must have been fifteen of the longest seconds of Labonte's life.

Labonte's older tires gave him less traction, and he was coming up hard on lapped traffic with Earnhardt right behind him. Something had to give. Would Labonte stop? Would Earnhardt lift off the throttle to avoid hitting Labonte? Rhetorical—and ridiculous—question. In turn 4, Earnhardt hit Labonte hard, turning him and knocking him right into the lapped traffic.

"I just kept my foot in it," Labonte said afterward. "I knew I could beat him to the line if I didn't try to save it," meaning that he just let the car skid of its own volition rather than kill momentum by trying to turn it the right direction. So Texas Terry spun, hit the lapped car of Ward Burton, and crossed the finish line sideways . . . just barely ahead of Dale.

After the race, Earnhardt was holding court with a few reporters, playing coy about how serious he'd been about spinning out Labonte, Speed, Cope, and Wallace. Right about then, a water bottle came flying over the crowd and hit Earnhardt in the face. Rusty Wallace followed right behind. He'd been riding around Bristol seething for the last few hours, ever since Earnhardt had spun him out a few laps into the race.

"I'll see you in fucking Darlington, Dale!" Wallace screamed. "I ain't forgetting this, and I ain't forgetting Talladega!" Referring, of course, to the infamous wreck two years before that may have cost Wallace a championship.

"Dale didn't do it on purpose," Petree, Earnhardt's crew chief, tried to tell Wallace.

"How the hell would you know?" Wallace shot back.

"Rusty," Earnhardt said, trying to calm the waters, "call me tomorrow."

"Yeah, I'll fucking call you," Wallace said. "It was thirty fuck-ing laps into the race!"

Just another night at the short track with Earnhardt.

THERE'S A PECULIAR element in NASCAR: drivers in the highest-level series can drop down and race in lower-level series. Sometimes it's for pride, sometimes it's for greed, sometimes it's for the love of racing. Regardless, Cup-level drivers usually have lit-tle trouble succeeding—and winning series championships, until rules changed in 2011—in the series known as Sportsman in Ralph Earnhardt's day and Xfinity today. Despite the unfair nature of the practice—it's not unlike a pro football player dropping in at a college game to throw around some underclassmen—Cup regulars bring undeniable juice to a lower-level race, and sponsors love that juice.

Way back in 1983, in the midst of his disastrous and expen-sive two-year run with Bud Moore, Earnhardt realized he'd lost some of the mojo from his championship season. Racing wasn't fun anymore, dammit, and Earnhardt decided that the best way to race better was to race more. Perhaps it was a lesson learned from his father, who once said, "A man learns something every race he drives, and I drive three times a week."

Earnhardt decided to run races in the second-tier series—then known as the Busch Series—and serve as his own boss. He hired his former brother-in-law, Tony Eury Sr., as crew chief. He named the operation the most obvious name possible: Dale Earnhardt Inc.

"In the beginning DEI was nothing more than Dale and his buddies from the Mooresville fire department just messing around," longtime driver Jimmy Spencer told *Sports Illustrated*. "Hell, Dale had more deer heads on the wall in his shop than trophies."

Busch/Nationwide/Xfinity Series regulars are generally young drivers on the way up or older drivers still hanging around.

Whenever a Cup-level regular descends to the series, it's usually about as unbalanced a fight as you'd expect, Cup drivers' superior ability apparent at every turn. Earnhardt had little trouble at the lower level, winning five of eleven races in 1986. He'd managed to drive for one owner while owning another team. It was a uniquely NASCAR way to extend his reach and his wealth.

By the mid-1990s, Earnhardt the racer and Earnhardt the businessman decided to align interests. DEI expanded into the Truck Series, the lowest of NASCAR's three national series and another venue for drivers on the way up or out. Earnhardt tabbed Ron Hornaday Jr. to drive a truck for DEI starting in 1995, then added a second full-time Busch car driven by Jeff Green.

A growing team demanded a larger facility, and in 1996 Earnhardt started work on his dream facility, the DEI headquarters. Located on a two-lane road midway between Kannapolis and Mooresville near Earnhardt's farm, the 240,000-square-foot facility featured everything from a fabrication and body shop to a paint shop to a trophy room to a restaurant-quality cafeteria. American and North Carolina flags flew outside the facility's mirrored exterior, and during the weeks after a DEI car won a race, a checkered flag would fly from the third flagpole. The facility also sported meeting rooms with the luxury and opulence that sponsors expected.

"It was a place to house your race team, but also a showplace to make your sponsors proud that they were associated with you and DEI," former Earnhardt crew chief Larry McReynolds said. Soon after its opening, Darrell Waltrip gave the magnificent facility the perfect name: "Garage Mahal."

One of Earnhardt's most sacred spaces was the Deer Head Shop, the garage so named because of the many stuffed deer heads that adorned the walls. It was Earnhardt's refuge, his own magnified version of Ralph's little garage on Sedan Street, and Earnhardt welcomed in anyone with the sense to turn a wrench the right way.

"We'd go down there every Monday night for what we called Monday Night Thunder, just talking racing and the weekend and whatever," Hornaday recalled. "We'd stay there till Teresa called Dale in, sometimes ten o'clock, sometimes two a.m."

Around this time Hornaday brought a young racer who was sleeping on his couch over to Earnhardt's to meet the man himself. The racer, a kid by the name of Jimmie Johnson, was awed to be in Earnhardt's presence and was delighted when Earnhardt reached into a drawer and presented him with a knife embossed with Earnhardt's own signature.

"Boy, now you've got to give me a gift back," Earnhardt said.

Johnson was dumbstruck.

"You've got to give me a gift back," Earnhardt continued, "or it's seven years' bad luck. I haven't won at Daytona yet, I don't need this working against me too."

Johnson would one day approach Earnhardt's career championship total, but on this day, he had absolutely nothing on him. No gift, no token, nothing. In a panic, he ran out to the parking lot and pulled a handful of change out of Hornaday's ashtray. He handed it to Dale, and that seemed to satisfy the debt.

Earnhardt enjoyed racing in the lower-level NASCAR series, but he always had his eye on something larger: leading his own team into the Cup level. It wasn't an easy transition. Jeff Green ran two Cup races and Robby Gordon one under the DEI banner, but DEI cars failed to finish any of the three races.

Racing at the Cup level wasn't a tough thing for Earnhardt's team to do; all you had to do was throw fistfuls of money at the problem. But competing? That took a lot more money, and a hell of a driver, which Earnhardt didn't have in 1996. Now where on earth could the most demanding man in NASCAR find someone like that?

CHAPTER 12

THE GUNSLINGER SLOWS

"I DIDN'T HAVE a vision," Junior once said of his early racing days. "I just wanted to drive race cars, and do whatever I had to do to get to that point."

Kelley Earnhardt had decided—or the NASCAR culture of the times had decided for her—that racing was no longer an option. Junior stuck with it, spending the mid-1990s on a grind throughout the Southeast, following the same paths and the same roads his father and grandfather had traveled two, three, four decades before. But the name preceded him. Whenever an Earnhardt showed up at a track, drivers expected him to be ready to slam their cars into the wall, and often responded preemptively.

It wasn't easy, being a kid with the name Earnhardt. Take, for instance, one race Junior endured while running Street Stocks, modified versions of standard showroom models. He brought his latest pride and joy to the track, a car he'd labored over for weeks and months. Another driver sized it up, saying, "Man, that car looks too good to be out on the racetrack," implying that Senior had paved the way for Junior with every advantage. Junior lasted exactly one turn before the other driver put his beautiful ride into the wall.

"I thought he was giving me a compliment," Junior said years later, "and then later on I found out that he'd told a lot of other drivers that he was gonna be the first one to run over it, because it was so good-looking. And he was jealous because here was an

Earnhardt coming in with a brand-new race car and he had to drive around in some ragged heap."

Purses at these tracks lacked the zeroes that Earnhardt collected at the Cup level. Winners of the forty-lap races would get $1,000, second place $600, and on down from there. Earnhardt wasn't funding Junior, so he cut corners where he could. On the way back from Myrtle Beach, he'd stop in Darlington, South Carolina, and sleep in the parking lot of a Huddle House not far from the same track where his father won so many races.

"Why are you sleeping in a parking lot?" Rudy Branham, a fellow short-track racer, once asked Junior. "Can't your daddy get you a bed?"

"Man, he don't give me enough money to get a damn hotel," Junior said.

By 1996 Junior had shown enough determination and skill to warrant a run at the big time. Let the record show that Dale Earnhardt Jr. first climbed behind the wheel of a DEI car—No. 31, sponsored by Mom n' Pop's restaurants—for a Busch Series race at Myrtle Beach Speedway in South Carolina on June 22, 1996. Junior started the Carolina Pride/Red Dog 250 in seventh, finished fourteenth, and walked away with a purse of $1,880. The next year Junior ran eight races at the Busch level, even posting a top-ten finish at Michigan.

That was enough for Senior to make the commitment to throw his full weight behind his son's burgeoning career. And Earnhardt's weight in NASCAR could tip the sport's gravitational axis. As Junior was making a name for himself on the track, Earnhardt had his eye on the souvenir market. He called Fred Wagenhals, former CEO of Action Collectibles and told him that there was a potential gold mine for the company, a driver who needed a licensing deal immediately.

"I have the next Dale Earnhardt for you," Earnhardt said.

"Okay," Wagenhals replied. "What's his name?"

Earnhardt laughed. "His name is Dale Earnhardt Jr." With-in years, Dale Earnhardt Jr. would be one of the most successful brands in sports history.

Needless to say, there's more to being a NASCAR driver than a heavy right foot and a licensing deal. You're also the face of an entire enterprise, a walking billboard not just for your team but for your sponsors and your sport. You go and act like a jackass in, say, a McDonald's car or a McDonald's fire suit, and McDonald's won't be very happy with you. Earnhardt knew this, and he wanted Junior to understand it long before he'd be tested with live cameras and microphones.

During one media outing at Bristol, he pulled aside Lori Worley, the local Bristol reporter, and instructed her to take Junior into a side room and begin grilling him as if she were conducting a real interview. Earnhardt wanted Junior to get some practice answering questions, to learn the athlete's delicate art of seeming to say plenty while actually saying nothing at all.

Worley sat down next to Junior and started with the most obvious question: "Tell me about your relationship with your father."

Junior's response was direct, honest, straightforward; he loved his dad, but would love more time with him, too. Worley asked her next question: "Tell me about your relationship with Teresa."

Junior began speaking, and Worley blanched. The relationship between Junior and his stepmother Teresa was "clearly tempestuous," she said, and here he was spilling it all over the table to a reporter he'd only just met. "Unless you want to get something started with everyone in your family," she told Junior, "you might not want to be so honest." Worley told Earnhardt of Junior's lack of discretion, and the tension between wife and son clearly pained him.

Nowadays, every driver undergoes media training, learning how to deflect uncomfortable questions and weave sponsor mentions in wherever possible. And Junior, particularly in recent years, has become one of NASCAR's best interviews, primarily because he still manages to inject more than a little honesty into virtually every interview.

Earnhardt also knew Junior could benefit from some of his on-track experience, and he began taking the boy around to various tracks on the circuit, pointing out the best lines and sharing the unique secrets of each track's concrete. You don't want to go into a fierce track like Darlington, for instance, without having at least some idea of what you'll be facing.

Darlington Raceway, located in the Middle of Nowhere, South Carolina, boasts a hallowed history. Back in 1949, when Bill France was just getting NASCAR off the ground, a landowner named Harold Brasington decided to get in on the action. Brasington had been talking about bringing a track to Darlington since seeing the 1933 Indy 500 in person. By 1949 he'd acquired the land and the guts to make his dream a reality. Manning his own bulldozer, Brasington carved a track out of the earth. His original plan miscalculated the position of a nearby landowner's minnow pond, resulting in the distinctive egg-shaped design Darlington has to this day. The 1.25-mile track is one of NASCAR's signature venues, and still hosts the Labor Day Southern Insert-Ever-Changing-Sponsor-Name-Here 500.

The very first Southern 500 featured seventy-five drivers—yes, really—and lasted six hours, so long that drivers were buying tires from fans in the infield just to finish the race. The next year, eighty-two drivers started the race; only one driver was within nine laps of winner Herb Thomas. Darlington earned the title of the Track Too Tough to Tame, and that was more than just marketing hype. Drivers at the track routinely received the Darlington Stripe—a gash in their sheet metal brought about by all-too-frequent contact with the wall—and anyone who came away from the track with a victory knew they'd achieved something special.

Earnhardt had no equals and few peers at Darlington. Over the course of his career, he'd win there nine times, second only in his career (with Atlanta and Bristol) to his ten victories at Talladega. Only David Pearson won more at the track. By the early 1990s Earnhardt had dominated Darlington for well over a decade and was in the midst of one of his many impressive streaks (winning three in a row from 1989 to 1990, placing 1-4-1-2-2-2 in six Darlington races from 1993 to 1995). It was time to pass along a bit of knowledge to the next generation.

Earnhardt rang up Russell Branham, then a PR associate at the track, and told Branham to reserve the track for him and him alone. This was in the days when NASCAR drivers could test at any track, any time during the year, a practice that has since been discontinued. Earnhardt gathered Junior and Hornaday into his plane, flew from Mooresville to Darlington, and took a helicopter into the track's infield.

Branham was waiting there in a Pontiac Bonneville, the kind of conservative four-door sedan beloved by rental companies for its utterly inoffensive character. Earnhardt ordered Junior and Hornaday into the back, then climbed into the shotgun seat so he could explain the track's nuances to the two young drivers.

Earnhardt looked at Branham and made a bone-chilling demand: "You drive."

"Dale, I can't drive this track," Branham replied. "If I wreck, I'll get fired."

"You won't wreck," Earnhardt replied. "If you wreck the car, I'll buy the car."

Branham breathed deep, wheeled the Bonneville out onto the track, and began turning laps. Branham had driven thousands of laps on the 1.4-mile track, mostly giving track visitors an up-close look at the Lady in Black. None of them had ever been quite as nerve-racking as this.

"I was rolling at about eighty miles an hour, thought I was doing all right," Branham recalled. "Then I hear this noise from the passenger seat."

"What the fuck are you doing, Branham?" Earnhardt barked. "Pick it up, pick it up. I can't show them anything going this slow."

Junior and Hornaday sat in the backseat, their eyes wide, taking in every word.

Branham swallowed hard and pushed the gas pedal down. The speedometer ticked past 90, 100, finally hitting 110 miles an hour. The car was starting to bump and hop over the old track, and Branham believed he'd done the impossible: driven well enough to impress Earnhardt.

"Move your leg," Earnhardt said, slapping Branham's right leg with one bricklike hand. Earnhardt lifted his left foot up and over the center console and jammed down on the gas pedal. He mashed the pedal to the floor and told Branham to steer. And that worked well . . . for a couple of laps.

"Goddamn, boy, don't you know how to drive this track?" Earnhardt said. "Haven't you ever watched me doing it the way I do it? You gotta drive it hard into the turn, then let it slide on up the track. Dammit, give me the wheel." That was how Dale Earnhardt taught his son and Ron Hornaday Jr. how to drive Darlington: while driving a bland sedan from the passenger seat, his left foot crushing the gas, his left hand steering them through every turn of the Track Too Tough to Tame.

"I was just along for the ride," Branham recalled. "But I did look down at the speedometer. We never dropped below 140 miles an hour."

They called the man Ironhead for a reason.

TALLADEGA, ONCE AGAIN. July 28, 1996. Earnhardt again
owned the track, again demonstrated his absolute mastery of
restrictor-plate racing. But then disaster struck, and this time, the
wave collected Earnhardt.

On lap 117 of the DieHard 500, the No. 3 got hit from behind,
skidded sideways along the wall, tipped over, and sat helpless in
the middle of the track as an onrushing pack raced toward its roof
at 180 miles per hour. Earnhardt had injured his sternum colliding with the wall. He leaned forward in the cockpit, holding tight
to the steering wheel to keep from being thrown around. Derrike
Cope hit the roof, collapsing it toward the dash. Robert Pressley
followed with a hit that cracked Earnhardt's left collarbone. As the
3 rolled back onto its wheels, Ken Schrader nailed it one last time.
It was as shocking a wreck as NASCAR had seen in many a year.

Earnhardt's radio wasn't working, so he couldn't reply to Childress. He clambered from the car and refused a stretcher that had
come to aid him—he was unable to lie down because of the pain.
A wrenching AP photo of the day shows Earnhardt climbing out of
the car and looking straight down at the ground, hand on his chest
as if trying to hold in his heart.

The verdict: a broken collarbone and a dislocated sternum. And
still the crazy bastard didn't want to take a day off. Against all
medical advice and common sense, Earnhardt climbed right back
into the car the very next week.

Earnhardt drove while broken for two reasons, one logical, the
other less so. First, NASCAR drivers amass championship points
in every single race. No race, no points. Even a dead-freaking-last
finish was better than putting up a zero. As a result, drivers did all
they could to remain on the track. Ricky Rudd once taped open
his swollen eyes. Davey Allison broke an arm at Pocono and had
his cast Velcro-taped to the shifter the next race. Richard Petty
once ran three races with a broken neck, also suffered at Pocono. It

wasn't until 2014 that NASCAR implemented measures to prevent drivers from racing while injured; until then, drivers raced with illnesses, concussions, and other ailments to avoid losing out on those precious points.

The other reason Earnhardt remained determined to strap in was more primal: he was a man, raised by a man who'd believed in doing one's job without fuss or complaint. Broken bones heal. Broken ambitions don't.

The next week's race happened to be at Indianapolis. The night before the race, Earnhardt watched old Clint Eastwood movies to amp himself up for the task ahead. Just before drivers fired their engines, Dr. Jerry Punch, a trauma physician who doubles as an ESPN commentator, tightened down the belts on Earnhardt and could feel the bones grinding in Earnhardt's chest. "I don't see how he withstood it," Punch said. "I told him he was ridiculous."

Earnhardt could withstand it only for six laps at the Brickyard before getting out of the car—getting hauled out, really. A wreck involving Robert Pressley and Ricky Craven in the rear of the pack was enough to convince Earnhardt that there was no percentage in remaining in the car any longer than necessary.

He radioed the crew to let them know Mike Skinner should finish for him. "The car feels comfortable," he said. "Tell Skinner he's going to have a fine ride."

Cameras followed his agony as he climbed out of the car. Earnhardt seemed to be fighting back tears—whether of pain or frustration it was tough to tell. He sat on the pit wall, watching Skinner get buckled in. Punch leaned over to ask a question, and Earnhardt held up a hand to block the inquiry.

After Skinner pulled off, Earnhardt shook his head in disbelief at his situation. He gave Punch a monosyllabic answer, then stepped away to catch his breath before confiding in the doctor.

"I wasn't in much pain driving along out there," he told Punch as viewers around the country listened in. "Our plan was to get [Skinner] in there in case something happened so I wouldn't hurt myself any more. Dadgum it, it's hard to get out of there, Jerry. I mean, you know, it's my life right here."

The next race fell at Watkins Glen, a road course that would require much more on-track movement and gear shifting, which increased the potential for grievous injury. Earnhardt was undaunted. Childress and Teresa had had quite enough of Earnhardt's tough-guy act, and before the race they asked Punch to come to Earnhardt's motor home to talk some sense into him. Earnhardt couldn't lift his left arm, and he was having tremendous trouble breathing.

He looked at Childress. "If you tell me, Richard, I'm going to hurt this race team by being in your race car," Earnhardt said, "I won't get in it."

It was a devilish trap, and Childress couldn't wriggle out of it. "Are you kidding me?" he replied. "You're Dale Earnhardt. I can't tell you you're going to hurt my race team by being in my car."

"All right," Earnhardt said, a winner once again, "it's done."

On qualifying day, Earnhardt buckled into the car and prepared to run. Punch spoke off-camera to fellow ESPN commentator Benny Parsons. "Let's hope he doesn't slide off this course and hit something," Punch said, fully aware of the gravity of the situation. "He might not make it back."

Childress had driver David Green on standby, but never needed him. Earnhardt went out and set a course record for qualifying speed, and he would go on to finish sixth in the race itself. He shifted and steered with his right hand, using his knees to hold the wheel. He insisted that he didn't feel the pain while he ran. "It hurts," Earnhardt said afterward, "but it's a good hurt."

"Just tell him he can't do something," McReynolds said. "Tell him he can't go to Watkins Glen and qualify with a broken sternum, or tell him he can't outrun you. That's all he needs to hear.

All you've got to do is tell him he can't do something, and he will flat prove you wrong."

Courageous or foolish, the forty-five-year-old Earnhardt was in a slide. He finished 1996 in unspectacular fashion: fourth place, only two wins. The picture turned even darker in 1997. For the first time in his career, the Intimidator wasn't particularly intimidating. Drivers who had once looked fearfully in their rearview mirror for Earnhardt's approach now looked back and watched him fade.

There were still moments. At the 1997 Daytona 500, Earnhardt once again fell short of a win—no real surprise there. A collision with twelve laps remaining sent his car flipping and forced Earnhardt into the care of track medical personnel. Sitting in the ambulance, Earnhardt took a look at his beloved, broken No. 3 and realized that the car's tires appeared intact and functional. He leaped out of the ambulance and hobbled over to the wrecker, where the 3 was already on the tow truck's hook.

"Will that car still crank?" he shouted over the noise of the crowd and the surrounding cars. It did.

"Get out," Earnhardt said to the tow truck driver hooking up the car. "I gotta go." Earnhardt climbed back into the car—which now looked like a dog's old chew toy—and finished the race, five laps behind winner Jeff Gordon, broken but unbowed.

At Darlington a few months later for the 1997 Southern 500, there was no room for a defiant gesture. As the cars circled the track for prerace pace laps, Earnhardt drifted up into the wall. He then began slowly winding his way side-to-side around the egg-shaped track as if lost.

"I can't find my way onto pit road," Earnhardt told his crew over the radio. For a driver as practiced as Earnhardt, this was as shocking as if he couldn't find his own driveway. His voice sounded distant and dazed on the radio. When he finally reached his pit stall, a coterie of track medical personnel helped Earnhardt from the car and loaded him onto a gurney, taking him first to the infield care center and from there to a local hospital.

"He's stable," Childress told assembled media as the race ran behind him. "I talked with him a bit and he was seeing double. He was real groggy before the race started. We were going to try to get him in before the race even started, and he couldn't hear us, couldn't communicate with us." Despite the fact that he was in shorts and barefoot at the start of the race, Mike Dillon, Childress's son-in-law and father of future NASCAR drivers Austin and Ty, would climb into the 3 and drive it the remainder of the race, allowing Earnhardt to at least gain some championship points on the afternoon.

Earnhardt would later recall that he had experienced some double vision as the race was starting, but he had shaken it off. He didn't recall anything after that for more than an hour. He spent some tense days after the race, wondering what the future held. "You always wonder, is there something there," he said at a later press conference, pointing at his head, "after you've been through so much in your racing career. . . . It's a dang thing to go through what we did [at Darlington] and really not have a solid answer of 'this is what happened.'"

As he prepared for an MRI, he wrestled with the possibility that his racing days were done. "You may not be able to go on from here as a driver," he would say later of his thinking in the moments before he learned of the MRI's verdict. "The important thing, in my time, was life itself, my family. If I can't drive, I'll be a car owner for Dale Junior and Steve Park. There's a lot more going on in life than racing."

The next week, at Richmond International Raceway, Earnhardt stood at a podium wearing a classic blue GM Goodwrench shirt and a relieved expression. The medical results had been good. Dr. Charles Branch Jr., a neurologist then with the Bowman-Gray

Medical Center, described the episode as "a temporary dysfunction of the brain," a migraine-like episode or a "short-circuit" related to an old injury. Branch believed there was no elevated risk of a similar event happening in the future.

"The one thing that concerned me was that my dad died of a heart attack," Earnhardt said. "I was concerned about my health and what I may or may not be able to do from here on. . . . I'm healthy. They've released me to race, which is great, but the greatest thing is that I'm confident in myself that it's not going to happen again or that I've got anything wrong with me. They did everything they could do," he said, adding with a forced smile, "Well, they didn't check me to see if I was pregnant."

When asked if he was going to return to a normal Dale Earnhardt–type schedule, he smiled and said, "No, I plan to return to a normal *winning* schedule."

It was the perfect Dale Earnhardt thing to say. It's just that no one could really believe him anymore.

CHAPTER 13

NO MORE MONKEYS

DALE EARNHARDT DIDN'T always have the easiest or most conventional relationships with his own children, but he had no trouble devoting time, love, and energy to other people's. At countless tracks he'd meet Make-A-Wish kids and spend precious prerace time chatting with them. Other times he'd use his celebrity and notoriety to bring a little unexpected joy into the lives of youngsters. In the early 1990s he gave his friend Gregg Dayvault's son Ryan a gift for his sixth birthday—a car-shaped No. 3 phone, the must-have accessory for young race fans of the late 1990s.

Dayvault's father and uncles, who had helped Earnhardt build that pink K2 so long ago, encouraged the boy to plug the phone into the wall socket in the kitchen. "Not two minutes later, the phone rings," Ryan remembered. "I answered it, and I hear this gruff voice saying, 'Whatcha doin', boy? I understand you got one of my phones.'" Earnhardt wished the young fan a happy birthday and created a lifetime memory for Ryan Dayvault, now a Kannapolis city councilman.

Earnhardt also had a dramatic effect on the life of young Austin Dillon, Richard Childress's grandson—a boy who would grow to play a significant role in the Earnhardt legacy. Dillon saw plenty of Earnhardt up close as a kid, and regarded the man as a superhero and a legend all wrapped into one. "He was our hero," Dillon said. "We would gather around the TV every Sunday or at the racetrack and pull for Dale Earnhardt."

Dillon once won a starring role in a slot-car commercial with Earnhardt and Jeff Gordon. Dillon and Earnhardt's daughter Taylor, both in grade school at the time, were supposed to be racing with replicas of the two drivers' cars. There was an argument about who would play with whose car, but, as Dillon recalled, "Dale settled it real quick." Dillon got to drive Dale's car; it would not be the last time Dillon got to run a No. 3.

"If you're talking about his own kids, he was hardheaded," Kelley would say years later. "If you're talking about other kids, he had a soft heart."

And a big one. Earnhardt invested countless hours and untold sums of money in charitable efforts without ever courting any public acclaim. He kept a low profile to prevent other requests for his time and money, but he also enjoyed doing good out of the public view. He'd help local farmers whose land was flooded; he'd make time in his overloaded schedule for a child confined to a wheelchair. He once helped a real-life little old lady at his church whose car failed to start; Earnhardt gave her a ride home and got her car fixed right up. He loaned Dale Jarrett his plane to help ferry thirty-four of Jarrett's family and friends to New York in 1999 to celebrate Jarrett's championship. When Jarrett sought out an invoice for the plane, a service estimated at about $30,000, Earnhardt sent a bill that read CONGRATULATIONS, NO CHARGE.

Fox Sports' Steve Byrnes told the story of the afternoon a local pastor came to see Earnhardt about Sunday services, although Sunday was a notoriously difficult day for Earnhardt to get to church. The talk turned to the church itself.

"What are you working on?" Earnhardt asked.

"Well, we're trying to raise money to get the parking lot paved," the pastor replied.

"How much is it going to be?"

"Seven thousand."

Earnhardt took out his checkbook and began writing. "If you tell anyone I gave you this," he said, "I'm coming over there with my front-end loader and ripping up that asphalt myself."

Thousands of kids sought Earnhardt's attention and benefited from his generosity. One little girl's love for Earnhardt, however, has earned her a hallowed place in Earnhardt lore. Wessa Miller was born with spina bifida, a spinal defect, and was given three days to live at birth. After she left the hospital, doctors predicted she wouldn't celebrate her second birthday. She made it to five, then to ten, and by eighth grade she was homecoming queen, a miracle in more ways than one. She came from tough beginnings; her father Booker left home at sixteen to work in Kentucky coal mines and stayed underground for most of the next twenty-six years.

Wessa loved NASCAR, and she especially loved Dale Earnhardt. In 1997, when six-year-old Wessa received a wish from the Make-A-Wish Foundation, she didn't hesitate to say she wanted to meet Earnhardt. Her mother wasn't quite so keen on the idea. She knew Earnhardt by reputation—the driver they called the Man in Black and the Intimidator. "I knew Dale from the TV, and was worried he'd be moody and mean to Wessa," Juanita Miller said. She still consented to the meeting, which was scheduled for the 1998 Daytona 500.

The Daytona 500 was Earnhardt's white whale, lurking on the Florida coast, waiting for him to come back around every February so it could torment him. He had pursued the whale for nineteen years and had held leads in seventeen of the nineteen races, and all he had to show for it was four second-place finishes and zero wins. The sport's greatest driver could do anything in a race car, could do things race cars weren't even supposed to do—everything except harpoon a victory at the world's most famous track.

"I told people that those things didn't bother me," Earnhardt said. "I lied. You don't come that close to winning the Daytona 500 and not feel it. It hurt."

Moreover, he was forty-six years old and hadn't won a race at all in nearly two years. During 1998's Speedweeks, he attended a celebration honoring the fifty greatest drivers in NASCAR history. Almost all of his fellow legends gathered there for the occasion—among them Richard Petty, Cale Yarborough, Buddy Baker, and Darrell Waltrip—gave him some degree of grief for not winning the big one.

"It just makes me want to go out there and dominate on Sunday," Earnhardt said. "Then we'll have to get all these guys back together again next year so I can bring my trophy with me and polish it up in front of them."

Earnhardt took inspiration wherever he could find it—just weeks before Daytona, John Elway had won his first Super Bowl after a career of frustration and disappointment on the NFL's biggest stage. "If Elway can win a Super Bowl, then I can win the Daytona 500," Earnhardt said. He needed to get himself off the long list of notable losers that included the likes of Charles Barkley, Ted Williams, the Buffalo Bills, and the Chicago Cubs.

The day before the race, the Millers waited anxiously in Earnhardt's garage as he finished his test runs. Wessa's father, Booker, who knew a thing or two about NASCAR, sensed that Earnhardt wasn't happy with the car. A dark cloud hung over his corner of the garage. Booker was nervous about his family's impending intrusion. Would Earnhardt break Wessa's heart?

When Earnhardt spotted Wessa, he immediately strode over and got down on one knee to speak quietly to her. Wessa held out her hand to him, and in it was a penny, a lucky penny she'd carried all the way from Kentucky. She wanted him to have it. He thanked her and took the penny, as he had taken thousands of gifts from fans before. As Wessa and her family were leaving, Earnhardt picked up some yellow glue and promptly glued Wessa's penny to his dashboard. With that penny in view, Earnhardt would run the 1998 Daytona 500.

"There was a real gentleness to him," her father said later. "He told her, 'Wessa, you can do anything you want.' He meant it. She's never forgotten that."

The day of the 1998 Daytona 500 dawned Florida-perfect, as it almost always did—the perfect antidote to the ugly winter gripping the rest of the country. Nearly 185,000 people filled the stands, front stretch, and backstretch, and tens of thousands gathered in the infield.

Earnhardt began the race in fourth and claimed the lead by the seventeenth lap. He surrendered it to Gordon about forty laps later, and the way that Gordon was running this particular afternoon, Earnhardt appeared to have little hope once again.

But the racing gods decided to throw a little good luck Earnhardt's way for once. At lap 123, Gordon hit a chunk of debris, damaging both his front end and his chances. Earnhardt slid by him, just as Cope had slid past Earnhardt eight years before. But this time, there were more than seventy-five laps remaining.

Earnhardt would lead five times, for 107 of the race's 200 laps. But after so much heartbreak, he tried to manage his expectations. Sure, everybody loved Earnhardt, or at least respected him, but nobody was going to lay back and hand him a Daytona 500. He tried to fill the entire track by himself, and for quite a while he was able to do it. The racing gods kept throwing bones Earnhardt's way: Gordon's engine died with three laps to go. Wallace couldn't stay connected with Jeremy Mayfield and slipped back to the pack. Mayfield and Bobby Labonte collided with one another while trying to get a run on Earnhardt.

With just over one lap remaining and Earnhardt in the lead, a yellow caution flag flew when John Andretti, Lake Speed, and Jimmy Spencer got caught up with one another on the backstretch.

Under current rules, NASCAR would halt the race immediately and restart with two all-or-nothing laps—a so-called green-white-checker finish. In 1998 the rules were different; drivers raced back to the line after a caution. The first one back to the start/finish line would win this race.

"I knew when I saw the white flag [for the final lap] and the yellow displayed together that I was going to win the race if nothing happened to my car by the time I got back to the start/finish line," Earnhardt said. He didn't take such a possibility for granted; a meteor could have hit Earnhardt's car in the backstretch of that final lap, and no one would have been surprised.

Earnhardt found Rick Mast, a lapped car, and used him as a moving pick to keep Labonte and Wallace behind him. He hit the line an eye-blink before the two of them, and after that there was only one final caution-speed lap to victory.

"Twenty years of trying. Twenty years of frustration," Mike Joy said in the broadcast booth. "Dale Earnhardt will come to the caution flag to win the Daytona 500! Finally! The most anticipated moment in racing!"

"I wasn't thinking about what could happen," Earnhardt would later say. "I was working to keep my car in front until somebody turned me over or we got to the finish, one of the two."

"Had it gone one more lap, would I have caught him?" Bobby Labonte said years later. "Maybe. But he was the hardest guy to pass at Daytona. I thought, 'Well, crap . . . if I have to lose, at least it's to him.' "

Final result: an average 172.712 miles per hour, the third fastest race in Daytona history at the time. The winner's share was $1,059,105, the first time in the Cup series that a single race win was worth more than a million dollars. "What's the five dollars for?" Earnhardt later said, laughing.

Many of Earnhardt's crew wept openly. When Earnhardt

turned down pit road, he was greeted by one of the most moving scenes in NASCAR history: every crew member from every race crew lined pit road, shaking Earnhardt's hand as he crawled down the strip. It went on for minutes, the first such reception in memory.

Earnhardt initially admitted that he "cried a little bit," the first time he'd done so on a track. "I don't think I really cried," he later corrected himself. "My eyes watered up." Either way, the black 3 turned right off pit road and into the front-stretch grass, where he carved one clockwise three-quarter turn, then another right next to it. No one at track level could see what he was doing, but the fans in the grandstands immediately understood: he was inscribing a 3 into the grass. Dale Earnhardt was autographing Daytona International Speedway. Fans would later head out to admire Earnhardt's handiwork, getting their pictures taken next to the 3. Some lay down in the fresh tracks. Others gathered up chunks of sod as souvenirs. Maybe somewhere, in some yard in Florida or Georgia or North Carolina, that grass grows still.

"They used to boo Earnhardt when he won too much," Joy said as the broadcast wound down. "That'll happen if you dominate any sport. But today, as they introduced the Intimidator, the crowd was full of cheers. If their favorite driver couldn't win the Daytona 500, they wanted this man to drive to Victory Lane."

"He did what he does every year here, except he kept doing it all the way to the end," Gordon said. "We all would have loved to have been in Victory Lane, but we're all real happy for Dale. . . . He's earned it, man. He deserves it."

Earnhardt hadn't just caught the whale. The win ended a fifty-nine-race losing streak, and ended any speculation that Earnhardt could no longer drive five hundred hard miles after the Southern 500 blackout in 1997.

"This win is for all our fans, and all the people who told me,

'Dale, this is your year,' " he said, and then, as if to convince himself, "The Daytona 500 is over. And we won it! We won it!"

Earnhardt entered the media center, ready to exult with the scribes who had followed him for so long. He reached inside his fire suit and with a dramatic flourish withdrew a stuffed toy monkey, once white, now gray and worn. He threw it on the floor, shouting, "I've got that goddamn monkey off my back!" Only Dale knew how long he'd been carrying the sodden thing around.

"This is it," he said. "There ain't nothing gonna top this. Well, maybe that eighth championship."

After the performance, the contemplation. Never again would anyone ask why NASCAR's greatest driver couldn't win its biggest race. "Now, I won't have to answer that question anymore," Earnhardt said. "The years of disappointment, the close calls, all the chapters have been written. Now, the twentieth chapter is in. . . . You can talk about it all day, but you can't put into words the feelings you have inside. It's everything you've ever worked hard to do, and you've finally accomplished it."

One of the quirks of the Daytona 500 is that the winning car stays in Daytona for the year after the race, displayed at the track's museum for fans to see. It's a tradition that can be a bit of a financial hardship on the rare small team that wins the race, but for Richard Childress Racing the donation was a pure delight. "I don't know about Richard," Earnhardt said at a winner's victory press conference the next morning, "but I'm very happy about it. Very excited. We're already planning for next year, since we've got to build a new race car for Talladega."

Richard Childress, who had also never won a Daytona 500, had difficulty containing himself as well. "I woke up about two o'clock this morning and couldn't get back to sleep just because of the excitement," he said. "The night before, I woke up about 1:30, and I couldn't go back to sleep worrying about engines and trying to think of anything that may go wrong the next day, so it was a great feeling to wake up and have that problem instead of worrying about something race-related. It's just an unbelievable feeling."

Earnhardt hadn't forgotten Wessa Miller and her lucky penny. A few weeks later, he invited the Miller family to Bristol and quietly presented them with a Chevy van to help with the drive from their home in Phyllis, Kentucky, to the University of Kentucky Medical Center—a 350-mile round trip—for Wessa's treatments.

In 2008 *Charlotte Observer* writer David Poole tracked down Miller, now in her early twenties, and detailed the difficulties Wessa and her family had suffered in the last ten years. Poole established the Pennies for Wessa Fund to help the family with their ongoing challenges, continuing the good work Earnhardt had started.

After the Daytona victory celebration, Earnhardt headed to New York City and *Late Night with David Letterman* to engage in the long-running winner's tradition of sparring with Letterman, a longtime race fan. Earnhardt, wearing a hideous red, white, and blue leather jacket, offered up his "Top 10 Reasons It Took Me 20 Years to Win the Daytona 500." The entries included "It took me nineteen years to realize I had the emergency brake on," and "Just figured out, if you mash the gas pedal all the way down, the car takes off like a son of a bitch," along with other now-dated references to the Spice Girls and Letterman's driving habits.

The circle was now complete, the last box checked. Earnhardt had done everything it was possible to do in racing. He'd succeeded far beyond his wildest hopes; he'd exceeded by several orders of magnitude what his father had done. The end of his career wasn't visible yet, but Earnhardt knew he only had so many turns left. Which meant it was time to start prepping the next generation.

CHAPTER 14

EARNHARDT VS. EARNHARDT

LISTEN AT ANY NASCAR track, and you'll hear it soon enough:

"Junior! JUNIOR! JOOOOOON-YERRRR!!!"

The fans are always there, just as they've been right from the start, right from the moment he began slinging his car around remote Carolina tracks. He was fast, but never fast enough to outrun his own name. They still call to him, even though they've seen him around the garage for nearly two decades. He used to disguise himself, moving among the crowds wearing jeans and a T-shirt, a cooler held on his shoulder. It was effective, since he looked exactly like his fans: pale, skinny, and clutching a beer. He doesn't do that anymore, but the crowds remain. It's part of the job, and only rarely is it a problem. (He once wore an expensive suede jacket while walking through a scrum of fans, and was dismayed to find that it had gotten ruined, covered with tiny dots from all the open Sharpies fans held around him.)

The only time the throngs of autograph seekers bothered Junior was early in his career, a time when he felt he hadn't earned that level of acclaim. The idea of running twenty-fifth on some backwater track and then seeing dozens of fans waiting for his autograph never sat well with him.

"I've always kind of understood there was going to be a certain amount of attention everywhere I went just because of my last name," Junior said in 2004. "That always made me very uncomfortable because I wasn't getting the attention for anything I did." However, despite the drawing power of his famous last name, or perhaps because of it, he made far more of a conscious effort to connect with fans than his father did. If you knew where to stand—and you were willing to stand there for hours on end—you could catch Junior for an autograph, each and every weekend.

THE CAR WAS a wreck, but what the hell—this was only practice.

Junior ran eight unremarkable races in the Busch Series in 1997. One afternoon during practice at Charlotte, Junior wrecked hard enough to put the body shop guys to work. There would be no more driving this day, but Junior could consult with the DEI garage guys, could stick his head under the hood, could learn something if he chose to stick around. But as an *ESPN: The Magazine* account noted, that didn't exactly happen.

"Screw it," Junior said to a few buddies. "Let's go back to my house."

"To do what?" one said.

"To get drunk!"

Many of Junior's early interviews document just how much beer the kid could drink—eight to get warmed up, a case if he was feeling rowdy, he claimed—and he had plenty of running mates willing to crack a few with him. The problem for Junior was that he was still living under his father's roof—legally if not necessarily literally. Senior took great pride in busting up Junior's gatherings, once swooping in low with his private helicopter's headlights glaring to roust a bunch of partygoers around the pool.

But this particular night, Senior came in through the front

door. "Get the hell off my property!" he growled at Junior's friends, and when the Intimidator orders you like that, you *move*. Then he turned his attention to Junior.

"Why you wasting your damn time over here?" he asked. "Why you drinking? You need to be tearing that car apart, getting ready for the next race."

"Really?" Junior said. "I'm gonna race again? I thought it was over with."

"Hell no, man! You just wrecked, it ain't no big damn deal." To Earnhardt, wrecks were a cost of doing business, like cleaning bills for suits.

His father's unexpressed but implied faith in him kicked something loose inside Junior. The two men went out onto Junior's back porch and talked for two hours, the kind of talk both men had needed their entire lives. "I want to show you what I can do, Daddy, and I keep screwing up," Junior said. "I know you're going to give up on me."

"I ain't ever giving up on you," Senior said, and for Junior, that little bit of cheerleading was all he needed. Junior spent 1998 and 1999 validating every bit of the faith his father had placed in him, winning Busch Series championships both years. He edged out Matt Kenseth for the victory in 1998, then ran away with the championship in 1999. That year he also made his debut in a Cup car, running under the No. 8 in the Coca-Cola 600 just like his father had more than twenty years before. For the record, Junior finished sixteenth in his debut race, while Earnhardt finished twenty-second at the same race back in 1975.

Junior had the skills to run at NASCAR's highest level. All he needed now was the right sponsor. As luck would have it, one was waiting right in the wings.

Today, Hendrick Motorsports is one of the most dominating teams in any sport. With eleven championships in its first twenty-nine years, Hendrick's success stands tire-to-toe against the dynasties of the Los Angeles Lakers, Boston Celtics, Chicago Bulls, Dallas Cowboys, Pittsburgh Steelers, and New England Patriots. That wasn't the case in 1998; even as Jeff Gordon was on his way to winning his third championship in four years, the No. 25 driven by Ken Schrader was foundering. Full-time sponsor Budweiser was not pleased.

"Hendrick has the magic potion now, but back then, it wasn't happening," recalled Tony Ponturo, who handled Budweiser's global media and sports marketing efforts in the 1990s and 2000s. "Ken Schrader was a wonderful guy, but he wasn't finding the winner's circle." That was a problem for Budweiser, then spending millions each year to serve both as the official beer of NASCAR and the sponsor of a weekly pole-position award. The sport continued to grow in popularity, and Budweiser understood that it needed to align itself with a new face to take its marketing into the next millennium. The stakes were huge; the right driver could propel Budweiser back into the spotlight, while the wrong driver could keep the company back in the pack for years.

After vetting every single young driver in the sport—even those several years away from running at NASCAR's top level—Budweiser executives narrowed their choice to two men: Matt Kenseth and Dale Earnhardt Jr. Kenseth may have been the more Cup-ready driver, but the choice was never really in doubt.

"Junior hadn't even won the Busch Championship at that point, but he had everything we wanted to see," said Steve Uline, group director of Anheuser-Busch's sports marketing efforts. "He looked like a guy who drank Budweiser. He had an edge to him. And he had that magic last name."

Budweiser knew all about that magic. For several years, the company had Earnhardt under a "personal services contract," which basically meant that Senior served as the grand prize in Budweiser's ongoing relationship with its wholesalers. Once a year, wholesalers from around the country got to go on a deer-hunting trip with Earnhardt. This wasn't an unusual arrangement for a sponsor and a celebrity; what was unusual was the verve and spirit Earnhardt brought the weekends hanging with the regular joes. "You'd see these guys come in all starstruck," Uline recalled. "But after a day or so, the thrill of being around the famous person wears off. It's then that you can see who's mailing it in. Earnhardt never did. He always stayed positive throughout the entire trip."

Earnhardt remained loyal to Childress, but he wanted to make his own race team competitive at the Cup level. You don't do that without sponsorship, even if you're Dale Earnhardt. Dale Earnhardt Inc. and Budweiser began a slow, stately courtship. Even though there was a clear benefit for both parties, neither was going to blink early. In August 1998 Uline opened negotiations with DEI executives Don Hawk and Ty Norris, and the two sides tried to determine how to merge the interests of two incredibly powerful American brands. Each side had grown accustomed to having contracts bend in its direction, and each side desired the last word in control.

Earnhardt, who had until this point remained above the fray, stepped into the breach. He, Uline, and several others gathered at a steak dinner following some testing at Gateway Motorsports Park in St. Louis.

"Dale was at one end of the table," Uline recalled, "and at one point in the meal, stopped everything and looked straight at me."

"Do you and I have a problem?" Earnhardt said in that familiar growl.

Uline, to his credit, stood his ground. "*You and I* don't have a problem."

"All right." Earnhardt nodded, and the dinner resumed.

"Not long afterward," Uline said, laughing, "the deal was

done." Final total: five years, $10 million a year, a deal that ended up paying off big for both sides.

The most lucrative sports partnership in Budweiser's history—and one of the most memorable of the 2000s—launched with a spectacle straight out of a very prosperous carnival. Dale Earnhardt Inc. invited the local media out to the Garage Mahal for a major announcement. With fanfare, a garage door opened to reveal the famous Budweiser Clydesdales, Junior himself holding the reins. It was supreme sponsor-love theater, and it worked perfectly. In gratitude for his years of service, Budweiser would later present Earnhardt with a Clydesdale of his own for his farm.

Dale Earnhardt Jr. began making thousands of appearances around the country—simultaneously. The army of Junior stand-ees, cardboard cutouts grinning in grocery stores and gas stations everywhere, established Junior as the brand's most popular spokes-man among wholesalers.

The Earnhardt-vs.-Earnhardt storyline was a natural hook, and it started early. Racing is far different from most other sports in that it's possible for fathers and sons to compete on a level playing field (or banked track, as the case may be) with both near the peak of their abilities. That's not going to happen in football or basket-ball; even in baseball and golf, the father is usually on the way out when the son makes his debut.

Junior's Cup-level debut happened in, of all places, Japan, where an exhibition called the Coca-Cola 500 would run at Twin Ring Motegi in November 1998. It would mark the first time father and son had taken to the track against each other in an official race. Well—*semi*-official. The Coca-Cola 500 was a NASCAR-centric showpiece, the third in Japan in recent years. It featured teams from all three major NASCAR series and the regional Winston West Series, as well as various Japanese drivers.

Junior was coming off a Busch Series championship, and his

father had won that year's Daytona 500. This would be an "exhibition" in name only. Both Earnhardts would be driving Coca-Cola-branded cars, Senior a Coke-red No. 3 with the classic logo on the hood, Junior a black No. 1 with one of Coke's stylized polar bears on its hood. At every turn, NASCAR and its broadcast partner helpfully pointed out that Action Collectibles had produced a wide range of Earnhardt-and-son-themed products for casual and committed collectors alike.

At a press conference unveiling the two cars, Senior told the story of the night when Ralph pushed him past a troublemaking competitor at faraway Metrolina Speedway. "I would have liked to have done more of it," he said. "It is exciting to see Dale Jr. grow into the sport, and it will be a great experience to race him in Japan. However," he added with a wink, "it wouldn't look very good for him to beat his good old dad, now would it?"

When a reporter asked Junior when the two had competed for the first time, he recounted the time they were out fishing, and each of them caught a crappie worth mounting. Problem was, they lost track of whose was whose. "And we still argue over which was which, 'cause one's a little bit bigger than the other. But I got a little bit better memory than him."

Turning NASCAR loose on Japan was funny in itself. At the drivers' meeting, Michael Waltrip offered advice to his fellow drivers for dealing with Japanese fans: "It doesn't matter how loud you yell at them, they won't understand any better." NASCAR's Gary Nelson added, "Michael, sometimes it works that way when the other guy speaks English, too."

During one of the cross-country trips on a 190-mile-per-hour bullet train, Helton recalls Earnhardt goofing around by playing "tour guide" and describing the sights of a country he'd never seen, delighting the NASCAR contingent and confusing the hell out of the locals, who had no idea who he was.

When the Earnhardts got down to business, Junior roared out of the gate with a faster practice time than his father. "The feeling I got being on the racetrack with my dad was far better than winning the Busch Series championship," he gloated. "The championship was special, but this is different."

He'd soon learn just how different. Senior had no intention of showing Junior every trick on the track. "It's an exciting deal getting to race Dale Jr. for the first time," Senior said. "I practiced pretty good. I didn't practice hard enough so I could beat him. I wanted him to beat me today so he'd get a 'thinks he can beat the old man' kind of thing in his mind."

Junior offered up a few shots at his old man for his advancing age, all of which Senior took in stride. "Because of Coca-Cola getting involved, this whole thing happened sooner than it would have otherwise," Senior said. "This was a great opportunity for him to get a feel of what it would be like. He didn't expect to win the Busch Series title, but he did. Now he gets to see how hard it is to run in Winston Cup."

The race featured most of the notables of the day: reigning champion Jeff Gordon, Rusty Wallace, Bill Elliott, Darrell Waltrip, and more. Despite the hype, the Earnhardts were largely unremarkable. Jeremy Mayfield won the pole, Gordon would lead sixty-nine laps, and Mike Skinner would win the race.

Midway through the exhibition, Junior decided to get chippy, thumping and then passing Senior. (Years later, Junior would laugh that Senior was so mad, he threw his shoe at his son after the race.) Junior would finish sixth and Senior eighth. Senior wasted no time bolting from the track afterward to prepare for the trip home, while Junior stuck around to enjoy Japanese culture.

Their father-son duels became common, and in 1999 both Earnhardts climbed behind the wheel at an International Race of Champions event at Michigan. IROC was designed to test a driver's pure driving skills without the benefit of a familiar car. Drivers could test practice cars, but prior to the race could only sit behind the wheel of their competition car for measurement purposes.

Earnhardt loved the challenge of racing in an unfamiliar environment and an unusual style. "The IROC guys thought he walked on water," Matt Yocum said. "He would always steer toward the guys working on the cars, rather than the suites or the hospitality tents."

Senior enjoyed himself at every IROC event, though never as much as in 1995, when he'd tormented Jeff Gordon. The IROC series began at Daytona that year, and while at practice, Gordon found himself on Ken Schrader's tail with Earnhardt right behind. Earnhardt gave Gordon a push to get past Schrader, then instantly dropped below Gordon to go three wide in Daytona's backstretch.

"I was just kind of a kid in a candy store, having a great time," Gordon said. "It just seemed like the longest back straightaway I'd ever experienced. It just seemed like that back straightaway went on for like five minutes, because the moment stood in time, and I was just there like taking it all in." Gordon looked to his right at Schrader. In those days, cars didn't have headrests or restraint systems, and he could see Schrader looking straight ahead, focused, trying to hold a three-wide line in Daytona.

Then Gordon looked to his left. "Dale is over here like"— Gordon leaned back in his chair, telling the story. "He's kicked back, he's got one hand over here, one hand on the steering wheel. He's looking at me with this big grin on his face."

They were approaching turn 3, which couldn't accommodate three cars side by side. Someone was going to have to pull up, and Gordon was determined not to be the one that bailed early. He waited . . . waited . . . and finally lost his nerve, pulling back just as Earnhardt swung up the track, floating up all three lanes to get ahead of Schrader. "It would have been a heck of a wreck," Gordon said. "But I'll never forget that look on his face, and just how relaxed he was in that race car at that moment, when I was freaking out because we're three wide."

Four years later, at the 1999 IROC event in Michigan, Senior had another upstart to torment—his son. With ten laps remaining in the race, Senior was in the lead, with Junior not far behind, pondering strategies for getting around the old man. On the final turn of the final lap, Junior got a good run and pulled neck and neck with him. The two hit each other once, twice, three times, and crossed the finish line almost simultaneously.

The margin of victory: 0.007 seconds.

The winner: you already know.

CHAPTER 15

CAGE-RATTLING

WOE TO THE reporter or driver who entered Earnhardt's domain on anything less than high alert. He was an incorrigible prankster, and the garage was his theater.

"You never knew what to expect from him, and that was deliberate," Matt Yocum said. "He wanted you off balance around him. I would be interviewing him and he'd be stomping on my foot or poking me in the ribs, out of the camera's view. I couldn't let on, of course, and he was having a great time."

Any cameraman who tried for the NFL Films–style "hero shot"—shot from below as the cameraman walked backward—was in for a treat. Earnhardt regularly walked those cameramen into people's legs or the backs of cars. He'd throw balls of tape at the camera, he'd grab a headset from a pit reporter and begin berating whoever was back in the studio.

"Every time you'd start laughing," Steve Byrnes said, "he'd say, 'Why aren't you taking this seriously?' "

ESPN reporter Ryan McGee found out the hard way that earnestness made you an easy target. As a young reporter in 1997, he was prepping for an evening out when his bosses asked him to swing by Charlotte Motor Speedway for some interviews. Earnhardt asked McGee why he was dressed so sportily, and McGee made the crucial mistake of mentioning that he was on his way to a date. As McGee was leaving, Earnhardt gave him a hearty slap on the back and wished him good luck. During the date, McGee discovered Earnhardt had dipped his hand in oil and left smears down the back of McGee's crisply laundered shirt.

In the early 1980s, Eddie Gossage—now the president of Texas Motor Speedway—was leaving Bristol, the track where he then worked as a promoter. He was driving sixty miles per hour down 11E—the Tennessee highway that runs past the track—when someone slammed his back bumper.

"I looked in the rearview mirror, and I saw those beady eyes," Gossage said later, laughing. "Earnhardt was right on me, an inch off my bumper. What was I going to do? I wasn't going to brake-check him, and no way I could outrun him." Earnhardt didn't leave Gossage alone until he reached his driveway.

Earnhardt even took his pranks international. He, Childress, Bill France Jr., and NASCAR president Mike Helton were on a trip to Monaco when Earnhardt decided he wanted to drive the famed Formula 1 course there. Problem is, the course runs on public roads, and those roads that day were very public. Earnhardt whipped their rental, a Volkswagen station wagon, through the streets of Monaco like some southern-fried James Bond. "No matter how he would drive," Helton recalled, "you always felt like he was in control. There was something serene about him behind the wheel."

Earnhardt tossed a rubber snake at Helton on a camping trip. He threw country music star Kix Brooks into the ocean off the coast of the Bahamas. At one champions' weekend in New York at the Waldorf, he and Ken Schrader raided the maids' closet and bricked up the doorway of NASCAR VP Jim Hunter with towels. He handcuffed Geoff Bodine to a hotel railing in Louisville. He left Budweiser on the bed of Rusty Wallace, who was devoted to his sponsor Miller Lite, every time Wallace stayed on Earnhardt's boat. He dumped a can of sardines under Wallace's seat just before the Southern 500 on a day when temperatures reached the 90s.

He'd hang out in the Talladega credentials office and tell unsuspecting reporters who called in that Talladega didn't need their coverage and they didn't need to bother coming to the track.

He also loved tweaking the fans. Many hung around outside the walls of the Garage Mahal, waiting for a glimpse of Earnhardt. He'd ride back and forth on his tractor, working the land and waiting to see how long it would take the fans to pick up on his presence. He once did a promotion for Darlington right in front of Daytona International Speedway, holding up a sign that read NEED TWO TICKETS TO DARLINGTON as astonished motorists drove by. While on hunting trips, he'd walk into a remote gas station somewhere in the middle of Alabama, and people would say, "You know who you look like?"

"When you would hang out with Dale," Larry McReynolds recalled, "you didn't need your brain. You could take it out and let it rest. I'd go have dinner with him, and it'd be, 'Don't sit there, sit over there. Eat more of that. Why do you eat that first? Teresa, get him some more of that. You need to drink water. Drink some more water.' I'd come back from dinners with him exhausted."

Earnhardt's rankest prank came at Bristol, when he spotted Childress entering a portable toilet in the infield. Earnhardt climbed into his truck, quietly rolled up to the plastic-walled toilet, and began gently tapping the front bumper of the truck against the door. Then he started striking harder and harder, until the entire toilet itself nearly fell over.

"DAMMIT, DALE," Childress shouted as he stormed out of the john. Soon enough he laughed along with Earnhardt, because, well, what the hell else could he do?

Earnhardt wasn't much for talking politics, though he generally had a conservative streak. Steve Waid, a journalist who'd known Earnhardt since his earliest days at the Cup level, recalls a conversation in which Earnhardt spoke out strongly against welfare.

Earnhardt's reasoning was straightforward: he'd been able to climb up from poverty with his own hands; why couldn't anyone else?

On other matters, though, Earnhardt could surprise. The Confederate battle flag remains an icon in NASCAR infields, second only to Earnhardt's 3, but Earnhardt himself was no fan of the symbol. There's a bumper sticker out there still on sale at just about every truck stop in the South. AMERICAN BY BIRTH, it reads, SOUTHERN BY THE GRACE OF GOD, usually with a rebel flag alongside. One day Earnhardt slapped one of these stickers onto the bumper of one of his trucks. He didn't think any more of it until his housekeeper, an African American woman beloved by Junior and Kelley, mentioned that the flag's implications made her uncomfortable.

Earnhardt immediately located a knife, strode out to his truck, and sliced off the rebel flag. The motto remained; the flag itself was trashed. "He didn't want to offend anybody or make anybody mad in that manner," said Kelley, telling the story on her *Fast Lane Family* podcast. "He had a good heart."

Years later Junior would take a similar stand—though, like his father, he was initially careful not to speak out too loud. "The rebel flag represents closed-minded, racist views that have no place in today's society," he wrote in his 2002 memoir. He followed that up with an even stronger denunciation in 2015 following a racially motivated mass shooting in Charleston. Calling the flag "offensive to an entire race," Junior said the Confederate battle flag "belongs in the history books, and that's about it."

The Earnhardts' stance against the Confederate flag put NASCAR fans on the defensive. The Confederate flag—and more specifically the spirit of rebellion it embodied in the minds of its supporters— decorated and defined NASCAR infields from the moment the first engines fired. Junior's stance forced NASCAR's hardcore southern base to choose between two icons, and reminded the rest of the country that NASCAR wasn't quite the homogenous redneck bloc it might appear.

IF EARNHARDT'S CAREER were a Western, by 1999 he'd become the grizzled gunfighter who took a little longer to get going. The new guns in town were faster, but were they craftier?

Earnhardt's last championship was nearly half a decade behind him. He'd established a multimillion-dollar empire that included a Lear jet, a home in Florida's Palm Beach Gardens, and the seventy-four-foot-yacht *Sunday Money* and the fifty-foot fishing boat *Intimidator*. A new crop of drivers was gaining on him, and his son was only a year away from his Cup debut. The talk that Earnhardt should think about hanging it up had gone from whisper to suggestion. (Not demand. Never demand.) What could be left for Earnhardt to do but to embarrass himself?

Plenty, as it turned out. Earnhardt's knack for thundering a car through a space half its width didn't decline with age. Nor did his thirst for immediate vengeance upon suffering any insult.

If the 1995 Bristol showdown between Earnhardt and Terry Labonte was single combat, 1999 was all-out war. The 1999 Bristol night race set up as one of the most competitive in the sport's history. Tony Stewart won the pole, and less than a quarter of a second separated him from the last-place qualifier in the forty-three-car field. Stewart held the lead for much of the 500-lap race's first 300 laps, but then Labonte stepped up, eased the youngster aside, and appeared to take total control.

He would've held it, too, were it not for that meddling 3. Labonte lost his hold on the top spot during a late caution with ten laps remaining when he decided to come in for fresh tires. He would start the final sprint of the race in fifth place, behind Earnhardt, Stewart, Jeff Gordon, and Mark Martin. Labonte passed Martin and Gordon with four laps left. Stewart was toast with three laps remaining. That left Earnhardt.

With two laps to go, Labonte raced Earnhardt the way Earnhardt would've raced Labonte: bare-knuckled and free-swinging. Labonte thumped the 3 twice, and as they passed the start-finish line for the final time, Labonte freed himself from Earnhardt. Fresh tires trump old ones every time at Bristol. But fresh tires don't trump a front bumper, especially Earnhardt's. As Labonte entered turn 2, Earnhardt drove straight into him, spinning him all the way around. Labonte took out Stewart, Martin, Ricky Rudd, and Sterling Marlin while Earnhardt scooted right on through to victory.

Right after Earnhardt crossed the finish line, a furious Jimmy Spencer slammed into Earnhardt's car. Earnhardt had broken the drivers' code. Anyone can win by wrecking the other guy, but it's dangerous as hell. That's why it's not done every week.

Earnhardt climbed out of his car in Victory Lane, ready to revel in the customary cheers and champagne bath, but this time he heard something different: boos, cascading down from all corners of the coliseum. This was an unprecedented show of disrespect, especially for Earnhardt. "Watch my back," Earnhardt told Rhodes as fans threw their Earnhardt T-shirts and other memorabilia over the fence and onto the track. They loved their Intimidator, but there were limits.

"I didn't mean to really turn him around," Earnhardt said with the kind of feigned innocence that made you either want to follow him into hell or try to send him there. "I meant to rattle his cage, though."

Labonte was livid, and Earnhardt's explanation was unconvincing. "Have you ever heard him say he means to spin anybody out?" Labonte said the next week. "He never had any intentions of taking anybody out. It just 'happens' that way."

Other drivers echoed Labonte's sentiments. "It wasn't right, it wasn't right," said Jimmy Spencer, who'd finished second. "I knew there was going to be a wreck," Ricky Rudd said. "In that situation, you've got to look at who you're dealing with."

"It was pretty amazing," Labonte would say years later. "I'd never seen Dale get booed like that. I think even some of his own fans were booing. Watching the look on Dale's face on some of the TV stuff, I don't think he really knew what to think about it, either."

"He shrugged it off, but I know it bothered him," Bristol's Lori Worley said. "He was proud that he won, but he wasn't proud of how he'd done it."

EARNHARDT SPENT MOST of the 1999 season suffering neck pain and numbness following a March wreck at Atlanta. He waited until December to undergo surgery to repair a ruptured disk and pinched nerve, having raced an entire season with the kind of neck injury that would sideline almost anyone else for weeks. Dr. Charles Branch Jr., the same surgeon who'd overseen Earnhardt following his Darlington blackout, removed the ruptured disk and fused the C6 and C7 vertebrae, which kept Earnhardt out of the car for more than a month.

"The surgery couldn't have gone any better," an unnamed DEI spokesman told the press, and Earnhardt would later say he felt invigorated and free from the pain that had plagued him for several seasons.

As the millennium arrived, Earnhardt was still as mean as ever, and now feeling better than he had in years. If NASCAR was on the cusp of a brand-new age, it didn't look like the old one was going to go quietly.

CHAPTER 16

FIND YOUR OWN WAY HOME

AS THE 2000s dawned, there was a sense that NASCAR was barreling headlong into a new era, ready or not. NASCAR's popularity, fueled in large part by Earnhardt, had grown large enough to attract mainstream national attention. And while that broadening base was exactly what NASCAR's brass had always sought, it came with a catch—the nation's growing disenchantment with cigarette smoking. This was good news for the lungs of America, but bad news for the Winston Cup and the flow of tobacco-company sponsor dollars to NASCAR. The days where cigarette companies could plaster their brand names atop NASCAR races and trophies were numbered, and the numbers were shrinking fast. The "Winston" adorning NASCAR's championship would soon give way to "Nextel" and then "Sprint," and even the most moonshine-soaked NASCAR infield campers could understand that metaphor.

The year 2000 wasn't shaping up to be an exceptional one for Earnhardt. He won in Atlanta in the season's fourth race, but results afterward were indifferent. He was running strong, but so were younger drivers like Bobby Labonte, Jeff Burton, and Gordon. Junior was starting to make his name alongside fellow youngsters like Matt Kenseth and Tony Stewart. Time was passing, and in racing, nobody slows to let you keep up.

In April, Junior won his very first career Cup race at the 2000 DirecTV 500 in Texas. As Junior rolled toward Victory Lane, fist pumping out the window, his father stood there waiting, wiping his face with a rag. Jade Gurss, Junior's publicist, moved toward Junior with the requisite Budweiser hat and towel for on-camera interviews. Before Gurss could reach Junior, a meaty paw threw him backward.

Dale Sr. leaned into the car and embraced his son. "I love you," he told Junior. "I want to make sure you take the time to enjoy this and enjoy what you accomplished today. You can get so swept up with what's going on around you that you really don't enjoy it yourself, so I want you to take a minute and celebrate how you want to celebrate."

It was a perfect moment—the culmination of decades of hard work to satisfy his father. As his team shouted the Budweiser catchphrase, "Wasssaappppp?," Junior understood that victory brought him a new level of connection with his father.

"In the past when I spent time with him, there was rarely a lot of conversation," Junior later said. "I didn't know what to say to him, and I didn't know whether what I had to say was worth a dime to him because I was just a child. But now that I'm more accomplished as a person and a driver I'm getting all sorts of attention in all areas. I'll say he respects me a lot more, he takes what I have to say into consideration more often, and we can relate more often than we did in the past."

Junior also won at Richmond a few weeks later, holding off none other than Terry Labonte. Less than a year removed from his cage-rattling at Bristol, Texas Terry apparently decided not to take out his revenge on Junior. Earnhardt, who finished tenth, once again found Junior in Victory Lane. This time the message was more succinct: "I love you. Find your own way home." Earnhardt didn't hang around at the track for anyone, even his own son.

Junior's ascent continued at the Winston, the Charlotte-based All-Star race. With the sounds of Smash Mouth's "All Star" echoing across Charlotte Motor Speedway, Junior and the crew of the brilliant red Budweiser No. 8 reveled in the cheers of "Joooonyer!" Only winning race teams could run in the Winston at that time, and Junior was only the second rookie—after Davey Allison—to make the elite field. Prior to the race, Humpy Wheeler, Ralph Earnhardt's friend from long ago, made sure everyone knew he was picking Junior, a layer of pressure that ticked off Earnhardt.

Wheeler's prescience paid off as Junior outran Jarrett, Wallace, and the old man himself to take a most unlikely victory. Junior whooped as the crowd roared and the confetti flew, even offering "Mr. Oreo"—the Oreo cookie mascot—a swig of Budweiser, a move that didn't go over so well with the execs at Nabisco.

That season—specifically, the Texas race Junior won—also saw the Cup debut of Adam Petty, a friend of Junior's who represented the fourth generation of Pettys to race in NASCAR. But Petty died just days after the Richmond race while testing at Loudon. Cause of death: a basilar skull fracture sustained when Petty's car hit the turn 3 wall head-on.

"I looked at him almost like a classmate," Junior wrote in his autobiography. "We grew up together, playing in the infield at racetracks with other kids like Jason Jarrett while our dads were busy racing."

The summer marked the Cup-level debut of another Earnhardt. At the 2000 Pepsi 400 in Michigan, Kerry Earnhardt joined his father and half-brother on the starting grid. At thirty, Kerry was a bit old to be making his Cup debut, and he was trying to draw notice in a year when Junior had become the hottest driver in the sport. Earnhardt had set up Kerry with the best possible chance to succeed, working with Dave Marcis, his old would-have-been-teammate with Rod Osterlund way back when, to field a DEI-backed team that included Hornaday's pit crew.

"Our goal is to stay out of trouble and to gain as much experience as I can," Kerry said before the race. "I hope we don't make any of the other drivers mad at us."

"Especially your dad," his dad said.

Kerry crashed six laps into the race and finished last, but that wasn't the point: Earnhardt was the first father to start a race with his two sons since Lee Petty did it with Richard and Maurice way back in 1960.

Junior wrote a column for NASCAR.com throughout the 2000 season, recounting the triumphs and travails of a rookie on the circuit. One night not long after that Michigan race, Junior decided to dig below the life's-pretty-cool-now surface. What emerged was a letter, "Through the Eyes of a Son," that was stark in its emotional honesty and outright hero worship.

Junior wanted to show it to his father prior to posting it online, and managed—against all odds—to catch his father alone in his DEI office. Junior handed the letter to his father. "He sat down to read it," Junior recounted later, "and got a strange look on his face. He got up and walked right over to me, right in my face. He gave me a hug and told me how much he liked it, and I thought for a second we were both gonna cry, which doesn't happen at all with the Earnhardt men."

I know a man whose hands are so calloused that gloves aren't necessary. Once, while cutting down a tree, he cut the back of his hand to the bone with a chainsaw. He didn't even stop to look until the job was done.

I've seen him get thrown from a tractor. The tractor, as large as a small home, was flipped by the trunk of a stubborn oak tree. His first thought was not fear, but how quickly he could get the tractor back on its tracks to complete the task. He has suffered broken bones and never had one complaint. Not to anyone, not even to himself . . .

The letter closed with hope for the days ahead:

I wonder what his future holds. He has so much to be proud of. To this point, he's only barely satisfied. His eyes see much more than my imagination could produce. He is Dale Earnhardt. Dad, the world's finest army awaits.

"This is too damn good to just be put on some Internet deal," Earnhardt told his son. "You need to save this for something big, like a book." The letter ran both on that Internet deal and in Junior's memoir of the 2000 season, and remains a powerful look at how these two men had finally begun to develop a true relationship after so many years.

Earnhardt was on the way to healing much of the damage he'd caused, intentionally and unintentionally, in the lives of his children so many years before. He'd helped out Kerry more than he had helped Junior and Kelley—setting him up with higher-quality equipment and financial backing—but he wasn't playing favorites. Rather, age and time had softened him.

Off the track, at least.

THE FALL TALLADEGA race in 2000 marked a transitional moment for the sport. A settlement with the federal government severely restricted tobacco companies' ability to market their products. The 2000 Winston 500 would mark the last time that a regular-season Cup race would carry title sponsorship from Winston.

October 15, 2000, was one of those classic Alabama fall Sundays, the sky wide, bright, and blue enough to touch, the flags in the infield rippling in a faint breeze. There was hope in the Alabama air; a hundred or so miles to the west, a generally woeful Bama football team had just thumped rival Ole Miss 45–7. Outside Alabama, Troy Aikman, Brett Favre, and Peyton Manning were suiting up for NFL games.

At Talladega, more than 170,000 fans filed, stumbled, or were dragged into the stands and infield. Joe Nemecheck had won the pole, and he led a field that ran smoothly and caution-free for the first 104 laps of the 188-lap race. Junior actually managed to lead the very first lap, but no more. Stewart, Gordon, Kenseth, and many others took a turn at the front; in all, there were forty-nine lead changes during the race.

There are two strategies at Talladega, and whichever one you choose, the other one usually turns out to be the better option. You can ride around in the back of the pack, hoping to avoid the inevitable chaos that comes from a dozen-car wreck euphemistically termed the Big One. The risk is that you'll be too far behind to make a move and challenge for the lead when you need to. Or you can race around in front, knowing that you're only a couple of degrees on the steering wheel from getting caught in a major pileup. Earnhardt ended up stuck with the former option. He'd qualified twentieth, and spent most of the afternoon back there as Bill Elliott, Junior, and others traded the lead. With less than twenty laps remaining, a wreck collected Martin and three other cars. After the requisite cleanup, the race restarted with fifteen laps remaining. Earnhardt was stuck deep in the pack, restarting in eighteenth.

As long as your car is running at Talladega, you have a shot at the win. One route to the checkers was a since-discontinued practice called tandem drafting, in which two cars bunch up nose-to-bumper and force their way forward, two cars being faster than one alone. The teamwork lasts until the final turn. Both the front and rear cars have weaknesses; the rear car can overheat, while the front car can suddenly lose speed when the back car releases to push ahead—the so-called slingshot move.

Earnhardt began slithering through the pack, heedless of anything but the clean air in front of him. Kenny Wallace followed

Earnhardt's lead, and before long, Earnhardt had forced his way right up to the front of the pack.

"How did he get through those cars?" ESPN commentator Benny Parsons said in disbelief. "How did he do that?" ESPN's cameras followed the black Goodwrench No. 3 on every turn, and on every turn it seemed Earnhardt had put another car behind him.

Cars stacked up four wide, then five wide as tension mounted. Every driver needed to make precision moves; one mistake on a turn could send the entire pack pinwheeling around. Nerves rode high, hearts choked throats, fear and anticipation hung in the air. In other words, it was Earnhardt's time.

"He's beaten and scraped," Punch said as cameras showed the side of the battered No. 3. "He will not be denied."

Coming around to the white flag marking one lap remaining, Earnhardt's teammate Mike Skinner was in first, with Junior second. Junior wobbled and slid down to the apron, losing his chance at victory. Earnhardt took a shove from Wallace to get past Skinner and out into the beloved clean air. From there, it was all over. Wallace was on Earnhardt's bumper but couldn't close.

Earnhardt won the race over Wallace by 0.119 seconds, four times shorter than the blink of an eye. (It wasn't anywhere near the closest finish in Talladega history; in 2011, Jimmie Johnson beat Clint Bowyer by 0.002 seconds.) As he took his victory lap, one huge fist stuck out the window in exultation, he passed brightly colored wreckage, the smoke rising from the cars' engines a fitting backdrop.

"Unbelievable," Childress said just after the checkered flag flew. "The race fans today got the race they deserved." The statistics told the story of a special race: with twenty-one drivers taking the lead forty-nine times, the day saw the most lead changes and most leaders in a race at Talladega in more than a decade.

Normally when a driver wins a race, a few scattered fans, some corporate guests, and the team wait for him in Victory Lane. On this day, the crowd ran two and three deep from the track all the way to Victory Lane. Earnhardt pumped his fist as he crawled past the crowd, then climbed out of his car into a blizzard of confetti. He hoisted crew chief Kevin Hamlin, who was suffering from an injured back, up onto the window ledge of the No. 3, mischievously slapping Hamlin's back and side all the way. To his credit, Hamlin kept his composure but hastily climbed down.

"It was wild," Earnhardt said in Victory Lane. "I didn't have any thought that I had any chance of winning this race, starting where I did on that restart. Boy, as we kept working away and got on the outside of Kenny . . . Kenny Wallace really worked hard with us and he done a good job. I don't think we could have gotten back up there without Kenny."

After he took a sponsor-mandated swig from a bottle of Coke, he delivered the kicker: "I hated to beat Mike Skinner, but I had to beat him for a million," he said, referring to a Winston program that paid a million dollars to drivers who met certain conditions while winning certain races. The Winston No-Bull 5 promised a million dollars to any driver who finished in the top five at one of five races that year—Daytona, Las Vegas, the Coca-Cola 600, Richmond, and Talladega—and won the next. Earnhardt had finished second at Richmond.

"This is the first time I've ever won it." Earnhardt smiled. "I've been close a couple times, but never won it. It'll be good going to Vegas with a million bucks in my pocket, huh?" The Winston 500 marked Earnhardt's seventy-sixth win, and his tenth Winston Cup victory at Talladega.

"If you were a NASCAR fan, you loved this," Punch said as the telecast wrapped. "If you weren't one, you became one today."

NO ONE KNEW it back in the late 1990s, but Jeff Gordon had single-handedly changed the entire broadcast future of NASCAR with one small turn at the road course at Sonoma. Fox Sports already enjoyed tremendous success with its *NFL on Fox* broadcasts, employing Terry Bradshaw, Howie Long, Jimmy Johnson and other notables to create a more in-your-face alternative to the staid broadcasts of CBS, NBC, and ABC. Fox Sports chairman David Hill was casting about for other sports properties. Hill, a voluble, profane Australian obsessed with ratings, knew that if he could take an underperforming property and turn it into even a modestly performing one, Fox Sports could reap significant rewards.

NASCAR remained a niche sport in the eyes of most outside the South. "I had little time for NASCAR," Hill recalled. "I was interested in Formula 1 racing. NASCAR? Come on." Hill happened to catch a broadcast of a road course race from Sonoma just as Jeff Gordon was approaching a hard right turn. "I thought this was just going to be a shame, watching these NASCAR cars on a road course," he said. "But as I watched, I could see how Gordon was approaching this same turn, over and over again, the way he set himself up [to enter and exit the turn with maximum efficiency] and I thought, 'Shit, this guy can drive.' . . . I realized I was totally wrong about NASCAR."

Emboldened by his discovery—both as a fan and as a broadcaster—Hill sought out Charlotte Motor Speedway president Humpy Wheeler, the same man who'd dined on slick-meat sandwiches in Ralph Earnhardt's garage all those years ago. Wheeler taught Hill the lingo of NASCAR—the difference between "too tight" and "too loose," the meaning of "four wide," and so on. Hill heard that Formula 1 driver (and fellow Australian) Alan Jones had described NASCAR as a "bloody black art" after driving at Charlotte, and that was enough to convince Hill. "NASCAR had those two key elements," Hill said, "the mechanical side of drafting and loose/tight and so on, and the mental attitude. It was perfect."

Hill turned his attention to the current NASCAR broadcast landscape, and what he saw galvanized him. At that time NASCAR was spread across seven networks—ABC, NBC, CBS, ESPN, TNT, and their subsidiaries. The tracks struck their own broadcast agreements, which meant that you might tune in to Daytona on one channel, to Rockingham on another, to Richmond on a third, and on through the season.

Fans tuned in despite the scheduling hurdles. "People were looking for this," Hill said. "They were seeking it out. We realized that we could pull these races together. You want to buy low and sell high when you take risks, and I was looking at NASCAR as one of the great low-hanging fruits."

Hill met with NASCAR president Bill France Jr. and talked him into packaging a portion of the season for Fox. Hill's bid to place NASCAR on an equal footing with the beloved, sanctified NFL delighted France. But how would NASCAR's garage ambassador take the news?

"In December 2000, I was going to get my hair cut for the year-end banquet," Matt Yocum recalls. He pulled up to Ellsworth Hair Design in Kannapolis and noticed something immediately. "There's this big old Chevy pickup there in the parking lot. The catalytic converter is still ticking. I know who's there, and I know he hasn't been there long."

Yocum walked into the barbershop, and sure enough, there was Earnhardt, getting a trim from Steve Ellsworth, his barber of seventeen years. Earnhardt ordered Yocum to sit and give him the details of the new Fox TV deal, end-to-end.

"He was the first person to understand everything about

NASCAR—the business side, the racing side, his image," Yocum said. "He understood the big picture. He could see the forest through the trees like no other."

NASCAR was entering a new era. And once again, Dale Earnhardt was set to be the face of it.

CHAPTER 17

LOST

THERE ARE MOMENTS you wish would last forever, and Daytona Beach in midwinter qualifies as one. It's warm enough to wear a T-shirt, but summer's hot-wool-blanket humidity hasn't arrived. In the late afternoon, when the shadows reach the infield at Daytona International Speedway, it's damn near perfect.

Three days before the 2001 Daytona 500, a couple of old-timers sat on folding chairs in the infield, trading stories of races past like so many of the other campers around them—laughing and drinking beer and shit-talking ahead of Sunday's race. The chief difference between these campers and the thousands around them: these two would be behind the wheel come Sunday.

Dale Earnhardt and Dale Jarrett were unwinding after that day's Bud Shootout, a race equivalent to a baseball spring training game but far more competitive. Earnhardt had finished second and Jarrett fourth. The two men had raced against one another for decades, from dirt tracks in Carolina to speedways in Japan. They'd swiped Daytona 500s from each other. They'd captured championships at the other's expense. Rivalry ran deep; respect ran far deeper. And on this afternoon, they just wanted to catch up.

"We talked about everything," Jarrett recalled long afterward, "but we talked a lot about safety."

Jarrett was planning on using a new piece of safety equipment, the HANS (Head and Neck Support) device, in Sunday's race. The U-shaped device, now mandatory, reaches over the driver's shoulders and attaches to the back of the helmet. The HANS holds a driver's head and neck immobile in the event of a crash. Combined with the closed-face helmet, it's a far safer option than the traditional open-face model, which Earnhardt favored. It also restricts a driver's head movement, sharply reducing peripheral vision.

Earnhardt turned Jarrett's HANS device over and over in his hands, asking questions all the while. Finally, he asked one that haunts Jarrett to this day.

"Are you afraid of dying?" Earnhardt said.

It wasn't asked in an accusing fashion, or a mocking one. "Dale was always inquisitive," Jarrett said, "and this incredible conversation was part of that. He was trying to get my feelings, to understand why I'd want to wear this device."

Earnhardt preferred freedom of movement that the HANS device did not allow. He adjusted his seat, his belts, his helmet, his wheel, everything he could to give himself the maximum room to move around and make adjustments on the fly—a throwback style dating to his very first days racing in the hills of Carolina.

Jarrett countered that the safety measures were necessary to prevent tragedies, that a time was coming when NASCAR might well force drivers to wear these safety devices.

"I don't think I can do it," Earnhardt said, and that was that.

THE DAY BEFORE the Daytona 500, Fox Sports brought Terry Bradshaw to Daytona for the short segment with Earnhardt. Bradshaw remains "the face of Fox Sports," as David Hill puts it, and matching him with Earnhardt was brilliant—a couple country boys who did good.

"He was strong, but he was a teddy bear," Bradshaw would

say of Earnhardt. "He was so frigging *nice*. I knew absolutely nothing about racing, but he showed me a respect I didn't feel I deserved."

Showing someone respect is one thing; going easy on them is another. When Earnhardt got Bradshaw in a pace car to tour the track, he showed no mercy. It takes an awful lot to rattle a four-time Super Bowl champion quarterback—a man who played with some of the toughest men on the planet—but Bradshaw had just met his match. Fifteen years later, Bradshaw could barely contain himself when telling the story.

"We were flying!" Bradshaw shouted. "He's there describing turn 1, and I'm going 'Oh my God . . .' Then we're coming around turn 3, and he says, 'There's going to be a big bump,' and then we're right up against the wall, and then we come flying down pit lane and burning out in the grass. He's celebrating like we won the Daytona 500, and I'm wetting my britches!"

Earnhardt and Bradshaw bonded instantly. Like Earnhardt, Bradshaw came from small-town beginnings—in Bradshaw's case, Shreveport, Louisiana—and both reached the peak of their professions through pure will. Drive recognizes drive.

"You meet a lot of people you don't connect with, a lot of people you don't get or don't get you," Bradshaw said. "Nobody would have put us together, but we connected somehow."

"Holy fuck, how good is this?" Hill thought at the time. "Terry loves NASCAR. Terry loves Dale. Dale loves Terry. Swagger and excellence. We were predicting great things for these two. We were going to have Terry on NASCAR, we were going to bring Dale in to talk NFL. You could see that these two guys had become best friends instantly. Dale fit in perfectly with what we were doing at Fox."

Earnhardt and Bradshaw laughed in the evening's fading light. The next day, the sun would rise on the 2001 Daytona 500.

AT 4:55 THAT afternoon, the ambulance rolled slowly out of Daytona International Speedway.

Back in Victory Lane Michael Waltrip exulted, scraps of red, white, and blue confetti falling all around him. "As soon as I find Dale Junior," Waltrip crowed, "I'm going to give him a big kiss!" Waltrip's three-year-old daughter Macy shrieked when someone sprayed her with Budweiser. This was also Macy's first experience in Victory Lane; unlike her father, she wasn't much liking it.

Waltrip exhaled again and again, a lifetime's worth of regrets and frustrations erased in a moment.

"I'm very happy for him," Darrell Waltrip said, looking down from the broadcast booth. His voice was somber. "I just wish he could enjoy it more, because his boss is not there."

After every win, the driver, his team, and his owner go through what's known as the Hat Dance—while cameras flash, the entire group wears the hats of one sponsor, then doffs them en masse and dons those of another. It's a way of showing gratitude and providing a triumphant photograph for every sponsor's annual report.

With the confetti still in the air and the Hat Dance well under way, Earnhardt's absence started to draw questions. He should have been there as the team's owner. DEI's Ty Norris held up the owner's trophy in his stead, smiling alongside Michael for the cameras.

Ken Schrader, who'd hit the No. 3 just before Earnhardt hit the wall, now made his way to Victory Lane. He'd already changed into a T-shirt and donned his M&M's cap and sunglasses. Schrader edged through the celebrations and put his hands on Waltrip's arms. Waltrip saw the expression on Schrader's face and made a halfhearted joke about how winning Daytona shouldn't be a cause for sadness.

Schrader leaned in close. "It's not good. I think Dale's hurt."

Waltrip understood immediately, and the light left his eyes. The rest of the Victory Lane photos from that afternoon show a man haunted by words he wished he hadn't heard.

FOX SPORTS WAS preparing to sign off from Daytona. The red flag from Stewart's wreck had swallowed up much of the race's allotted time, and the network was going to enforce a hard 5:00 p.m. eastern cutoff time. The race was over, and there was no timetable for information on Earnhardt's condition. Sensing the growing dread, Mike Joy tried to keep Darrell Waltrip and McReynolds focused on the nuts and bolts of race strategy.

Joy wrapped the broadcast with a balance of hope and trepidation. "We're jubilant for the Waltrips," he said, "and our prayers are with the Earnhardt family."

The rest of the nation cut to local news or syndicated programming, with *The Simpsons* on tap later that evening. Joy, Waltrip, and McReynolds took off their headsets and joined hands to pray.

TWO MINUTES LATER Earnhardt's ambulance arrived at Halifax, a sprawling medical campus that looks more like a beachfront condo development than a hospital. The ambulance had run a gauntlet of fans unaware of its passenger's grim condition. The car carrying Teresa and Junior arrived five minutes after Dale's ambulance. Junior raced into the hospital through the ambulance bay, still in his red-and-black fire suit; Teresa followed slowly.

Tony Stewart was in the emergency room, recovering from the hard hits he'd taken during his own catastrophic wreck. He was in a wheelchair, more as a precaution than as a medical necessity. He had a brutal headache and sore ribs, but other than that he was fine. He'd just taken a dose of pain medication and gone through a battery of tests, including X-rays and a CT scan, when he heard that Earnhardt was in the hospital. With no televisions anywhere on the floor, Stewart had no idea who'd won the race, or that Earnhardt had been in a wreck.

Stewart was ready to do a little bench racing with the Intimidator when an attendant rolled Stewart into the same room as Earnhardt. The two men had a mutually respectful relationship; Earnhardt recognized the fire in the young defending champion, and Stewart held the icons of NASCAR in the highest regard.

Someone realized the mistake immediately and rolled Stewart out of the room. "You could have left me in there," Stewart said. "I know him real well. It's okay."

"No," the attendant said, "I don't think so."

NASCAR's elite gathered in the waiting room. In addition to Junior and Teresa, Childress, Mike Helton, Dale's brother Danny, and members of the France family stood nearby. Darrell Waltrip and Rusty Wallace later showed up as well.

At 5:16 p.m., a doctor appeared and delivered the news.

"We did the best we could."

Junior wailed. The long, wordless, wrenching cry of pain echoed in the hospital's halls. For a long minute, no one moved. Some bowed their heads. Helton realized he needed to address the media, and issued an open invitation for anyone to come with him. No one took him up on the offer. Childress sat in one corner, Waltrip later recounted, weeping and talking to himself. Bill France Jr. and Wallace locked eyes; they'd conversed about Wallace retiring before something bad happened, and Wallace would later say this was the moment he decided to begin winding down his career.

Teresa sat quietly in the middle of it all. "Will somebody," she said softly, "please tell me what to do?"

HELTON SAT WITH Brian France and NASCAR senior vice president Paul Brooks in a small room near the garage. "What do you say," Helton said, "to tell the world we've lost Dale Earnhardt?"

"Say that," France replied. Helton gathered himself, walked to the media center, and began to speak. "This is undoubtedly one of the toughest announcements I've ever had to make," Helton said to the silent group of reporters. "After the accident in Turn 4 at the end of the Daytona 500, we've lost Dale Earnhardt."

There were no sounds of shock, no audible sobs. These were professionals, though many wrote with tears in their eyes. The Internet would carry news of Earnhardt's death within minutes. With no Twitter or Facebook to compete against, there was still time to compose a few thoughts—to try to make sense of the impossible.

Outside the media room, the Flying Aces and other crews embraced one another or stared into the sun setting on the backstretch. Fans gathered in small groups around the track. As the news spread—slowly, without the benefit of smartphones—they scrawled tributes on the backs of signs, lit candles from their campfires in the infield.

Tony Stewart left the hospital as the day's last light turned orange. A police escort took him from the hospital to the Daytona Beach airport, directly behind the speedway. He could see fans leaving the track. As he approached the tarmac, there were only two planes still there: his and the late Dale Earnhardt's.

CHAPTER 18

IT DIDN'T LOOK THAT BAD

IT JUST DIDN'T look that bad.

All these years later, that's what you're still thinking. You watch the final turn of the 2001 Daytona 500 again and again. Maybe this time, what looked like a minor wall scrape will end up being just that. The car will slide down to the infield, the window net will drop, and Dale will climb out, pissed off that he got wrecked, but prouder than hell that he just put his team 1-2 in the Daytona 500.

Look again, though, and you see the inescapable.

Dale Earnhardt Sr.'s car was traveling in the fourth turn at more than 170 miles per hour, with Marlin's car behind and below him. Earnhardt cut downward to block Marlin, and that's when his left rear quarter-panel caught Marlin's right front bumper. Earnhardt swooped low toward the infield, then as he fought to correct—the final racing move he'd ever make—the car knifed back upward toward the high turn 4 wall. Just after Schrader's car piled into the No. 3's right side, Earnhardt hit the wall. His hood ripped loose, flapping in the wind like a sheet of paper. Earnhardt and Schrader slid back down toward the infield as cars rushed below and around them, Earnhardt's right front tire ripping loose and spinning away into the grass.

Networks played the wreck over and over again. The original Fox broadcast showed the view from Earnhardt's car, the track ahead, the spotter's voice saying "Side . . . side . . ." in Earnhardt's ear, the wall coming closer and closer, then finally blackness as the hood obscures the camera's lens.

Your memories of other wrecks that drivers walked away from—plus the optical illusion caused by a tight camera angle that doesn't give a feel for the cars' true speed—make his collision seem like a fender-bender. In truth, Earnhardt hit the wall at somewhere between 157 and 161 miles per hour. He almost surely died instantly from what the Volusia County medical examiner's office would initially call blunt force trauma to the head. The autopsy would show that Earnhardt also suffered eight broken left ribs, a broken left ankle, abrasions in the clavicle and hip areas from the seat belts, and a sternal fracture that may have been the result of CPR attempts.

By the time Waltrip crossed the Daytona 500 finish line, the Earnhardt story was no longer a rescue mission. The postmortem investigation was already under way, and every movement, every moment, would be scrutinized and examined with two questions in mind: *Why did this happen? Could it have been avoided?* Earnhardt had been in so many wrecks before. Why hadn't he walked away from this one? Something must have gone wrong. There must be something or someone to blame. It was inconceivable that the greatest driver in American history could die because of what track old-timers would call "one of those racing deals."

The hunger for news on Earnhardt's death—for answers—was unrelenting. Five days after his death, NASCAR officials held a press conference to release preliminary findings on the wreck. Dr. Steve Bohannon, the track's director of emergency services and one of the first to attend to Earnhardt, initially speculated that a faulty seat belt had caused Earnhardt's chin to impact the steering wheel, transferring impact to the base of his skull.

The possibility that failing equipment had cost NASCAR's greatest star his life sent the organization—and the media covering it—into a frenzy. Bill Simpson, president of the company that had manufactured the seat belts, received death threats from infuriated NASCAR fans. The pressure would eventually force him to resign from the company that bore his name.

A malfunctioning seat belt made for an easy scapegoat, but not necessarily a correct one. If Earnhardt's head had struck the steering wheel, would a closed helmet—the very helmet he had rejected in at least two separate conversations before the race—have saved him? The *Orlando Sentinel* began seeking Earnhardt's autopsy records with the intent of hiring independent investigators, contending that the public's right to know the truth about Earnhardt's death—and whether that death was preventable—prevailed over the family's right to privacy. That would set in motion a chain of events that turned a racing story into a referendum on the freedom of the press.

The *Sentinel* claimed that it had no intention of publishing the photos, but wanted an independent expert to review them for clues to Earnhardt's death. The newspaper received thousands of enraged calls and e-mails, including a letter from US House Majority Leader Dick Armey (R-Texas), who wrote, "Please count my voice among those who believe your efforts are outside the bounds of common decency."

The Volusia County medical examiner had performed the autopsy on Earnhardt on February 19, the day after the wreck. The county took the unusual step of notifying NASCAR and Teresa Earnhardt prior to releasing the records and any associated autopsy photographs. Teresa Earnhardt filed a legal brief in the Circuit Court of the Seventh Judicial Circuit that blocked the release of the photographs until a hearing.

Four days after Earnhardt's death, Volusia County Circuit Court Judge Joseph G. Will kept the photos sealed, noting that "many of the photos not yet released . . . may have no bona fide newsworthiness, and are not the subject of legitimate journalistic interest. . . . Further release of said photographs would cause Mr. Earnhardt's family additional anguish and grief, and would inflict further emotional distress upon them."

Teresa offered a rare public statement with Junior at her side at Las Vegas Motor Speedway. "The trauma we have suffered has only grown since that tragic day two weeks ago," she said. "In fact, I have not even had time to caringly unpack Dale's suitcases from Daytona, let alone have time to grieve for him. The main reason is because we have been caught up in an unexpected whirlwind as a result of efforts to gain access to the autopsy photographs of Dale."

She continued, "We can't believe, and are saddened that anyone would invade our privacy during this time of grief. I want to let you know that if access to the photos is allowed, others will demand them, too. And make no mistake, sooner or later the photos will end up unprotected and published . . . and most certainly on the Internet."

The *Orlando Sentinel* released a statement in response emphasizing its sympathy for the Earnhardt family, and indicating that the photos could provide a clue into the reasons behind Earnhardt's death. "Newspapers are not always popular," the statement read. "Sometimes newspapers have to ask hard questions; this is one of those times."

Furthermore, the *Sentinel* noted, the newspaper's request for the photos was not uncommon or illegal; in fact, Will's sealing of the photos was unusual. "I think the general community needs to understand that I can walk into any medical examiner's office in any county in the state of Florida and look at any autopsy photograph," *Sentinel* attorney David Bralow said.

Florida politicians paid lip service to the idea of freedom of the press, but took a far more ardent stance against releasing the photographs. Moving with impressive legislative speed, the Florida legislature enacted a law in late March entitled the Earnhardt Family Protection Act. Sponsored by Republican state senator Jim King of Jacksonville, the law amended Florida's entire open records law, barring media organizations from viewing autopsy photos absent a court order, with a retroactive provision that would keep Earnhardt's photos sealed. Florida governor Jeb Bush signed the bill into law on March 29, 2001, with Teresa Earnhardt in attendance in Tallahassee.

The Earnhardt family did agree to allow Dr. Barry Myers, a professor of biomedical engineering at Duke University, to investigate the circumstances of Earnhardt's death. Two days before Bush signed the Earnhardt bill into law, Myers spent a half hour studying the forty-seven autopsy photos. Following Myers's examination, the floppy disk containing the photos, as well as the videotape of the autopsy, were placed in a lockbox and taken to an undisclosed location

The *Orlando Sentinel* withdrew from the legal proceedings after Myers performed his examination. Two other entities stepped into the vacuum, continuing to push for release of the photos. The *Alligator*, the University of Florida's student newspaper, challenged the assertion that Teresa acted on her own in requesting that the photos be sealed so soon after Earnhardt's death.

"These circumstances strongly suggest that NASCAR, motivated by its own fear of a lawsuit for wrongful death . . . urged Teresa Earnhardt to file this suit to seal the photographs at issue because of what they might reveal," the newspaper's attorney, Tom Julin, wrote in a memorandum filed in Volusia Circuit Court.

Also seeking access to the photos was Michael Uribe, a photojournalist and owner of the site WebsiteCity.com. Uribe had gained notoriety from publishing autopsy photos of drivers Neil Bonnett and Rodney Orr online. Uribe claimed a higher purpose in posting those autopsy photos, to bring to the public's attention the horrors inherent in racing, and it was certainly possible that he would publish the photos of Earnhardt if he gained access to them.

Judge Will presided over the Volusia County hearing to release the photos in June 2001. Teresa recounted with heartbreaking detail the events of February 18, as well as the days afterward, in testimony often carried live on cable. Television cameras had hovered over her home, and at least one reporter had hidden in bushes during private memorial ceremonies. She said she had attended every single race of Dale's career since marrying him, including the one at which he was killed.

"Dale was part of me," she said on the stand, "he was half of me." To Uribe, she vowed to keep the autopsy photos sealed "because of what you've already done."

Uribe countered that he was only seeking to shine a light on misdeeds, not commit them himself. "I wasn't responsible for [the deaths of Earnhardt, Bonnett and Orr]. It's the violent sport," Uribe said. "NASCAR wants you to see the fancy cars and sell you a jacket. When it comes to the death and carnage, the public has not connected with that."

A widow at forty-three, Teresa drew praise for her performance on the stand. "Like a prizefighter," the *Daytona News-Journal* wrote, "Earnhardt sat slightly sideways on the witness stand, her left shoulder out front and her right farther back, rocking in the swivel chair, ready for a showdown."

Teresa had allies in the court system, in state government, and in the medical profession. Bohannon, the doctor who had ridden from the track to the hospital in the ambulance with Earnhardt, testified on her behalf. He described Teresa's wailing grief when a hospital attendant tried to cut off Earnhardt's wedding ring. "I tried to explain to her that this was policy," Bohannon said at trial. "Under the circumstances, though, I told [the attendant] to leave the ring on."

He added that there was no pressing reason for release of Earnhardt's autopsy photos. "They depict images that are very personal," Bohannon said. "To anyone other than a medical professional, they would be gruesome and inappropriate for public dissemination."

The hearing ended with the court upholding the county's right to block the photographs' release. A series of appeals and rejections led all the way to the US Supreme Court. On December 1, 2003, the Supreme Court declined to hear the appeal of the decision, and the photos have remained sealed ever since under the Earnhardt Family Protection Act.

A year after Earnhardt's death, singer Lisa "Left Eye" Lopes of the group TLC died in a car crash in Honduras. Shortly afterward, images of her autopsy circulating on the Internet were a grim reminder of what could have happened had Earnhardt's photos been made public. In an expression of sympathy and solidarity, all three DEI cars sported a black stripe underneath the left headlight during the 2002 Pontiac Excitement 400 at Richmond.

THERE WAS STILL the matter of what exactly had killed Dale Earnhardt. The report filed by Myers, the independent expert, absolved the restraint systems of culpability, indicating that—despite NASCAR's initial claims—the belts' position and integrity had no impact on the crash's outcome. Earnhardt hit the wall so hard that his neck could not have withstood the force no matter where the belts had been positioned.

The collision whipped Earnhardt's head forward and downward in a circular motion, causing the mortal injury: a basilar skull fracture. In such cases, a small quarter-sized, doughnut-shaped bone at the base of the skull known as the foramen magnum cracks. The hole in the foramen magnum serves as a conduit for the two critical carotid arteries and part of the brain stem. If the bone cracks, the carotid arteries can rupture, leading to death in seconds, or the brain stem can suffer trauma, affecting breathing and heart functions. Blood had been found in Earnhardt's ears and breathing passages, indicative of a basilar skull fracture. Myers's verdict: tragic accident, unavoidable given the terrible circumstances and the current safety standards.

The medical examiner's report indicated that death was instantaneous; at most, a basilar skull fracture would have allowed Earnhardt a few more moments. Either way, Earnhardt was surely gone before his car returned to the infield dirt.

NASCAR spent six months and more than a million dollars creating its own 300-page report, which it called "perhaps the most thorough, comprehensive investigation in U.S. motor sports history." The report attributed Earnhardt's death to a variety of factors: the impact with the wall, the collision with Schrader's car just prior to impact, the movement of Earnhardt's open-faced helmet on his head, and—despite Myers's determinations to the contrary—the failure of the left lap belt.

In crafting its report, NASCAR performed computerized modeling tests with the data obtained from the cars of both Earnhardt and Schrader, as well as live tests with replica cars and reenactments of the crash scene with two of the paramedics involved. (The third declined to participate on the advice of his attorney.) The tests showed that Earnhardt had hit the wall with his car positioned at a heading angle of between 55 and 59 degrees (where 90 degrees is head-on) and a trajectory angle (the route the car was traveling as a result of momentum) of 12 to 15 degrees. The car lost 42 to 44 miles per hour of velocity at the instant of impact.

Just before the impact from Schrader's car, Earnhardt's car was angled at 26 degrees relative to the wall, and just starting to reorient down the track. Schrader's car turned Earnhardt's car clockwise toward the wall, changing the heading angle from about 26 degrees to about 55 degrees and greatly increasing the amount of force upon impact. Even two or three degrees fewer would have reduced the force on Earnhardt by 25 percent or more. As it was, the force exerted on Earnhardt's body was the equivalent of a vertical drop from a six-story building.

The persistent questions about the seat belt—had it been intact, broken on impact, or cut by the paramedics?—had still not been answered. While the belts were loose, the paramedics said, they appeared to be intact. However, under later questioning, they described the off-center position of Earnhardt's belt buckle, a position that in theory would not have been possible had the belts done their job. But Earnhardt had slid to the right because of the impact from Schrader's car, further stressing the lap belt.

Earnhardt himself may have had a role in the belts' positioning; he had always liked to give himself more room to move, potentially in violation of the belts' standards. Moreover, Earnhardt had a habit of bringing the crotch belt up over the seat rather than through the centering slot, allowing more give in the belt and perhaps allowing for the possibility of failure. Earnhardt had liked to ride low in the seat since his days at the dirt tracks, looking out the left side of the windshield. He had, on occasion, requested the left lap belt be placed as far as eight inches behind its typical location.

"The conclusion is clear," Helton said in announcing NASCAR's report. "There was no cutting of the belt after the accident. It separated during load [i.e., the load placed on it during the accident]." NASCAR did not assign blame to either the belt's manufacturer or Earnhardt himself for adjusting the belt's fit. In response to NASCAR's report, attorneys for Simpson indicated that Earnhardt had incorrectly mounted the belts, adding that Simpson himself had warned Earnhardt about using the belts in their proper fashion.

"Simpson warned him about it the same way he warned me about the way I was wearing my belts," Jimmy Spencer told *USA*

Today. "It was common for Simpson to look around this garage at these cars and make suggestions as to how it could be safer."

Childress ripped Simpson and his attorneys for blaming Earnhardt, calling those statements "undeserved and unfair, especially when Dale is not here to defend himself." Both Childress and NASCAR pointed out that Earnhardt had survived many a vicious crash with the seat belts in the same position.

"There's a tendency to want to have a single finding that you can say, 'Ah, that did it. That's what it is and that's what's at fault,'" said Dr. James H. Raddin, one of the experts who conducted the NASCAR report. "But typically, with something that normally works well, if just one thing goes wrong, it tends to still work pretty well. When multiple things come together and go wrong together, that's when you have problems."

IT'S A GRIM irony that Earnhardt's death probably saved the lives of several other drivers in later years, thanks to the safety improvements mandated and fast-tracked in the wake of Daytona 2001.

"Before Earnhardt died, all safety was reliant on the driver," ESPN writer Bob Pockrass said. "Drivers weren't even required to wear gloves."

Shortly after Earnhardt's death, drivers switched from five-point to six-point harnesses—belts that have six points of contact with the car rather than just five. Teams installed more protective cocoon-like fiberglass seats. NASCAR instituted the placement of SAFER barriers, a series of foam-braced walls that collapse upon impact and disperse force. That force dispersal is the key, both inside and outside the car. It's simple physics: a car in motion builds up kinetic energy, and when the car itself suddenly stops, that energy leaves through the path of least resistance. If the car and the wall don't absorb enough of the impact, the energy exits through the body of the driver.

The racing industry had been familiar with kinetics for decades—it was the reason the earliest drivers belted themselves in with ropes, after all—but it wasn't until the early 1980s that researchers began diagnosing the effects of force on the human neck. Dr. Robert Hubbard, a professor of biomechanics engineering at Michigan State, began diagramming the basics of what would become the HANS (Head and Neck Support) device after the death of a friend in a racing accident. Hubbard conceived of the U-shaped device designed to fit over the driver's shoulders and attach to the helmet, preventing the head from snapping forward. Hubbard's initial prototype, first tested in 1989, reduced the kinetic energy absorbed by the neck by 80 percent.

The racing elite had little initial interest in the HANS device, considering it either unnecessary, uncomfortable, or both. That all changed in 1994, when Formula 1 legend Ayrton Senna died of a basilar skull fracture. Formula 1 began evaluating the device more closely, but it would take another seven years—and many more deaths—for the device to become mandatory.

Earnhardt's death was the fourth in just over a year—following those of Adam Petty, Kenny Irwin Jr., and Tony Roper—that was the result of a basilar skull fracture. Even with the mounting death toll, few drivers had adopted the HANS device by the 2001 Daytona 500.

One who did was Kurt Busch. "At the end of every year, I always look to what we can do for more safety in the car," he said. "I had heard about the HANS device, and I liked its direction and feel. The Daytona 500 was my first race using it."

It is worth noting that neither NASCAR's report nor Myers's indicated whether a HANS device could have saved Earnhardt's life. Regardless, drivers warmed to the device after Earnhardt's death. At the time NASCAR's report was released on August 21, 2001, forty-one of the forty-three drivers were using a HANS device. Blaise Alexander died in a wreck at Charlotte Motor Speedway late in 2001—also of a basilar skull fracture—and that was enough. NASCAR began requiring the use of HANS devices for all drivers. All other racing series, including Formula 1, CART/IndyCar, and ARCA, required the device within a few years after Earnhardt's death.

The list of NASCAR drivers involved in catastrophic wrecks since 2001 encompasses nearly every major figure in the sport: Dale Earnhardt Jr. Jeff Gordon. Jimmie Johnson. Tony Stewart. Mark Martin. Denny Hamlin. Elliott Sadler. Ryan Newman. Carl Edwards. Brad Keselowski. Kyle Busch. These drivers and more suffered major, grandstand-silencing wrecks in the late 2000s and early 2010s—wrecks that they might not have survived without the safety improvements enacted in the wake of Earnhardt's death.

"I wouldn't be here if it weren't for that [wreck]," said Sadler, who hit a wall in Pocono head-on in 2010, the strongest impact ever recorded in NASCAR. Sadler walked away from the wreck with only soreness. Five years later at Daytona, Kyle Busch would hit an inside concrete wall—one unprotected by SAFER barriers—at a nearly head-on angle. He suffered severe injuries to both legs, but was back to racing later that season thanks to the car's safety protections.

Earnhardt "was never scared in a car, to his detriment," Petree said. "When he got killed, everything changed overnight. NASCAR got 70 percent safer overnight. The technology for seat belts and head restraints was already developed, and seat technology was coming along. Nobody used it until Dale was gone."

CHAPTER 19

THE DAYS AFTER THE DAY

THREE DAYS AFTER Earnhardt's death, the family gathered for a tiny, private service at St. Mark's Lutheran Church in Mooresville. Rev. Johnny Cozart spoke to the small group of family members and loved ones, telling stories of the Intimidator's compassion and reverence.

"Dale knew what he believed in," Cozart said, as Michael Waltrip recounted in his autobiography. "He believed in the Lord. He sinned. He fell short like all of us do. But he loved Jesus Christ. He had such a positive influence on everyone. . . . Whenever I'd visit with him, I'd always leave with a spring in my step."

A much larger crowd gathered the next day for a twenty-two-minute service at the 6,200-seat Calvary Church in Charlotte. A stark modern megachurch, Calvary had three levels of seating. A national television broadcast of the Earnhardt funeral, *Dale Earnhardt: A Celebration of Life*, featured Mike Joy and Ken Squier seated at a desk with dark paneling and a stylized Earnhardt portrait behind them.

"The family has agreed to this one-time live telecast service," Joy told the audience, "because the Earnhardts wanted to reach out to Dale's many grieving fans, to help you achieve closure, and allow you a look at the ceremony." Squier added that there would be "no fancy camera angles."

Randy Owen, guitarist for the group Alabama, began the nationally televised ceremony playing Alabama's "Goodbye." A large red, white, and black flower arrangement in the form of Earnhardt's stylized "3" stood before the podium—the only indication that the man being honored and mourned had once raced cars.

Twenty-five hundred invited guests showed up, including Marlin, Junior Johnson, and the brothers Allison and Labonte. Dale Beaver, the chaplain who traveled with NASCAR for much of its schedule, urged the crowd in attendance to do three things: tell stories of Earnhardt, laugh and listen to those stories, and pray. Beaver recounted his own story of meeting Earnhardt and asking his permission for his daughter Taylor to join a church camping trip. Beaver had interrupted Earnhardt's lunch, and he feared the consequences. "I half expected to find a man eating a bear, tearing it apart with his bare hands. I thought, 'He's eating bear, and I'm going to be dessert,'" Beaver said, drawing the day's only mild laugh. "I saw a man eating an orange, who with a very warm demeanor welcomed me into his presence. I didn't come into the presence of a racing icon or an intimidating figure. I came into the presence of a dad, a father, who was concerned about his daughter."

Teresa walked to the pulpit as the ceremony ended, looked out over the congregation, and blew a kiss. With both hands extended outward, she whispered, "Thank you, thank you," to the skies. She and Taylor were escorted out immediately afterward.

Tracks all over the circuit held individual memorials, some scheduled, some impromptu. Hundreds of people turned out at vigils at Indianapolis Motor Speedway, Talladega, Bristol, and others. "Like you, I long to see that No. 3 roll by one more time, I long to have one more shared conversation," Ed Clark, president of Atlanta Motor Speedway, said at an AMS vigil. "And somewhere in heaven today, Dale and his dad Ralph are having a long conversation, catching up on all the victories that Dale's experienced."

"As a rule, I don't get that close to the drivers just because of things like this," Bill France Jr. said. "But some of them just jump out and grab you. Dale was one of those."

By midweek, fans began gathering at the grave of Ralph Earnhardt in the Centergrove Lutheran Church cemetery in Kannapolis, expecting that Earnhardt would be interred near his father and other family members. Ralph's tombstone bears a No. 8 car with the names of his three sons—Danny, Randy, and Dale—on its hood. It stood to reason that Dale would be buried here as well, but the grass around Ralph's grave remained undisturbed.

In order to throw fame-seekers off the trail, the Earnhardt family had in fact consulted with three different funeral homes in Kannapolis. A sweep of Kannapolis's other churches turned up no evidence of a recent burial. The *Kannapolis Independent Tribune* only added to the mystery by quoting an unnamed Earnhardt relative saying, "I can't make a statement on behalf of the family, but we did not attend a burial service for Dale Earnhardt in Kannapolis on Wednesday."

The location of Dale Earnhardt's final resting place became a guessing game. Was Earnhardt going to be buried at another date? Was the service scheduled for another day? Had Earnhardt already been buried in a city other than Kannapolis?

The answer to the last question was yes. Earnhardt was interred in a mausoleum on his farm in nearby Mooresville. Burial in Kannapolis was never a realistic option; the Centergrove Cemetery, located along Kannapolis's main thoroughfare, has only a single narrow road in and out. As soon as word got out that Earnhardt might be buried there, cars clogged the driveway throughout the week, and well-meaning mourners tromped over other gravesites looking for Earnhardt's.

The family's concerns were not confined to issues of gridlock and disrespect for the cemetery's other residents. Nearly a quarter century earlier, barely two weeks after Elvis Presley was buried in the Forest Lawn Cemetery in Memphis, police foiled an alleged plot to steal the singer's body. Family members had the body removed and reinterred on the grounds of Presley's Graceland estate, where it's now the final stop on the Graceland tour.

Earnhardt, like Elvis, was laid to rest on his own property. By the time fans gathered to pay their respects on Thursday, Earnhardt's body was already locked away from the world. It remains there to this day, within an ornate mausoleum with space for six caskets. Earnhardt was gone, and in a sense so was Teresa, who barricaded herself behind the walls of her estate, declining every interview request. Her own father had to go through a secretary to reach her, and he told a *Los Angeles Times* reporter that he would go weeks without talking to her.

"DALE'S DEATH DID more for the sport of NASCAR than anything else possibly could," Fox Sports' David Hill said. "I was fielding calls from every media outlet, everywhere, and the weirdest conversation I had was with this guy from New York, worked for *Time* or *Newsweek*. He asked, 'Where has this been? Why didn't anyone tell me [NASCAR] was so big?' "

Fox Sports executives saw an opportunity to honor both Dale's memory and the spirit of NASCAR by continuing their mission to rewrite public perception about NASCAR. They began the very next weekend in Rockingham.

February 25 dawned gray and ugly, a reflection of the mood that consumed the garage and the grandstands. "Everyone was walking around like a zombie," Kurt Busch recalled.

The hours in a garage before a NASCAR race are normally charged with energy as fans and crews mingle in shared anticipation. But fewer corporate tour groups wandered around the garage. Fans still waited for autographs; crews still prepped for the race. But nobody's heart seemed in it. Everyone's mind was elsewhere.

Crew members on every team wore black No. 3 caps. Gordon's team handed out black-and-red tribute ribbons. Richard Childress Racing's two cars and DEI's three bore a special logo, a number 3 with Earnhardt's signature and "1951–2001" emblazoned on it.

Throughout the week, fans and drivers had offered suggestions for how to honor Earnhardt. Some asked that the pace car be painted black, others suggested that the first stall in the garage—traditionally reserved for the remaining champion—be kept open. The idea of retiring the No. 3 entirely, a practice not done in NASCAR, drew discussion.

It was time to race, but the weather would not cooperate. Darrell Waltrip spoke to the Rockingham crowd during a short rain delay. "Our hearts are hurting right now," he said. "We've lost a great friend, and it all seems so unfair." He asked each member of the audience to grasp the hand of the person beside them, to bond as a family.

Heavy cloud cover prevented three F-15 Strike Eagles from nearby Seymour Johnson Air Force Base from conducting a fly-over in a missing-man formation to honor Earnhardt. While the national anthem played, the three crews from Dale Earnhardt Inc. stood on the pit walls, lifting their caps in gratitude to the crowd and in farewell to their departed leader. On the parade lap, pole sitter Jeff Gordon dropped back and left a space for Earnhardt's memory.

"We came here to win the race," Childress said. "But we just want to get it over with." The black Goodwrench No. 3 had become a white Goodwrench No. 29. An unknown rookie by the name of Kevin Harvick, a twenty-five-year-old running in his very first Cup race, had replaced the icon.

It didn't take long for this race to remind everyone of the

tragedy just a week before. On the very first lap, in an eerie echo of Earnhardt's fatal wreck, Ron Hornaday ran into the back of Junior, who turned sideways and hit the outer wall as Kenny Wallace hit Junior in the side. NASCAR nation held its breath until Junior climbed out of the crushed car. "Tell everybody back home I'm fine," Junior said afterward. "The lap belt was a little too tight," he added, a comment unintentionally chilling in light of the ongoing Earnhardt seat belt investigation.

As the race proceeded, Junior stared at the wrecked remains of his car, oblivious both to the media around him and the cars still running out on the track.

"People didn't understand why I could go back immediately and race," Junior would say later. "If I had sat home, there's no telling where I'd be today. I don't think I would ever have gotten back in the car and I probably would have ended up a total failure at anything I tried to do, so I had to get back in the car."

The race ran for fifty-one laps before rain made it impossible to continue. The remainder of the race was postponed until Monday under prettier skies. As fate would have it, Steve Park, one of DEI's drivers, found himself in the lead in the closing laps, with Bobby Labonte in his rearview mirror. Park was weeping openly as he neared the final lap, sensing the import of what could be about to happen. He needed to fend off Labonte, the defending Winston Cup champion and as fierce a competitor as still remained on the track. Labonte hammered away at Park's rear bumper, looking for that one crucial edge.

He wouldn't find it. Inspired by his departed leader, Park blocked Labonte hard right into the wall on turn 4 and won by two car lengths. "I threw a block on him because I was trying my hardest to win this race," Park said afterward. "I did what Dale Earnhardt would do."

It was an emotional moment—the DEI car winning the first

race after the death of the most inspiring figure in NASCAR history. Park grabbed the No. 3 hat he'd hung around his gearshift lever and waved it out of the car window. He spun out in front of the grandstand, found Michael Waltrip, exchanged an in-car high five, and wheeled into a long burnout, so long that he ran out of gas and needed a shove into Victory Lane.

Perhaps Labonte decided that aggressive driving wasn't necessary in such a powerful moment. "If it wasn't him, we probably both would have wrecked," Park said. "But he checked up and he gave me the opportunity to win, and I want to thank him."

Teresa Earnhardt was not at the track. She was watching from Mooresville and called Park to offer her congratulations. He characterized her words as "emotional but happy."

Park would run another ninety-one races at the Cup level, but would never again win a race.

Tributes to Earnhardt poured in from around the world. The Foo Fighters' Dave Grohl played a Dale Jr.–embossed guitar at a concert. At the Grammys, U2's The Edge wore a No. 3 jersey. Jimmy Buffett paid tribute to Earnhardt in a Charlotte concert days after Earnhardt's death. Olympic skier Picabo Street dubbed her skis "Earnies" in Earnhardt's honor. On March 3, just prior to the Evander Holyfield–John Ruiz fight at Mandalay Bay, the bell tolled ten times, a traditional boxing honor rarely granted to anyone outside the world of boxing.

"He was the last connection to the working man," Wheeler said, "the welder, the painter, the shrimp boat captain, the backhoe operator, the bulldozer guy. Usually when a driver dies or retires, his fans go to somebody else. In this case, there was nobody else out there like him."

"It's like waking up one morning," David Poole said, "and seeing that the mountain you'd seen out your window every day was gone."

CHAPTER 20

THE SAVIOR'S BURDEN

WHEN YOU BUY your kid a go-kart for his kindergarten graduation, you never know if you're about to create a monster or a prodigy. Mike and JoNell Harvick put their five-year-old son Kevin behind the wheel of a go-kart in 1980, and ended up with a little of both.

Born in 1975 in Bakersfield, California, Harvick would grow into one of NASCAR's most notable drivers, uniquely positioned between the sport's illustrious past and its corporate-driven future. You have to be driven to reach the Cup level of NASCAR—pardon the pun—beyond all reasonable limits. Harvick came from a racing background; his father had a bit of cachet around Bakersfield as a driver. Behind the wheel of his go-kart, Harvick won national championships throughout elementary school. While still in high school, he debuted in the NASCAR Featherlite Southwest Series, NASCAR's equivalent of Single-A minor league baseball.

Broad-faced, with a wry smile, Harvick still looks like the Big Man on Campus he was in high school, a multisport athlete who never outgrew his first athletic love. He rose rapidly through NASCAR's ranks, winning first in western regional series, then in the Busch series. He signed with Childress for a full season in 2000, the year after Junior won the Busch series championship. Aggressive and hardheaded, Harvick was a driver in the Earnhardt mold, and Childress appeared to be grooming him for future stardom. The early signs were encouraging; in 2000 Harvick took the No. 2 AC Delco Chevrolet to three wins and the Busch Series Rookie of the Year award, beating out a fellow Californian named Jimmie Johnson.

The plan was set going into 2001: Harvick would drive the No. 2 in the Busch series, along the way entering a handful of Cup-level events in the No. 30 AOL Chevrolet. He'd then make the jump to a full-time Cup series run starting in 2002. Daytona changed all that in an instant, and Childress made the decision to rush Harvick into the Cup series driving Earnhardt's cars.

Childress and Earnhardt had discussed contingency plans for continuing onward should either of them die. "We talked about what would happen if I was in Africa and got run over by a elephant or fell off a mountain or if something happened to him in whatever manner, what we would want and what we would want to do," Childress said, "and it's to go on."

Childress put Harvick in the No. 29, reversing the paint scheme from black to white. "This will undoubtedly be the hardest thing that ever happened in my life," Harvick said after it was announced he'd be driving one of Earnhardt's own cars. "I would hope that you don't expect me to replace him, because no one ever will."

Years later, Harvick would remember, "It all happened pretty fast. It happened on a Wednesday before Rockingham for me. We had the funeral on Thursday and then went to the track Friday."

Harvick started in the back of the pack at Rockingham, but finished fourteenth. The next week at Las Vegas, he brought home an eighth-place finish. Then came Atlanta, and the Cracker Barrel Old Country Store 500.

Atlanta is one of the fastest tracks on the circuit, its high banks and cracked asphalt combining for a driving experience as nerve-racking as any superspeedway. Not even Ralph Earnhardt could conquer its steep slopes. Harvick qualified fifth, and afterward addressed the media's concerns about Atlanta's high speeds with a line that could have come straight from Earnhardt himself.

"If you want to race, that's what you do," Harvick said. "If you think it's too fast, maybe you ought to go do something else."

With five laps remaining in the race, he put Dale Jarrett and Jerry Nadeau behind him to take the lead on a daring three-wide pass. Harvick now had an exceptional car and a side window full of Jeff Gordon, who wasn't going to let sentiment get in the way of his own victory. Harvick held the low line as he tried to block Gordon. On the final lap, Harvick went high as Gordon dropped low. The two approached the finish line, side by side. Gordon couldn't quite get past Harvick, who won by 0.006 seconds—one of the closest finishes in NASCAR history—becoming one of a handful of drivers to win a Cup race in just their third start.

Harvick held three fingers out the window as he circled the track. Earnhardt's former team wept openly and embraced. Crews from all teams lined pit road to congratulate Harvick, just as they had for Earnhardt during the 1998 Daytona 500. "I don't even know how to put it into words, to tell the honest truth," he said in Victory Lane. "It took an extra cool-down lap just to get through the emotional part of it. I don't know how you could script it any different."

"I know he is up there looking down," Childress said. "I could see his mustache break out with that big old smile."

Success brought the crushing weight of expectation. Fans wanted Harvick to be something he wasn't—the second coming of the Intimidator—and he chafed under the burden. "Everybody wanted it to be like it was," he recalled much later, "but I didn't. I didn't like it. It just didn't feel good, didn't feel comfortable." The Childress team did all it could to insulate Harvick, but he was inexorably stuck in a groove carved by Earnhardt—a groove too deep for him to see out of. He lobbied for a different sponsor,

231

a different paint scheme, anything to differentiate himself from Earnhardt. "Goodwrench" would remain on the car through the 2006 season.

AS TOUGH AS it was for Harvick, the burden of the Intimidator's legacy was far heavier elsewhere. In July 2001 Junior had to return to the scene of the worst moment of his life and strap himself into a car just the way his father had five months before. He had to circle the same track in the same way, seeing that same turn over and over. How in the hell was he supposed to do that?

NASCAR visits Daytona twice a year, once for the 500 and again during the week of Independence Day. It's a biennial reunion for fans—a chance to get comfortable in one of the sporting world's true marquee locations and maybe work in a visit to a local beach or $5-cover strip club. Daytona accounts for two of the year's four restrictor-plate races, along with Talladega, offering opportunities for anyone in the field to drive away with a victory if the fates break just right.

It would be a living hell for Junior, who felt as if he had spent the last few months shouldering the pain of everyone in NASCAR. Everywhere he went, people wanted him to know the depths of *their* grief, to share what his father meant to *them*. Every story he heard was like being jabbed in a still-open wound.

"At autograph sessions or in the garage area, people meant well, but they'd bring odd items for me to autograph, like photographs of Dad," he wrote in his autobiography *Driver #8*. "Some days I was fine, and then one of these moments would just set me back days and send me into depression." The fans trying to get him to sign bootlegged merchandise were the worst of all, unable to understand why asking Junior to sign something that read "1951–2001" would be in the worst possible taste. Junior also loathed the mawkish 3s with halos or angel wings that sprouted up on bumpers and rear windows all over the country.

"Publicly he'd handle it well," says Jade Gurss, Junior's publicist, "but when things got quiet, he would ask, 'Why would someone bring me a photo of my father and ask me to sign it?'"

Junior knew that at Daytona he would peppered with painfully inappropriate questions: *What does it feel like to be back here? What does it mean to drive at this place? How are you going to handle driving in turn 4 again?*

"He did everything he could to steer away from [melodrama]," Mark Martin said. "He said he likes coming to Daytona and he was looking forward to it. He didn't start crying and say, 'I can't believe I have to come back here and race.'"

Junior walked his sister Kelley down the aisle a week before the Daytona race. He and friends changed clothes in the church parking lot and drove to Daytona, renting a secluded house where they could decompress in private. He drove to the track a few days before the race, working up the courage to face turn 4 with friends at his side.

"I took them around the 2.5-mile track and into turn 4, where Dad's accident occurred," he said. "I looked at the skid marks that still hadn't been washed off the track and I looked at the point where his car hit the wall. I sat and thought quietly for a while. I somehow felt closer to my dad at that moment." That was a private story, one he wouldn't share until later. Junior instituted a total media blackout. He didn't speak to the press and didn't have much to say even to close associates and his team.

His car did the talking for him. DEI had been perfecting its superspeedway strategy for years, and it paid off with the 1-2 finish earlier that year at Daytona. Junior kept the beat going by leading the entire pack for most of the race. The only real drama came with seventeen laps remaining: Kurt Busch and Mike Skinner set off a twelve-car accident in the middle of green-flag pit stops. Junior exited pit road after his final stop in seventh place.

Crew chief Tony Eury Sr., bespectacled and gray-goateed, groused on live television that there was no time for Junior to make up that many places, but Junior put the entire pack behind him with four laps to spare. He made his final pass for the lead on Johnny Benson's right between turns 3 and 4, the exact spot where his father had died.

Michael Waltrip repaid the favor Junior had shown him back in February, tucking in behind the No. 8 and serving as a rolling defense. Three laps later, Junior won the race. For a moment, Earnhardt Nation was whole again.

"I wanted Dale Jr. to win so bad," Waltrip said. "And I wanted to be part of it. I didn't want to finish tenth or twelfth. I was committed to Dale Jr. just like he was to me in February." Waltrip questioned his own commitment only for a moment, when Junior head-butted him in celebration.

Just as the first trip to Daytona had marked the initial NASCAR race for Fox, this marked the first broadcast for NBC Sports. Network executives had asked team PR reps to make sure their drivers showed plenty of emotion after the race—this was right in the heart of the reality-TV era—but a Dale Earnhardt Jr. victory made such requests unnecessary. Junior leaped off the car and stage-dove into the arms of crewmen from multiple teams reveling in the moment.

Schrader, Park, Jarrett—all figures from Earnhardt's past, all there in the infield to offer congratulations. "That reminded me of someone I once knew," Jarrett said as he embraced Junior.

The storybook ending seemed a little too perfect for some. Both Johnny Benson and Jimmy Spencer hinted that it was an awfully convenient way for a race to end. Junior didn't get wind of the controversy until he arrived in Seattle to help promote baseball's All-Star Game, which would be played three days after the race. A media session was proceeding uneventfully—the usual questions and angles—when a reporter mentioned the possibility that the race was fixed. Junior was stunned. His first instinct was to knock the hell out of the questioner—that's what his father might have done—but Junior showed admirable restraint. For the moment.

"It's really bothered me pretty badly," he admitted a couple of days later. "A lot of people have told me not to let it upset me any. But that was the biggest race of my career, that was my biggest win. Other than the wins I had when my father was there, that'll be the day I always remember. And for somebody to be questioning its credibility, questioning my credibility, I feel that's a slap in my face and a slap in my father's face and a slap in Tony Eury's face."

Jeff Gordon leaped to Junior's defense. "That's when you know you really did a good job, when they start saying it was fixed," he said the next week. "That's when you should sit back and be extremely proud of what you accomplished. I've been there. The Brickyard 400 [where Gordon had won in his hometown in 1994]—everybody thought that was fixed. The 13-win season [in 1998]—everybody thought that was fixed. You know, the greatest compliment you can ever get is when people think you're either cheating or NASCAR has given you an unfair advantage."

Other drivers offered up support. "If anybody had passed the word to let Junior win, they sure forgot to tell a lot of folks," Jeremy Mayfield said. "I'd say people could spend their time a whole lot more constructively trying to figure out if aliens really did land in the New Mexico desert in the 1950s than why a great race team won a race."

Everyone got a glimpse of the temperamental difference between father and son. If Senior had bothered with critics at all, he would have told them to go fuck themselves, and he might not have been that polite. But the rumors of race-fixing gnawed at

Junior—the idea that anyone could think that the finest race of his life wasn't legit burrowed under his skin. "I feel like everybody I talk to about the race, I have to prove it was real," Junior said. "That's a shame. I don't know how it'll go away. But it was a great moment in NASCAR history and it has been [ruined], basically."

This wasn't the first allegation of race-fixing in NASCAR history, and it wouldn't be the last. Big Bill France's early tendency to reshape race results based on whims and favoritism had bred a distrust of authority in NASCAR fans. Anything benefiting a driver other than your own had to involve some underhanded intervention, of course. As writer Jeff MacGregor put it in his book *Sunday Money*, "What was suggested, in the grandstands and garages and press box alike, was that Dale Earnhardt Jr., unwittingly and without volition, was being allowed to drive a marginally hotter car than anyone else. The community was in mourning, and maybe a tech inspector, only human after all, and wanting so much to help heal all that hurt, might look away at a crucial moment. What Junior might be able to do with incrementally better equipment was solely up to him."

Tiny modifications in the No. 8's engine—increasing the size of restrictor-plate holes to improve air flow and therefore power, for instance—would not be difficult to perform, even though the restrictor plates were handed out randomly and winning cars were inspected immediately after the race. But consider what NASCAR would be risking: it had just signed multiyear, multibillion-dollar contracts with Fox and NBC, and any complicity in rigging races would mean financial ruin for the entire sport. If NASCAR were caught tampering with the results of a race, the sport would never recover.

"I am 100 percent certain beyond a shadow of a doubt that Earnhardt's win at Daytona, Harvick's win at Atlanta, Steve Park's win [at Rockingham]—those cars were legal, those drivers played by the rules," Fox Sports commentator Dick Berggren said. "It would be totally impossible and too many people would have to be in on it."

Plus, race results indicated that DEI engineers and drivers had figured out how to run extraordinarily well on restrictor-plate tracks. Earnhardt was a master of the wide-open racing, and he'd passed along his knowledge to his team—knowledge that would pay dividends for several seasons to come.

The simplest answer is the most accurate: just as sometimes sports can break your heart, sometimes everything ends exactly as it should.

TWO MONTHS AND four days after that Daytona win, two planes slammed into the World Trade Center, rendering sports irrelevant. NASCAR officials spent their first hours of 9/11 trying to locate all their personnel and those of every race team. Several teams had been testing at the brand-new Kansas Speedway on the morning of the eleventh, and were using rental cars to get home. Other drivers were grounded en route to appearances for sponsors. No one involved with NASCAR had been on any of the ill-fated planes.

"We had to figure out what we were going to do as a sport," NASCAR president Mike Helton would say years later. "The next scheduled race was in Loudon, New Hampshire. We were supposed to be on the track that Friday and we knew we had to make a decision." The criticism leveled at the NFL for playing just days after the 1963 assassination of John F. Kennedy was on everyone's mind; former NFL commissioner Pete Rozelle maintained that it was the worst decision of his entire career. After consulting with other sports leagues, NASCAR postponed the Loudon race to late November, the Friday after Thanksgiving.

The first race scheduled to run after Loudon—the Cal Ripken

Jr. 400 at Dover on September 23—posed its own problems. Located less than 160 miles from the site of the World Trade Center and 100 miles from the Pentagon, the city of Dover, Delaware, is home to an Air Force base where drivers customarily arrived on their private planes. After 9/11, the base was being used to identify remains of the dead from the Pentagon and unavailable for nonessential travel.

With terrorism a staple of news broadcasts now, it's tough to remember the time when America was in shock from the unprecedented attack. The Dover race was overrun with paranoia and security concerns. The attendance of 140,000 people would be the largest single gathering of people since 9/11. The usual flyover was canceled, as were aerial helicopters. NASCAR and the track urged teams to drive, not fly, to Dover. Soldiers and police were everywhere, searching everyone and everything, running down rumors that ran from the suspicious to the absurd.

NASCAR drivers adorned their cars with a range of flags, messages, and patriotic iconography. Ken Schrader's Pontiac 36 was completely covered in an American flag paint scheme—no M&M sponsorship visible at all. On the morning of the race, those 140,000 fans were patted down, their belongings searched. No coolers or large bags were permitted. The track distributed 130,000 small American flags to fans, according to ESPN reports.

Tanya Tucker sang the national anthem and "God Bless America." Lee Greenwood joined in to sing his anthem of faith and patriotism, "God Bless the USA." As each driver walked out to the cheers of the crowd, an announcer read out the driver's designated charity pledge.

Cal Ripken Jr. was in the final days of his legendary career, making his farewell circuit of ballparks, receiving gifts at each stop. Major League Baseball and Delaware-based credit card giant MBNA, a longtime track sponsor, had coordinated efforts to put his name atop this particular race. He obliged by serving as grand marshal, waving the green flag to start the race.

"It takes a lot for one day or one moment to stand out from that year, especially as numb as we all were at the time," Ripken said afterward, "but I will never forget being in the flag stand over the track. As the cars came around, I nearly forgot to wave the green flag because I got so caught up in the 'U-S-A' chant that was going on behind me." Ripken scooted a few miles down the road to play the Yankees in Baltimore, where he would hit a three-run homer that night—the final one of his career.

Junior would take the lead on the third lap of the Monster Mile and remained strong throughout. He led a race-best 193 laps and cruised to a victory over Jerry Nadeau. NASCAR dispensed with the customary white flag to signal the final lap, to avoid any symbolism of surrender.

Juan Pablo Montoya had won his first career Formula 1 victory in the Italian Grand Prix a week earlier, and his celebration was muted. "They handed me the champagne and I just set it down," he said later. "Going crazy at that moment was not the right thing to do."

Junior had been watching and taking notes. He radioed his team right after the victory: "Hey, where's that big American flag at?" A crew member brought it to him, and Junior took it with him on his reverse victory lap, circling the track in front of the fans waving flags of their own. "I remember thinking, okay, we're back at the track now," Junior said. "We're all happy again, even if it was just for a few hours. Maybe now it's okay to smile again. To feel normal again."

CHAPTER 21
FREE BEER

BEING DALE EARNHARDT JR. brought pain and heartache and pressure. But there were also ample opportunities for insanely good times. As the events of 2001 faded, Junior began to stretch out and revel in the perks of fame. Junior was too shy for the showmanship of a Jeff Gordon, who hosted *Saturday Night Live* and subbed for Regis Philbin on the *Live with Regis and Kelly* morning show, but he dipped his toe into the world of celebrity, most notably with two appearances on MTV's *Cribs*.

The first *Cribs* show, filmed just weeks after Daytona 2001, took viewers inside Junior's property in Mooresville across the street from DEI. Sporting a backward baseball cap, he showed off his now laughably archaic "computer room," featuring four networked desktop computers so he and his pals could race online. The rest of the home's upstairs looked like it had been bought wholesale from an IKEA catalog.

The purple-neon-lit "Club E" downstairs was clearly the brainchild of a guy with a lot of money and a desire to carve out a safe space for himself. Club E featured a big-screen TV; a fully stocked bar with stools, tables, and chairs; a neon JR's PLACE sign; and several floor-to-ceiling poles with spotlights. The beer cooler held nearly a dozen cases of beer, and according to Junior, up to 250 people could cram into the space.

"I like to go to clubs, but when I go to clubs, I like to get trashed," he told the camera, a line that surely had some Budweiser

241

and DEI execs cringing. "Driving home is always hard because we live about thirty minutes from all that good stuff."

At one point in the segment, Junior pointed to a photo of himself and Senior in Victory Lane after the Winston All-Star race in 2000. "This was probably the best moment me and him had last year at a race that I won. He was pretty happy," Junior said, adding, "I never really had pictures of him around until then, so it's good to have him around and see his face whenever I want to."

A few years later, *Cribs* returned to check out Junior's sprawling new estate in Mooresville. The furniture selection appeared more personal, but the overall aesthetic was still Wealthy Southern Bachelor Bro: fish tank in the foyer, dining room whose centerpiece was an eight-seat poker table ("There's a top that goes on this table if you want to eat on it, but we never do that"), fridge filled with Amp, Budweiser, and Jell-O Pudding pops.

Junior also appeared in videos by Sheryl Crow ("Steve McQueen"), the Matthew Good Band ("Anti-Pop"), and 3 Doors Down ("The Road I'm On"), as well as a Jay-Z video with Danica Patrick. He played celebrity photographer for *Playboy*, snapping shots of the Dahm triplets in January 2003. ("They were buck-ass naked," he later said. "I was really nervous, but it was just a job for them.") He also shilled for Drakkar Noir cologne—it's tough to imagine Senior would have endorsed any scent other than burnt rubber—and did stints on *People*'s Most Beautiful People and Sexiest People in the World lists, alongside luminaries such as Jennifer Aniston, Brad Pitt, and Orlando Bloom. For one such issue, *People* writer Michaele Ballard interviewed Junior in his motor home, surrounded by buddies and not overly concerned with presenting an image of sophistication.

"If you could only take one beauty item to a deserted island," Ballard asked, "what would it be?"

"Q-Tips," Junior replied, as his buddies howled. "I love to clean my ears, even when they're not dirty." Junior was clearly better suited for some markets than others.

Junior took full advantage of the doors that open for celebrities in America. A devoted Redskins fan, he had unprecedented access to the team's sideline, locker room, and skyboxes. Celebrities such as Jon Bon Jovi, Kenny Chesney, Neve Campbell, and Mötley Crüe traveled to the unfamiliar confines of racetracks in search of one person: Dale Earnhardt Jr.

He also took shots at the silver screen, but carried on the dubious tradition of Earnhardts in Hollywood. Ralph is visible in the background of the early-1970s Jeff Bridges movie *The Last American Hero*. Dale Sr. appeared in only a couple of films: first as a NASCAR driver—big stretch—alongside one of his favorites, Burt Reynolds, in *Stroker Ace* (he pushed Kyle Petty in a room-service-cart race), and next as a maniacal cab driver in the film *BASEketball*. ("Excuse me, driver," one character asks, "can we go any faster?" Earnhardt grins and puts on his helmet.) Junior didn't overstep his modest acting abilities either, voicing an animated car in *Cars* and appearing as himself in *Talladega Nights* ("Ricky Bobby, can I get your autograph?" he asks. "I think you're awesome, just don't tell any of the other drivers").

Celebrities like Ludacris, Third Eye Blind, and boxer Arturo Gatti Jr. helped liven up Junior's thirtieth birthday party in 2004—a throwdown so legendary that some partygoers may still be suffering from hangovers. The party began at a nightclub near Mooresville and then segued back to Club E and its full-size boxing ring—a present from someone at Budweiser who had heard that Junior liked the sport. The ring proved an irresistible temptation that night for Junior and his friends—the "Dirty Mo' Posse," named for Mooresville—and Junior showed up at his next race with a black eye.

Although Budweiser was pleased with Junior's everybro image, he needed an occasional reminder of exactly how the brand relationship worked. After a practice session at Pocono, Junior wheeled the car into the garage, where Budweiser liaison Steve Uline was horrified to see the letters DMP spray-painted on the car.

"Junior," Uline said, "what is *that*?"

"DMP, man!" Junior replied, glowing. "Dirty Mo' Posse! Ain't it cool?"

"No, it's not cool!" Uline said. "It's graffiti!" That was the last time "DMP" appeared on a Budweiser car.

On another occasion, Junior instructed a crew member to slide a skull-and-crossbones decal into the car so that it would be visible on the in-car camera. The decal ended up right next to a Budweiser logo, making it look like Budweiser might be poisonous. The decal soon vanished.

Junior, shy by nature, didn't need to be aggressive to attract female attention. (Sample sign spotted in Talladega: DALE JR I'LL SIGN A PRENUP.) His status as an eligible, club-trotting bachelor generated countless rumors and put him square in the tabloids' crosshairs, often forcing Uline to do damage control. Junior in truth was an introvert who, by dint of his celebrity, could hopscotch right over the usual get-to-know-you dance of dating. Junior once confessed that he actually had a copy of *Dating for Dummies* in his house.

"Me and dating? I ain't no good at it," Junior said in a revelatory *Playboy* interview in 2001. "I ain't married, am I? If I was real, real good at it, I'd probably been married by now. . . . I like having a girlfriend. But you know, it seems to go for about three months, and gets to a point to where they're trying to drive the boat instead of me. I run the damn show. You know what I mean? I'm the boss."

Women threw themselves—or their daughters, or granddaughters—at him. In his father's time, these enterprising women were dubbed "pit lizards," always on the lookout for a (usually indulgent) driver. By the 2000s a new term had emerged: "waffle bellies," named for the waffle imprint left on young women's bare midriffs by the chain-link fences that separated them from the objects of their desire. It wasn't just flesh that fans sought; they took everything from Junior's pit box and hauler that wasn't bolted down—tools, clipboards, even tires. Such is life in a sport where fans can mingle with the stars before, during, and after the event.

JUNIOR WAS EVERYWHERE—Racing on Sundays and

staring out from magazine racks and beer cases every day of the week. Teresa, by contrast, had become a virtual recluse. A quiet woman even in the Intimidator's heyday, she now observed DEI's operations from a distance. Journalists coming to the Garage Mahal for press announcements would report her looking down on the garage floor from behind glass in a room above, standing with Taylor, always watching, rarely participating. Reporters who interviewed Teresa—and there were not many—said that her answers seemed rehearsed, as if she didn't want to show the world any pain. More than one journalist described her as one of the most painful interviews of his career. "That woman," remarked another after interviewing her, "has ice water in her veins."

Teresa finally broke her silence in 2003, consenting to a long, flattering *People* article about life after the Intimidator. The article painted the picture of a woman keeping the many Earnhardt business interests moving, trying to stay one step ahead of the demons of mourning and sadness.

Teresa spoke of the heartbreak of being unable to share moments and news with Dale. "I don't have a lot of time to dwell on any thoughts," she said. "I don't have time to dwell on anything."

That image jibes with Junior's assessment of Teresa as perpetually consumed with protecting Earnhardt's legacy. The article's perspective of Teresa being the steadying influence in the family—Kelley called her "the rock"—either indicates that some significant changes occurred in the subsequent years, or that the entire Earnhardt team was putting forth a brave and composed public face in 2003.

The article further notes how Teresa fiercely protected the Intimidator's image –she rebuffed Humpy Wheeler's desire to play "The Last Red Dirt Racer," a "mournful" song dedicated to Earnhardt's memory, at Charlotte Motor Speedway—and was determined to use the Earnhardt fortune in philanthropic ways. She created the Dale Earnhardt Legacy Program and Foundation, designed to support children's charities and wildlife conservation. Earnhardt had long prized his meetings with children such as Wessa Miller, and his affinity for working and hunting outdoors was legendary; this seemed a reasonable means of perpetuating those connections.

The *People* article depicted a woman who has remained steadfast in her determination to preserve and present a specific image of Dale Earnhardt to the world. Granted, *People* is not a sports-oriented publication, but the article doesn't even mention DEI by name. Whether by design or circumstance, the article served as an early indication of the hands-off role Teresa would play in the ongoing existence of DEI.

DEI CYCLED THROUGH a series of third drivers to accompany Junior and Waltrip, including Steve Park, Kenny Wallace, John Andretti, Ron Fellows, and Jeff Green. Waltrip won four times between 2001 and 2003, including a second Daytona 500, but could never translate those big-stage wins into long-term success—he never finished higher than fourteenth in a season after Earnhardt's passing.

On the other hand, everything was jelling for Junior. He ended

2003 ranked third—behind only his old buddy Matt Kenseth and Jimmie Johnson—and headed into 2004 thinking his time had come around at last.

There was reason for optimism. Years before his death, Earnhardt had recognized DEI's weakness at restrictor-plate tracks, and set about ensuring that the team started running like its boss. Back in 1999, Earnhardt sat down with Norris and Park to develop a specific superspeedway strategy. Earnhardt won thirteen Cup-level races in Daytona and Talladega, and he saw no reason why cars bearing his own damn name couldn't be reasonably competitive.

The root problem: DEI wasn't in charge of its own equipment. DEI leased engines from Childress and used only a small team to oversee testing and operations. After the meeting, Earnhardt decided to invest in the restrictor-plate program, creating an in-house fabrication and engine-building shop with the express purpose of crafting restrictor-plate engines.

Earnhardt, Richard Childress, and Andy Petree had formed one of NASCAR's first technical alliances shortly before Earnhardt's death. While such alliances are now common in NASCAR, RAD was one of the first to focus on the aerodynamic engineering necessary to win at the restrictor-plate tracks. DEI's commitment to a restrictor-plate program turned perpetually losing Waltrip into a two-time Daytona 500 winner, and turned Junior into one of the best restrictor-plate racers in the world. From 2001 to 2004 Junior and Waltrip won eleven of sixteen regular-season races at the two restrictor-plate tracks, Daytona and Talladega.

"The reason behind all that, in my opinion is, that's Dale," said Tony Eury Jr., son of Dale Jr.'s crew chief and cousin to Junior himself. "He knew the importance of a fast car at Daytona, and that was the culture he built at DEI. We were going to have the best speedway cars, and anything else was unacceptable. When he left us, everybody just took that to heart."

"Dale Sr. absolutely loved the plate races," former DEI director of motorsports Richie Gilmore said in 2004. "His comment always was, 'Let's get the best stuff and not lease it to anyone else.' I remember he'd usually come into the engine shop at seven thirty in the morning, after he'd been working on his farm, and if we weren't busting our tails, we'd soon be looking for new work."

"If anybody was ever set to leave this [world], it was Dale," Tony Eury Sr. said in 2004. "He had everything laid out the way it needed to be when he left. He told all of us, 'One of these days I might not be here. You don't ever know. You all have to carry on.' That's what we've done."

THE MERCHANDISING OF Dale Earnhardt Jr. rolled on. ESPN created a gauzy, slightly dramatized-for-TV biopic entitled *3*, starring Barry Pepper as Dale and J. K. Simmons as Ralph. NASCAR Media and CMT produced their own documentary, *Dale*, narrated by racing enthusiast and competitor Paul Newman.

Ryan McGee, now with ESPN, wrote the screenplay for *Dale* with legendary Pulitzer Prize–winning journalist Richard Ben Cramer's help. The author of comprehensive biographies of Ted Williams and Joe DiMaggio, Cramer dove deep into Earnhardt's history. He couldn't help but be impressed by Earnhardt, in particular the grace of his final days. "He was working so hard to mend the fences he'd torn down," Cramer told McGee. "He was working hard to fix the flaws he knew he had."

EVERY DAYTONA CARRIES with it memories of Daytonas past. The calendar syncs up again and again. The 2004 race ran six years to the day after Dale Earnhardt Sr. won his only Daytona

500. Junior had seen the many ways his father somehow lost the race over twenty years. So although DEI cars brought heavy weaponry to the track, Junior didn't allow himself to get his hopes up too high.

Every single race blends past, present, and future due to the longevity of NASCAR careers. The 2004 race featured future NASCAR fixtures like Jimmie Johnson, Kasey Kahne, and Greg Biffle running against longtime stars like Dale Jarrett, Rusty Wallace, and Terry Labonte. Stars like Jeff Gordon, Tony Stewart, and Junior himself were right in the middle.

Shortly before the race, Air Force One descended and landed at the Daytona International Airport just past the backstretch, and President George W. Bush entered the speedway amid a throng of post-9/11 security to give the command to start engines. It was the first time a sitting president had attended a NASCAR event since Ronald Reagan came to Daytona for Richard Petty's two hundredth career victory twenty years before.

Junior had caught Stewart by lap 181, and began sizing up the 2002 Cup champion. The absolute worst place to be at superspeedways is in the lead with a fast driver closing; there's almost no chance of holding off a driver who knows how to use the draft.

Superspeedways reward drivers with the requisite timing, reflexes, and balls to pull off a move known as the slingshot. Essentially, a driver rides in the draft of another car, and uses the lack of air resistance to build up momentum before pulling out for a pass. Both Earnhardts mastered this technique and its associated high-low fake, the equivalent of a basketball player's head fake that leaves the defender grasping at air. Junior and Stewart had each attempted this maneuver to win a race more than once, but never with more on the line than right now. Junior feinted high on the front stretch. Stewart had to respect the attempt. When he went high to block, Junior dropped low and hammered down. The bait-

and-switch was right out of the Intimidator's mold, and it worked to perfection. Junior wouldn't stop driving until he'd finished a burnout and parked at the start/finish line.

Junior removed his helmet, tears in his eyes. The crew members who swarmed over him were hardly dry-eyed themselves. Junior blew a kiss in the direction of the grandstands. "Every time we come to Daytona," Junior said afterward, "it feels like I'm closer to Dad. But at the same time it's a reminder of losing him. So I wanted to come down here and win."

"Considering what this kid has gone through, losing his father here, it's nice to see him get his victory," said Stewart, respectful in defeat even though he lacked (and, as of 2015, still lacks) a Daytona win of his own. "I think his father's really proud today." You can want to beat the hell out of a man and yet still respect him, and that's exactly how NASCAR's drivers felt about Junior. The win unified the garage like no other event possibly could. Every driver expressed pride and satisfaction with this closing of the circle. With a single victory, Junior had validated himself in the eyes of everyone who'd wondered if he was really anything more than the self-indulgent offspring of a legend.

"Maybe all those things that happened in the past is what made us work harder, to try to win this race more than any other," Junior speculated at the press conference immediately after his victory. "I'm not ashamed to say I put more emphasis on coming down here and winning this race, just because of what I've been through down here."

Junior stopped to take a phone call in the middle of the press conference. He spoke briefly with the person on the other end, agreeing that this was the most exciting race of his entire life. He finished with a "Glad to see you today. Take it easy." He made sure to note down the number, in case he ever wanted to call the president of the United States.

Earnhardt would go on to five more wins that year, and he seemed ready to assume his father's mantle sooner than anyone had expected. He already had far more Cup wins at the age of twenty-nine than his father, 14 to 1. But when Junior headed to Sonoma, California, in July to run practice sessions for an American Le Mans Series race, Fate warned him about flying too close to the sun.

In Sonoma, Earnhardt wrecked his Chevrolet Corvette C5-R when a combination of cold tires and a slippery racetrack caused him to lose traction. He slid hard and backward into a retaining wall, breaking the fuel filler neck. The wreck came early in the run, while there was still substantial fuel in the car. As he sat in the car, dazed from the impact, the fuel exploded into flames that quickly covered his body and head. The car's sensor would record that the interior of the car went from 115 degrees to at least 750 before the device burned out.

"I could die here," Junior would remember thinking. "This could be how I go. This would really suck if it's the way I'm going out." It took him fourteen seconds to get out of the car, by which time he suffered second-degree burns on his chin, neck, and legs—he carries the scars to this day. NASCAR fire suits are engineered to specifications that protect a driver subjected to open flame from suffering second-degree burns for a minimum of ten seconds; clearly, Junior's wreck and subsequent explosion exceeded those tolerances.

When Earnhardt was brought to the infield care center, he immediately began calling for whoever pulled him out of the car. Junior swore someone had him underneath the arms and had hauled him out of the car. "Nobody helped you get out," said a befuddled track PR man.

Much later, Junior recounted the incident with Mike Wallace on *60 Minutes*, saying he believed that his father had something

251

to do with his escape: "I think he had a lot to do with me getting out of that car. I don't want to put some weird, you know, psycho twist on it like he was pulling me out or anything, but he had a lot to do with me getting out of that car. . . . From the moment I made to unbuckle my belt to lying on the stretcher, I have no idea what happened. Freaks me out today, just talking about it. It gives me chills."

EARNHARDT WOULD WIN three more races in 2004 after Sonoma, but he'd win only three more races over the next *eight years*. Did the Sonoma wreck alter the trajectory of Junior's career? Many racing fans attributed his mediocre late-2000s performance to that day at Sonoma. *He got scared*, they said. *Lost his edge.*

The reality was different. Junior ran well the rest of 2004, totaling six wins on the year. His problems from then on stemmed from a wide range of sources—from internal team squabbles to off-track business distractions to changing car specifications. The Sonoma wreck had absolutely nothing to do with any of that.

"I promise—and I've been asked that a lot—it really doesn't have an impact on my career as far as stock cars go," Junior would say years later. "I feel completely, overly safe in that [Cup] car." Not that the wreck didn't make an impression. "It's probably not healthy to daydream about situations like that. I never realized it would be as hot and crazy as it was."

DALE EARNHARDT OFTEN won championships with several races remaining in the season. NASCAR, trying to keep future seasons competitive right up to final race, introduced a new championship system in 2004: the Chase for the Cup. The Chase was basically a modified playoff system, where a select number of drivers who excelled during the first two-thirds of the season would win the right to race for the Cup over the final ten races. Junior was part of the initial Chase field, even briefly leading in the standings, but he found himself in trouble for the unlikeliest of reasons.

Earlier that year, Janet Jackson's bustier had "malfunctioned" during the halftime show at Super Bowl XXXVIII, exposing her nipple for less than a second. This set off a wave of prudishness that seemed reactionary at the time and ridiculous more than a decade later. At the time, television networks were terrified of any impropriety that could draw a six-figure fine from the Federal Communications Commission.

The fallout from the Janet Jackson scandal ended up taking a big bite out of Junior's championship chances when he had a language malfunction that fall at Talladega. He was already tied with Darrell Waltrip, Buddy Baker, and Bobby Allison for second-most wins at Talladega with four. In the hours before the race, Junior had talked with reporter Matt Yocum about what a win would mean. After Junior went ahead and won the race, he and Yocum continued their chat in Victory Lane while cameras rolled.

"What does it mean to win here not only once, but to win here five times?" Yocum asked.

"It don't mean shit right now," a grinning, champagne-soaked Junior said. "Daddy's done won here ten times. I gotta do a little more winning."

Suddenly NASCAR had a real—if ridiculously overblown—problem on its hands. For a sport in which competitors had been *killed*, NASCAR was oddly squeamish about a single word's potential to harm the brand. It was hard to fathom: the Great American Race Car Driver could shoulder the sorrow of millions of fans, but wasn't allowed a single four-letter word on the air? Junior got hit with a 25-point penalty, which knocked him out of his first-place spot in the Winston Cup standings. Kurt Busch would eventually claim that year's championship. It was a rough way to go out. But the way that DEI in general, and Junior in particular, was running, surely the Budweiser No. 8 would be back in the championship hunt in 2005, 2006, and years beyond.

CHAPTER 22

THE SCHISM

WHEN TIMES WERE good at DEI, they were very, very good. Junior, Kelley, Teresa, and crew wizards Tony Eury Sr. and Jr.—they were family both in name and in spirit, a family that had faced tragedy and come through the other side, scarred but smarter.

But as February 2001 receded, DEI's shine faded. "It was such a great atmosphere when Dale was alive," recalled one DEI crew member. "He knew everyone's name. He'd goof around with us every now and then, giving us the Vulcan neck pinch and stuff like that. He expected a lot out of us, but he could be genuine too." Now he was gone, and the absence from the DEI garage was palpable.

The No. 8 team followed up the six-win 2004 season with an ugly mess of a 2005. Junior racked up just one win, at Chicagoland, and finished the season ranked nineteenth. He grew ever more exasperated: "DEI is like this big-ass dam and there's all these guys standing there with their fingers in these holes and every time you plug one, you're taking your finger out of another one. . . . When every cylinder is firing, they're badass. I know, I've won races with them. It's just hard to get all those cylinders firing sometimes."

According to Junior, Teresa's attention wasn't focused on DEI as a racing organization. "When you go into her office and there are stacks of paper, most of it is dealing with my father and whatever they're doing with his name and whatnot," he said. "So, we don't talk a lot. We don't have a lot of sit-downs about racing and the team and ownership and stuff because that's not at the top of her list. When Dad was alive, we didn't really discuss anything business-wise. I talked to Dad about the race teams and racing, and talked to Teresa about personal stuff, like, 'Hey, I'm going to buy a boat. What does that entail?' She knew about stuff like that. Now, she's the owner, and I've got to talk to her about race teams and race cars and what I expect out of her efforts and the company."

Junior and Tony Eury Jr. were bickering with ever more intensity. Prior to the 2005 season, DEI brass tried to jump-start its foundering teams by switching pit crews, removing Eury from the 8 team and upsetting Junior in the process. According to his publicist Jake Gurss, "Publicly he handled it well, but privately he thought this might have been the last chance to work with his cousin. Up until 2005, he and the team had that swagger. But by 2005, that swagger had disappeared."

Business had begun to trump family at DEI, just as it had at Richard Childress Racing twenty years before. Junior didn't have his father's clout within the organization, a fact he learned when he discovered that he didn't even have the rights to his own name. "Dale Earnhardt Jr." belonged to Teresa through DEI as both a brand name and a trademarked signature.

Dale Sr. had signed the first trademark filing for Junior's name. When Senior died, the rights to Junior's name transferred to Senior's estate, and eventually to Teresa, the executor of that estate. Complicating matters was an April 3, 2002, consent letter in which Junior—who had previously raced in his father's company with just a handshake agreement—signed over the rights to his name: "I, Dale Earnhardt Jr., hereby consent to RDE [Ralph Dale Earnhardt] Administrative Trust's use and registration of the name DALE JR. as a trademark."

Whether Junior knew what he was signing at the time, that consent form meant he couldn't license anything with names like

"Junior" or "Dale Earnhardt Jr." in the title. So when he decided to follow in his old man's footsteps by starting his own lower-level race team, Junior had to go with "JR Motorsports." He and Kelley insisted the name was pronounced "Jay-Are," despite the obvious evidence to the contrary.

Workarounds weren't enough; Junior and Kelley thought that the least Teresa could do was give Junior his own name back. "In the world we're in, other people usually don't own the rights to a living person's name," Kelley said in 2006. "As it got out [that] this was an issue between DEI and Dale Jr., the business world started asking, 'What's going on with that?' "

In June 2006 Junior finally won from Teresa the rights to his own name, and the trademark is now the property of DEJ Holdings, LLC. "It's my name," he told ESPN.com's Wright Thompson soon afterward. "I want to feel like I'm not somebody else's. I felt like I was still being raised under her roof somehow, some way. So it was a way for me to really be on my own. . . . I wanted to have it because it was rightfully mine and I could rightfully use it as leverage how I rightfully should be able to."

That year, the newly emboldened Junior rebounded in the standings, finishing the year in fifth place. His public stock continued to rise. He was now one of the most popular athletes in America, regardless of his performance on the track.

Shortly after Earnhardt's death, Junior, on the advice of Kelley, turned down Teresa's offer of a lifetime contract with DEI, instead signing a five-year deal. That contract was up for renewal at the end of the 2007 season. There was strife within the DEI camp, but everyone involved expected the negotiations to end with Earnhardt once again driving for the company that bore his family's name.

Then Teresa spoke. On December 14, 2006, a *Wall Street Journal* article about Max Siegel, DEI's new president, contained this line from Teresa regarding Junior:

"Right now," Teresa said, "the ball's in his court to decide on whether he wants to be a NASCAR driver or whether he wants to be a public personality."

It was the garage-gossip equivalent of "Gentlemen, start your engines." Suddenly anyone and everyone was revved up and commenting on the Junior-Teresa divide. The easy angle was hopeful-son-thwarted-by-cold-stepmother, and neither Junior nor Teresa did much to soften that perception.

Junior stayed silent until after the new year, when he began discussing the *Journal* article during the initial round of driver interviews in January 2007. Consciously or not, he ran a masterful two-pronged campaign, publicly offering Teresa the benefit of the doubt while also reminding the world of who was, quite literally, in the driver's seat.

"Right now," he said, "I want to drive for my father's company and drive the No. 8 Bud car. That's what I do. That's what I'm known for and how I want things to be." He admitted that he "didn't really appreciate" Teresa's comments, pointing out that "it should be every owner's dream to have a driver that's so easy to market." He allowed that Teresa "might have been having a bad day or something."

He confessed that he would like to own DEI one day if Teresa were to sell the business. Privately, he confided to associates that his relationship with Teresa had not changed since he was six years old, when he was the kind of kid who'd get in trouble for hiding cereal bowls under his bed.

"Mine and Teresa's relationship has always been very black and white, very strict and in-your-face," Junior said. "It is what it is . . . it ain't a bed of roses. . . . It's always been the same. It hasn't gotten worse over the last couple of years or the last couple of months."

Although Junior's relationship with Teresa hadn't changed much over the years, Junior and Kelley had. They were no longer those two kids being left alone while Daddy raced; their father was gone, and they had grown into successes in their own chosen professions. They were a thriving family of their own, independent of Teresa. Soon after he started making real money in 2000, Junior had moved his mother, Brenda, and her husband from Virginia to Mooresville to help with Kelley's family. The first Earnhardt fan was back, and very much in Junior's camp.

"With a family business, what you see on the outside is not always what's happening inside," says Kyle Petty. "You can't leave your work at the race shop. It follows you right to Christmas dinner."

For the most part, Junior walked the proper PR walk, and it fell to others to throw the poison darts. Before the start of the 2007 season, Kevin Harvick unloaded on Teresa during the January media tour: "It's hard when you have what I call a deadbeat owner that doesn't come to the racetrack. Richard [Childress] is one of the best owners in the garage. You always see Richard Childress. You always see Chip Ganassi. All these owners, they all come to the racetrack. It's not just a money pit that somebody says, 'Well, I can make money off of Dale Jr. I can make money off of Dale Earnhardt. You have to be at the racetrack and you have to play the politics of the sport and you have to be a part of your team and you have to understand what's going on. To me, from the outside looking in, it doesn't look like that's happening."

Junior cringed at Harvick's shots, calling them "ridiculous" and defending Teresa publicly, saying that she'd had a "full plate" to deal with ever since Earnhardt's death. Childress also praised Teresa: "It's tough for women in this business. For her role, to be able to do what she's done since 2001, she's done a phenomenal job. She's in a tough position. I think she's done well with it."

"Where's Teresa?" became a recurring theme nonetheless. Richard Petty himself even called her an "absentee owner."

Teresa's decision to remain out of the public eye meant that the Junior story moved on without her input, often to her detriment. "When it's raining, the sun doesn't get equal coverage," writer Monte Dutton said. "Teresa didn't get equal coverage because she didn't speak to the press."

Teresa—or her handlers—tried to walk back the *Journal* quote. "I think it was taken out of context," former DEI motorsport director Richie Gilmore said. "Our main focus every time we talk to Teresa, she wants Junior back. That's what's best for the company, that's what's best for Junior, and that's what's best for DEI."

Jeff Gordon wasn't so sure. "They better figure out a way to come to terms, because Dale could write his own ticket," he said. "He's in the best seat that you could possibly be in this sport, and I don't know if Teresa is really recognizing that."

Teresa wasn't alone in failing to acknowledge her stepson's value. Kelley had been trying to convince Junior of his high standing in the sport, but it took the actual negotiations for him to realize his worth to DEI and NASCAR. "When you guys write about the position I have and the leverage I have," he said, "it sort of helps me understand what my sister . . . has been trying to explain to me the last five or six years."

Junior made it clear that he wanted controlling interest in DEI at some point, with other shares going to Kerry, Kelley, and Taylor. "I'd love to take over DEI," he said. "Me and Teresa will talk about that when the time comes."

Ed Hinton of the *Orlando Sentinel* noted that several people at DEI "have privately expressed enormous frustration with [Teresa's] management style—which is largely, it seems, to let matters sit, and sit, and sit, while Dale Jr. stews on the back burner." This "absenteeism with a refusal to relinquish control," as Hinton put it, seemed to characterize the entirety of the negotiations. The two sides agreed to an outside mediator, but by then it was already too late. There was too much bad blood, too many hurt feelings, and a growing awareness that Dale Earnhardt Jr. did not need DEI nearly as much as DEI needed him.

"What happened to Teresa was, when she was married to Dale Earnhardt, she had all of the chips," Dutton said. "She didn't realize that this was now a battle she could not win. She owned the team. Her stepson owned the *sport*."

MEDIA GATHERED AT JR Motorsports in Mooresville on May 10, 2007, to hear an announcement they knew was coming. "At thirty-two years of age, the same as my father was when he made his final and most important career decision," Junior said, "it is time for me to compete on a consistent basis and contend for championships now. It is time for me to continue his legacy in the only way I know I can, by taking the life lessons that he taught me: be a man, race hard and contend championships. Since that is what I plan to do, I feel strongly that I would have my father's blessing." He said he believed it was Senior's intention for him to have "a huge role in the company," but that "me and Kelley came to the understanding that this was not in the cards."

It was a deft public relations move, invoking Dale Earnhardt's legacy while simultaneously sticking it to the institution that still bore his father's name.

"I do believe that for Junior it was important, in his mind, to be a part of DEI, so it takes a brave person to step out of that," Kyle Petty said. "It had to be the hardest decision of his life."

"I think there was a sense of guilt," ESPN's Ryan McGee said. "I'm sure he was conflicted about the relief he felt at leaving. He knew he was the face of DEI. But he knew their cars sucked. He knew he was jumping off of the *Titanic*."

DEI president Max Siegel tried to put a positive spin on the devastating split. "Obviously, our No. 1 priority was keeping Dale Junior and we're disappointed. I think that there's always been a real possibility that he could go somewhere and there were other options. Everyone remained extremely committed to the process. Much like Dale Junior, we're exploring all the opportunities to enhance our company, to grow to four cars and to be strong in competition and diversify the company."

Junior's departure from DEI set off a free-agent bidding war unlike anything NASCAR had ever seen. "I bet there's a lot of car owners licking their chops right now," Darrell Waltrip said.

Not everyone was in the game; Junior would only drive Chevrolets, and at the time, only three top-flight teams were running Chevys: Hendrick Motorsports, Richard Childress Racing, and Joe Gibbs Racing. In theory, Earnhardt could also have taken the reins himself, moving his own JR Motorsports up to Cup level, but that would have required an expenditure of resources and a gathering of expertise he knew he didn't have.

The solution appeared obvious: Junior would move to Childress, the team where his father had won six of his seven championships, and take over driving the No. 3. Junior didn't dismiss the idea of heading to Childress, but cautioned that he wasn't necessarily thinking in the storybook terms of others.

"I've got to do a little soul searching about how I feel about driving the No. 3 car," he said, "but I don't personally know if that's what I want to do specific to that number."

He had another reason to shy away: Childress remained in business with Teresa Earnhardt, both on the merchandising and the automotive fronts. Bringing money in for Childress would be supporting Teresa, and Junior wanted to make the break in every way possible.

In the end, Junior decided to go with a man who offered him a father figure—a man who also knew the searing pain of sudden loss.

CHAPTER 23

SECOND CHANCES

WHEN YOU ACCOMPLISH enough in this world, you can bring your memories back to life exactly how you want them.

On the campus of Hendrick Motorsports—one of the most successful teams in any sport—sits a building unlike any in NASCAR, or America, for that matter. Here, in the Hendrick Heritage Center, Rick Hendrick has painstakingly reassembled his history, brick by brick, image by image. Model storefronts line the walls: the JR Hendrick General Store, his grandfather's business. The firehouse from Palmer Springs, Virginia. The ice cream shop where Hendrick met his wife, Linda. The Bank of Virginia, where Hendrick's mother worked. The first dealership of what would become Hendrick's automotive empire. All memories of one man, all perfectly re-created and preserved, all utterly off limits to the public.

Hendrick would peer through a fence at Martinsville as a kid, trying to catch a glimpse of his NASCAR heroes like Richard Petty and Rex White. As he grew older, he tried his hand at racing himself—starting with drag racing at age fourteen—but he had a better touch under the hood than behind the wheel. He also possessed an uncanny gift of gab and a relentless will. He parlayed these skills into buying and franchising auto dealership lots. For Hendrick, the old NASCAR manufacturers' saying "win on Sunday, sell on Monday" was an opportunity to keep his customers in a closed loop: cheer for a Hendrick driver on Sunday, buy a Hendrick automobile on Monday.

Hendrick worked his way into car ownership in the early 1980s, pairing with Robert Gee to sponsor cars in what's now the Xfinity Series. Hendrick's first NASCAR win with Gee came in 1983 at Charlotte, and the driver was Gee's former son-in-law—fellow by the name of Dale Earnhardt. The young champion continued to help the budding owner get his own Cup and Busch series teams off the ground by testing Hendrick's cars in late 1983.

Hendrick's All-Star Racing had an auspicious start in 1984, but early top-ten finishes faded fast. By the season's eighth race—back at Martinsville—Hendrick had reached a win-or-pack-it-in point in his career. He didn't make the trip to Martinsville that day; he'd promised his wife he'd attend a church service with their children.

"When it was over," he recalled, "I found a pay phone and called my mom. She said, 'Oh, you didn't hear? They blew an engine.' I was just crushed. Then she started laughing and said, 'No, I'm joking. You won.'"

Martinsville was the first of three races All-Star Racing would win that season. The Hendrick train was rolling. Earnhardt himself wasn't going to jump ship from Childress. But Earnhardt's rivalries with Hendrick drivers like Tim Richmond, Darrell Waltrip, and Jeff Gordon would help Hendrick Motorsports—the "All-Star Racing" name didn't last long—ascend to the sport's highest levels. Hendrick teams would regularly venture into the season's final top ten, but it wasn't until 1995 that Hendrick captured his first Cup title with Jeff Gordon. Nine more Hendrick championships (and counting), and well over two hundred wins, would follow over the next two decades.

Hendrick would surely trade them all to change what happened on the morning of October 24, 2004, when his son Ricky boarded a small plane bound for Martinsville Speedway. The plane, a Beechcraft Super King Air 200, was ferrying Ricky and nine others to Martinsville for the weekend's race.

Hendrick was driving home from a visit to his mother's house when his cell phone rang.

"Where are you right now?" Hendrick Motorsports vice president Ken Howes asked.

"I'm driving."

"Pull off a minute."

Howes told Hendrick the plane was missing. At first, Hendrick wasn't certain who was on board, but then Howes ticked off the passengers' names. Hendrick called his wife, Linda, and headed home, where family members had already begun gathering. That afternoon, he received the call from NASCAR president Mike Helton. The plane had been found in shards on Bull Mountain near Martinsville. There were no survivors.

Ricky Hendrick: gone. Rick's brother John and John's two daughters: gone. Six other Hendrick employees and friends: gone, all gone.

The loss was unimaginable on both personal and professional levels. More than a week passed before Hendrick could manage to return to Hendrick Motorsports. When he arrived at the HMS campus, the first person he spotted was Jeff Gordon, whose eyes welled with tears. Hendrick spoke to all of the hundreds of employees, thanking them for sticking together and pledging that HMS would survive. Afterward, he shook the hand of everyone in the room.

Barely two years after that meeting, Jimmie Johnson, one of Ricky's best friends, won the first of his six-and-counting championships for Hendrick Motorsports. Every year when he flies into Martinsville, Hendrick sees Bull Mountain. In late October, Hendrick takes his son's black 2004 Chevy Tahoe for one short drive. Ricky drove that same car to the airport on the final day of his life, and behind its wheel, Hendrick told ESPN.com's Marty Smith, he feels close to his son once again.

The father who had lost his son. The son who had lost his father. Junior and Hendrick had known each other since Junior was a boy; Hendrick once signed Junior to a "contract" written on a cocktail napkin when Junior was fifteen. But the intervening years and tragedies had left both men staggering. By 2007 it was clear that each saw in the other more than just a potential business partner.

Gordon, who'd grown into an elder statesman in NASCAR, caught wind of the negotiations and sought out Junior to offer some counsel. Robert Edelstein recounted their exchange in his book *NASCAR Legends*:

"Rick told me you were talking to him about driving for him," Gordon said.

"Yeah," Junior replied, "we're talking a little bit."

"Don't fuck with that guy," Gordon warned. "If you're fucking with him, I'll kill you. You're putting hopes in that man's head. If you're playing around, that's bullshit."

Junior wasn't playing around, and he was impressed by the loyalty Hendrick inspired in a towering figure like Gordon. On June 13, 2007, Hendrick happily announced that Dale Earnhardt Jr.—the most notable free agent in NASCAR history—would be joining Jeff Gordon and Jimmie Johnson in the Hendrick Motorsports stable.

Once Junior secured his deal with Hendrick, the next question arose: What number would he use? It wasn't an inconsequential question; numbers in NASCAR are de facto driver trademarks.

It's impossible to overstate the symbolic connection between a driver, his number, and his fans. Drivers use numbers as shorthand out on the track and in postrace interviews, even when talking about their close friends and teammates ("The 14 was crowding me going into the turn, and that's when I got into the back of the 11.") When it comes to the sanctity of numbers, fans are even more devoted. They'll get the number of their favorite driver tattooed onto their body, which is quite a show of faith as drivers do change numbers. They'll also actively avoid the numbers of their rivals whenever they can, passing up grocery cart no. 24, parking space 48, or seat 18.

By 2007 Junior's name, face, and brand were inextricably linked with Budweiser and the number 8. The 8 had a long history behind it—in more than 1,300 Cup races, beginning in 1949, eighty-six different drivers had used the number—but the Earnhardt family made it iconic.

Ralph Earnhardt had driven the 8 way back on the hardscrabble tracks of North Carolina, eventually running his fifty-one Cup-level races with it. Dale Earnhardt Sr. debuted at the Cup level with the 8 in the 1975 Coca-Cola 600. Almost a quarter century later, Junior made his own Cup debut in the 8 at the same race. Junior had gotten DEI to purchase the rights to the 8 from Stavola Brothers Racing, a small outfit that happened to hold the number at that time. DEI now owned the rights to the number, and if Hendrick wanted it, Hendrick would have to pay.

Teresa brought some of her old Intimidator tactics to the negotiating table. She demanded not only payment for the 8 but also a cut of all licensing revenue related to it going forward, as well as the stipulation that Junior would return the number to her after he retired.

"Just ridiculous kinds of requests," Junior said. "We just wanted the number, but I was willing to give the number back when I was done driving. I wouldn't have any use for it personally." Before that day came, Hendrick would have to pay Teresa a percentage of every T-shirt, every ball cap, every die-cast car sold with an 8 on it. That would be a gargantuan sum—Junior merch was the best-selling of any active driver in the NASCAR stable. The deal would also put Junior and Hendrick in business with Teresa. Junior's success would be Teresa's, with no risk to her whatsoever.

"She either feels too personal about the number, or the rift between me and her is too personal," Junior said in August 2007, while still racing for DEI. "I'm not going to sit here and get personal about this. It's upsetting as hell and unfortunate, but that's just what happens sometimes."

"I say this with confidence," Larry McReynolds, Dale Sr.'s former crew chief, said. "Teresa Earnhardt would have burned that number before she let her stepson have it."

Hendrick and Junior rejected Teresa's terms, leaving Junior, who had won seventeen races with the 8, the next-best option: the 88. If nothing else, the choice proved a great boon to Junior's fans, who could just add another 8 to their existing tattoos. An ad campaign poked fun at the change, claiming that Junior was the same Junior, but the number was just a number. "Maybe it's for the best," he said. "Maybe it's sort of a blessing in disguise to really make a clean break. I have to let it go." (Worth noting: in a 2014 Mountain Dew commercial, Junior appeared in a basketball jersey featuring only a single, nonstylized 8.)

After time had passed and it was clear who'd come out the winner in the court of public opinion, Junior was able to be a bit more courteous. "If I was in her shoes, I probably would have done the same thing," Junior would say a couple of years later. "I don't have any malice about Teresa's decision on keeping that number. I really wasn't as upset about it as everyone thought I was. It wasn't as ugly a situation as a lot of people felt like it was."

Junior had every reason to be gracious; he'd won in every way possible short of holding on to the number. After Junior left the 8 behind, Teresa and DEI discovered that without Junior, the number was useless to them. Budweiser decided against continuing its sponsorship of the 8 soon after Junior's departure, opting instead for Kasey Kahne at Gillett Evernham Motorsports. DEI brought the US Army on board as a sponsor, and Mark Martin and Aric

Almirola took over, running the number through the 2008 season and the first part of 2009. Neither was able to return the 8 to Victory Lane, and the Army withdrew its sponsorship at the end of the 2008 season. The 8 finally gave up the ghost after seven races in 2009. The number's last race to date came at the 2009 Samsung 500 in Texas. Wrapped in a Guitar Hero: Metallica sponsorship, Almirola's No. 8 finished thirty-third, six laps down.

"I'm pretty sad about it," Earnhardt said that next week. "But I don't think it will be gone for long. That number has a lot of history. The 8 will be back, and someone will add to it."

The number 8 has not returned to the track. In a corner of the DEI gift shop in the Garage Mahal, you can still find Junior-branded memorabilia bearing the 8, on sale as if nothing had ever changed.

THEY'D BEEN THE best of childhood friends, cousins, accomplices, and partners. Dale Earnhardt Jr. and Tony Eury Jr. had spent their young lives imagining what it would be like to race together, and then had lived the dream together, first at DEI and now at Hendrick Motorsports. They were a package deal—the Junior-Junior duo, Earnhardt Jr. driving the car and Eury Jr. serving as crew chief. It paid immediate dividends with a victory in the 2008 Bud Shootout—Junior's very first time behind the wheel of a Hendrick car.

A couple months later, Junior had the lead late at Richmond, racing hard against Kyle Busch, a mercurial young talent and the very driver he'd replaced at Hendrick. Going hard into turn 3, Busch collided with Junior's driver's-side door and spun Junior out in a haze of smoke. It was an aggressive, win-at-all-costs move reminiscent of another Earnhardt.

"No! No! No!" Darrell Waltrip screamed in the booth, sounding like he was in physical pain. "Boys, I tell you what, that's not going to go over too well there."

Maybe Busch turned his wheels up into Junior. Maybe Junior chopped down too far on Busch. Either way, Busch effectively humiliated Junior in front of NASCAR nation, and cost Junior what could have been his first Cup win in a Hendrick car.

Busch was unrepentant. "That was just a product of good hard racing," he said. "I apologize that it happened. I hate that it did . . . I didn't feel that I slipped."

So how was Junior going to respond? With an Intimidator-style on-track whipping? Hardly. "I was in position for a win," he said mildly. "I ran hard. And got wrecked. I had a top-three car. I should have finished in the top three." He later admitted that he "really wanted to kill" Busch, but added, "There are some that do appreciate you taking the high road and being the better man about it."

While his sponsors may have appreciated Junior's restraint, fans heard the message loud and clear: there were now drivers in the garage who were more Earnhardt than Earnhardt.

Junior would have his revenge; he spun Busch at Richmond later that year in a move that may or may not have been intentional. "I wreck somebody, I ain't going to leave him in good enough shape to come back and get me in the same race," Junior said. Early in 2015, Busch noted that Junior fans with elephantine memories continue to give him grief even now for what happened back on that Richmond track.

The 2008 season devolved into a grind after the near-win at Richmond. Junior couldn't get aligned properly, and while he had one win—a fuel-mileage gamble that paid off at Michigan in June—he just barely squeaked into the Chase. Junior ended up finishing dead last among the twelve Chase drivers. The Michigan victory and a second-place finish at Talladega couldn't keep the first Hendrick season from looking like total roadkill. First-season jitters, right?

Earnhardt had established himself at Hendrick Motorsports by 2009, but the entire team seemed to be settling for mediocre. Junior set off a nine-car accident at the Daytona 500, and the year didn't get much better from there. Sniping, disregard, and careless errors were the order of the day in the 88 pit box. The 88 team stumbled to terrible finishes in race after race. Junior was consistently running in the mid-pack at best, having trouble breaking into the top ten. He could only watch as fellow Hendrick drivers Jimmie Johnson, Jeff Gordon, and Mark Martin all won races, redemption, championships. This was NASCAR's preeminent driver on its most decorated team, and the 88 shop was running a half-assed operation with ever-dwindling results.

Junior tried hard to defend Eury from the mounting criticism, but by the late spring, it was clear that the team was damaged almost beyond repair. "Frustrated," Junior repeated over and over—frustrated over starts, finishes, setups, races. After a fortieth-place finish at the Coca-Cola 600 in Charlotte, the 88 team was mired in nineteenth place, nearly 500 points off the lead. Hendrick dropped the hammer.

Family's family, but business is business, and Eury Jr. was out of the crew chief's position. "It seemed the harder we pushed, the more it unraveled," Hendrick explained at the time. "We need a new reason to get up and go to the track each morning, and the chemistry had broken down between them to the point where we just needed a fresh start."

The fresh start ended up looking like the mess that had come before. Junior didn't record a top-five finish for the rest of the 2009 season. He ended the year in twenty-fifth place overall, his worst as a full-time driver.

Jimmie Johnson pounded onward to yet another championship.

Harvick, Kyle Busch, Denny Hamlin, and Carl Edwards claimed ever greater shares of the sport's interest. Junior was thirty-five, and farther from the mountaintop than he'd been in his entire career.

IN THE SUMMER of that very same year, the very No. 3 that Senior himself had driven to victory in Talladega in 2000 turned up in, of all places, merry old England. An Earnhardt was behind the wheel, but the one people would least expect: Taylor Earnhardt, Dale and Teresa's daughter, who was only eleven years old when her daddy won that Talladega race.

The event was the annual Goodwood Festival of Speed in Sussex, England—an auto and aviation extravaganza that includes an exhibition of cars from motor racing history as well an uphill race. It's the English equivalent of a Talladega infield, everything coming together at once in a spectacle of racing, danger, and a damn good time. In 2009 the festival had prepared a slice of NASCAR history as a special treat: an Earnhardt racing Rusty Wallace once again.

Earnhardt's old nemesis had made the trip to England to run an old chassis from one of his No. 2 Miller Lites. The 2 and the 3, among others, would compete to race the fastest time up a 1.16-mile hill on the grounds of the Goodwood estate. Former Earnhardt Flying Aces Danny Lawrence and Rich Burgess took Earnhardt's old Talladega car and prepped it for the twenty-year-old Taylor. "I was told there were about 125,000 fans here today so it had to be a little intimidating," Lawrence said. "But she knows a thing or two about intimidating. So it didn't seem to bother her any."

Wallace set a speed record, and Earnhardt won acclaim. The Goodwood organizers invited Childress to send another Earnhardt car the next year, and in 2010 another Earnhardt traveled across the ocean to pilot it.

"It's amazing how much folks over here know about NASCAR,"

Kerry Earnhardt said before getting behind the wheel of the Monte Carlo that his father drove to victory at the 1995 Brickyard 400 at Indianapolis Motor Speedway. It had been one of Dale's proudest moments, and Kerry understood what an honor it was to be driving the car fifteen years later.

Dale Earnhardt's famed cars were now only relics. Dale Jr.'s cars were fading fast on the track. The message could not have been clearer.

OVER AT DALE Earnhardt Inc., cracks had widened into gaps, and the gaps were becoming chasms. In the wake of Junior's departure, only Martin Truex Jr. and Paul Menard remained to drive at DEI. A few weeks after Junior's press conference announcing his departure, DEI completed a merger with Ginn Racing, which brought Mark Martin and Aric Almirola under the DEI banner. About eighteen months later, DEI would merge with Chip Ganassi Racing and Felix Sabates to form Earnhardt Ganassi Racing.

Truex, Almirola, Jamie McMurray, and Juan Pablo Montoya would combine to run 367 races under the Earnhardt Ganassi banner. The team notched five victories, four by McMurray and one by Montoya, as well as eighty-four top-ten finishes. It was a respectable run, though only one driver—Montoya in 2009—ever made the Chase for the Cup.

McMurray, the driver at whom Will Ferrell flicks the bird in *Talladega Nights*, became Earnhardt's unofficial and unlikely heir at Talladega. McMurray's frosted tips and high-pitched voice couldn't be any less reminiscent of the Intimidator, but during the late 2000s McMurray was one of the sport's best restrictor-plate track drivers. He's one of many drivers whose career could have gone in a very different direction had DEI remained a fully functional organization.

Teresa remained reclusive—hidden from the public and even her own employees. She made appearances at the company Christmas party, but rarely at the track, which left those in business with her to defend her with the same rationalizations that had been used for a decade.

"It's obvious to me that at the death of her husband she could have walked away and nobody would have said a word. Instead, she hung in there," her partner Chip Ganassi said in 2009. "She stayed in the business and built her business. All I know for sure is that she's put a lot of her own money into the sport of racing and doesn't get any credit for it. That's a complete travesty for her to take the kind of heat that she does for being such a great supporter of NASCAR and the NASCAR community."

Teresa's rare public appearances drew controversy. Before the 2008 Daytona 500, she went public to promote a new die-cast replica of the famous Goodwrench No. 3 Chevy. The replica was the current "Car of Tomorrow," a car that featured a wing on its rear deck lid. Fans loathed the Car of Tomorrow's style, and saw Earnhardt's 3 on one of those boxy little monstrosities as something akin to American flag toilet paper.

DEI itself also had significant upper-management turnover through the 2000s. Don Hawk, Ty Norris, and Max Siegel all left the team over the course of the decade, keeping their reasons for leaving to themselves. (Most former DEI employees remain bound by nondisclosure clauses in their contracts.)

Richard Childress, seeing the faltering fortunes of his late friend's company, sent executive and former driver Bobby Hutchens to oversee the team's racing operations in August 2008. The move brought some improvement to the team's performance. But the US Army and Menards nonetheless ended their sponsorships with DEI, following Budweiser and NAPA out the door and leaving little behind but echoes.

"It's sad what that building [the Garage Mahal] is now, just a bunch of memories," says a former DEI crew member. "But it's her building. She's in charge."

Faltering in the boardroom, faltering in the public eye, faltering on the track . . . DEI couldn't succeed in any venture beyond merchandising the Intimidator. Tony Stewart summed it up perfectly in the end: "What's DEI without Dale Jr.? A museum."

CHAPTER 24

EULOGIES AND MEMORIES

APRIL 29, 2010, would have been Dale Earnhardt Sr.'s fifty-ninth birthday. Junior and Teresa gave him the gift of peace, however fleeting. Earnhardt Ganassi Racing, Richard Childress Racing, JR Motorsports, and Wrangler came together on that day for a historic announcement. To honor Dale Earnhardt Sr.'s induction into the brand-new NASCAR Hall of Fame, Junior would drive a Wrangler No. 3 in the Daytona summer Nationwide Series race on July 2, 2010.

"I just want to go to the racetrack and run it once before I retire, and this will probably be it," Junior said. "After this, I'll probably never drive a car with a 3 on it again. I can pretty much say I'm ninety-nine percent sure that will never happen again."

That news surely came as a crushing disappointment to all the Earnhardt holdouts who'd hoped Junior would one day take over his father's number and continue the legacy. Junior had his reasons: "It's not [my number] to take and use whenever I feel like using it," he said. "You just don't grab the car keys off the counter and go run out the door and haul down the road with your dad's car. I didn't do it when he was alive, and I won't do it now."

Junior offered a prediction that would prove prophetic another few years down the line. "I'm borrowing it once, and then maybe sometime down the road some kid will come up, and he'll have a connection to the 3—whether it's through my father or whether it's what his number's been since he was playing tee ball. Whatever, you know, that will be his. It will be someone else's."

Wrangler's involvement seemed like a sentimental one, but nobody in NASCAR does anything for sentimental reasons alone. JR Motorsports was struggling, and Junior was learning the hard lesson that other Cup-level drivers had learned when trying to run their own team: your name may be enough to interest potential sponsors, but if you aren't the one driving the car, it's not enough to induce them to reach for their checkbooks. JR Motorsports needed sponsors, and Daytona was one of the races without a designated sponsor on the car. Junior had an existing personal-services contract with Wrangler, and so he leveraged that deal into a sponsorship for the Nationwide race.

Making the whole thing happen had been a group effort: Hendrick Motorsports supplied the car's engine; Childress supplied the use of the number; and JR Motorsports and Teresa supplied the rest. It was a triumph of cooperation, even if no one really expected the car to show up in Victory Lane on July 2.

Except Junior, of course. He had a way of winning races when the spotlight was brightest. He won that first return to Daytona after his father's death. He won the first race after September 11. But since his last win in 2008, he'd run eighty-five Cup-level races without a victory. Did he have anything in the tank?

Everything set up well enough for Junior; the level of competition in the Nationwide (now Xfinity) Series didn't quite match that of the Cup. This was the level where Junior had had his most success, and where he would certainly feel more comfortable.

As the Subway Jalapeno 250 began—sponsors' names always have a way of undercutting the significance of races—Junior's loud blue-and-yellow Wrangler 3 seemed anachronistic, a car out of time. The race wore on, and the 3 kept pace.

This being Daytona, plenty of Cup regulars were in the field and looking for a victory of their own. On the final two-lap shootout for the checkered flag, Kevin Harvick got off to a poor start. Newcomer Joey Logano pushed Earnhardt to the front but was unable to get around him. Earnhardt held on for a victory in the 3 at Daytona. It all fit together perfectly.

"Victory Lane's like when you're a little kid and you've got a tree house or you and your buddies got a clubhouse in the woods," Junior said afterward. "That's what Victory Lane is to me, and I like going there. You miss it really bad, but you know it's there and you can get back there again if you try really hard. It's not gone, but it's very difficult to get into."

Later, Junior talked about the win's deeper meaning. "I was so worried that I wasn't going to win, because nothing but winning was good enough," he said. "If you didn't win, what a waste of time. I worked hard to try to win it, not only for Daddy . . . just all his fans. He had so many great fans. Not just mine. This is for his fans. Hopefully, they enjoyed this."

Eury Jr. turned to an ESPN camera and said quietly, "We lost everything here. To come back with that number and do this, it means everything."

AT THE INAUGURAL Hall of Fame induction ceremony later that year, Dale Earnhardt Sr., Richard Petty, Bill France, Bill France Jr., and Junior Johnson formed the Hall's first class. Childress told a classic Earnhardt tale about his response to drivers complaining about the high speeds at Talladega: "He said, 'If you're afraid to go fast, stay the hell home. Don't come here and grumble about going too fast. Dip rags in kerosene [and wrap them] around your ankles so the ants won't jump up and bite your candy ass.'"

The centerpiece of Earnhardt's induction was a sight he rarely saw in life—a reunion of his children and his third wife. Unlike inductions at the Rock and Roll Hall of Fame, where drama surrounding long-feuding groups can flare up onstage, the ceremony saw the Earnhardt family—Teresa, Kerry, Kelley, Junior, and Taylor—stand as one to honor Dale.

"When Dale Earnhardt had his hands on the steering wheel," Teresa told the assembled crowd, "he felt and saw things that you and I will never see. He could see the wind. Even moving at two hundred miles per hour, he could see things more clearly than most of us could ever fathom, and thrill us all when he was doing it." She quoted from half a dozen luminaries honoring Earnhardt before turning the podium over to Kerry.

The Intimidator's oldest son sported a full mustache like his father's. Like Teresa, he was ill at ease behind the microphone, but more candid. "There were a lot of times Dad wasn't around," Kerry began, "and I wondered what was so important to him that he had to be gone all the time." The remainder of Kerry's speech focused on the fans. "Dad would always take the last minute, plus some, to associate with the fans," he said before introducing his sister.

Kelley spoke in the strongest, most assured voice of the five, and also for the shortest time. She mentioned Earnhardt's charitable side—the way that he would offer help without seeking public acclaim.

Then it was Junior's turn. He was relaxed—he wore an unbuttoned Oxford over a white T-shirt beneath—and he earned the majority of the evening's laughs. "There were a few times I got public advice," he recalled, telling the old story of racing against his father in Japan in 1998. Junior tried and failed to make a clean pass on his father, who retaliated by slamming into his rear bumper and lifting his car off the ground. "That was the day I met the Intimidator," he said to a room full of laughs. "He let me go and I ran from him like I had an F on my report card."

Taylor's reminiscence was the final and most poignant of the five. When she didn't want to clean her room, Taylor would enlist her father to take her around their farm, showing her how to care for wildlife and respect the outdoors. "We all had different experiences with him," Taylor said, finishing, "but we all look like Dad. We're driven, determined, and stubborn as a fence post." Teresa ended the evening with another quote, this one from Earnhardt himself: "I've had a great career. If it ended tomorrow, I'd have no regrets."

The evening was nostalgic but somber, and not just because the Intimidator wasn't present to join in the celebration. When it was over, they all went their separate ways. As of the 2015 season, the five had not been seen together in public since.

THE HALL OF FAME sanctification of Earnhardt had the feel of a eulogy for the Earnhardt name. His victory in the No. 3 at Daytona notwithstanding, Junior was on a Cup-level losing streak that had darkened his entire career. JR Motorsports fired the Eurys, severing a family tie that went back decades. Teresa remained cloistered on the farm or on *Sunday Money* as Earnhardt Ganassi continued its slow slide downward. Like the Pettys before them, it appeared that the best days of the Earnhardt family were in the past.

"It's sort of like when the NBA doesn't have the L.A. Lakers or Boston—a couple of their key historic franchises—in the race," NASCAR CEO Brian France told the *Charlotte Observer* in 2009. "That impacts the league. We're in the same boat."

Junior didn't respond well to France's comments. "Damn, dude. I can barely get my ass in gear on the racetrack, much less try to win races," he said. "I'm so far off from being competitive I can't even imagine trying to carry, trying to bring excitement to the sport every week." It was an ugly streak, uglier than your grandmother's sofa. It grew and mutated, running through 2009 and 2010 and 2011, and Junior slipped deeper and deeper into despair.

The fans grumbled, but interest remained as strong as ever. Year after year, Junior won NASCAR's Most Popular Driver award. "Covering Junior," said *USA Today*'s Jeff Gluck, "is like covering the home team. No matter how he finishes, you write it up." No matter how deep in the pack that finish might be.

Gluck recalled talking a walk with Junior after yet another disappointing finish at Dover. His head was down, his shoulders slumped, his body language that of a lost man.

"Where do you go from here?" Gluck asked.

"I don't know," Junior said, honestly bewildered. "What do you think?"

There was even talk that Junior should hang it up as a driver, focus on JR Motorsports, and move into an ownership role. What was the point? Running around in twenty-fifth every week, cruising on the fumes of a good name? But he wasn't really asking Gluck for advice; Junior had never let quitting cross his mind, even when his father died. "Quitting was never an option," he'd say much later. "If I'd quit in 2009, 2010, I would have regretted it the rest of my life. You can't quit what you're doing. You never get over it if you give up."

The 2011 Daytona 500 marked the ten-year anniversary of Earnhardt's death. Junior slouched on a stool amid a crush of reporters. His hat was pulled low on his head, his chin was down, his voice barely audible. Everything about his demeanor indicated that he would have rather been anywhere on earth than right here at NASCAR's annual preseason media circus, held just outside Daytona International Speedway in a series of makeshift tents. Junior hadn't won in ninety-three Cup races, and now he had to bare his soul, reopen old wounds yet again. Who could blame him if it affected his driving this weekend?

During qualifying, Earnhardt surprised pretty much all of NASCAR by running fast enough to win the pole. That small victory struck at least one observer—Tony Kornheiser of ESPN's *Pardon the Interruption*—as somewhat curious. "Well, it's a great American moment, isn't it, when Dale Earnhardt Jr. at Daytona can have the pole position," he said. "There are people in and around the NASCAR world, not just drivers but people who cover the sport as well, who are winking at this one, who are wondering if this wasn't a set-up because it's the pole position, it's not winning the race. It's just getting on the pole, having the lead and bringing the viewers in. Dale Earnhardt Jr. is the most popular driver for the last seven or eight years and he can't win a race. This is a good set-up moment, is it not?"

"He probably shouldn't challenge the credibility of the sport," Earnhardt replied when told of Kornheiser's comments. "My teammate [Gordon] was second. We've got good stuff. . . . If anything kind of like that was going on in this sport, man, it would be so hard to hide it. [The media] would uncover that in no time. The fallout, they would never recover. I know the two guys that do that show [*PTI*, referring to Kornheiser and Michael Wilbon] don't know much about racing, so it don't really bother me."

Kornheiser's ESPN colleague Dale Jarrett—Earnhardt's old Daytona rival—wasn't nearly as diplomatic. "It pisses me off that somebody thinks that," he said. "Dale Earnhardt is in a very good race car down here. He's always run well here. He's my pick to win this race. Was it because it's the tenth anniversary of his father's death? No. It doesn't have anything to do with that. It aggravates you that that perception is out there. I can assure anyone and everyone that it can't happen within this sport to set something up, there's too many people that would have to be involved, and you couldn't keep anything like that quiet."

After three lackluster years, Hendrick had gone all-out to

surround Earnhardt with every possible element that could lead to victory. The 88 moved into a shop alongside the 48, in the hope that some of Jimmie Johnson's championship mojo would rub off on Earnhardt's team. Hendrick also brought Earnhardt the man he needed at exactly the right time. Shortly after the 2010 season Steve Letarte, Jeff Gordon's crew chief, was summoned to the Hendrick offices and informed that he would be working his magic for a new team—Dale Earnhardt Jr's. It would be Letarte's responsibility to craft a fast car, and Junior's responsibility to drive it well. Earnhardt exhaled.

"It was always, 'What's wrong with me? What's wrong with me? What's wrong with me?'" Earnhardt said. "For the first time, it was, 'We're going to get all these pieces and put them together. It's not just you. It's a lot of different things to make it work. And we're going to get them all right.' That made me feel good. It won't all be on me."

Junior quickly discovered that he needed to refocus. Prior to the 2011 season, Letarte gathered together Junior's armada of PR people to inform them of a new status quo: everything else in Junior's life would take a back seat to racing. That meant Junior would have to be at the hauler an hour before practice began, and he'd stay at the hauler until Letarte no longer had use for him that day. Until Letarte laid down the law, Junior had been accustomed to doing business with Eury Jr. and others in a more relaxed fashion. He'd show up right around the time practice started, hop in the car, and bail as soon as practice was done. He'd rather hang out in the motor coach, and those video games weren't going to play themselves.

Letarte needed Junior at the track for legitimate competitive reasons. A crew chief is only as good as the information he gets from his driver about handling, mechanics, *feel*. A driver is only as good as the car his crew chief crafts for him. Each needed the other—even if Junior didn't realize it and didn't much like it. "I was like, goddang, man," Junior recalled. "Man, fuck, this ain't any fun." Early in the season, Junior found himself in the hauler with a moment to himself. He thought about going back to his RV to goof off. As he would later recall, he looked deep inside and told himself, "I am not leaving this trailer. . . . I'm going to be a part of trying to figure out why we're running like we're running."

NASCAR haulers—those gargantuan tractor-trailers that bear drivers' names, numbers, and sponsors on the side—are self-contained mobile headquarters. They transport the car and its backup from track to track, and they also serve as private clubhouse and conference room. They seem larger on the inside than the outside—a testament to efficient design. Each hauler has a small but surprisingly comfortable room at the front where the driver, crew chief, engineer, and others can meet to plot strategy. Junior had decided at long last to dive into these strategy sessions and start making his team better.

Letarte's new, more focused approach struck the right chord within Junior, building him up and inspiring him rather than breaking him down and insulting him. "Say two guys are saying the same thing," Earnhardt says. "One guy, you're thinking, 'Man, I don't want to take any shit from you.' And the other guy you're thinking, 'I like what you're saying, let's do it.' But they're both saying the same thing. Steve had that connection with me."

Letarte knew just how to handle Junior. At Texas, during Letarte's first year, Junior bitched up a storm about how hot it was in the car. "I bet you'd like to get in your pool, wouldn't you?" Letarte deadpanned.

"Yeah. Yeah, I would," Junior muttered, trailing off, the air quickly going out of his protest.

He was running better in this new environment, but not well enough. He picked up his first win in four years at Michigan in

2012. He made the Chase, but ended up finishing twelfth in the field of twelve after suffering a concussion in an enormous wreck at the Talladega fall race. Tony Stewart set off a wreck that collected more than two dozen cars in one last-lap pileup. After the race, Junior tried to send a message to NASCAR and the fans.

"It's not safe wrecking like that," he told Yahoo Sports while sitting on his hauler's back bumper, visibly rattled by the carnage he'd just seen. "It's ridiculous, man. It's bloodthirsty, if that's what people want. . . . If this was how we raced every week, I'd find another job." It was a far cry from Richard Childress's assessment of Dale Earnhardt Sr. twenty years before—"Dale would probably vote to race at Talladega every week"—but Earnhardt would probably concede that Junior had more awareness of consequences than his father. Junior missed the next two races with a wreck-induced concussion, marking the first time in thirty-three seasons a NASCAR race ran without an Earnhardt in the field.

Progress continued in 2013. Junior notched twenty-four top tens—four second-place finishes among them—the most without a win since Jamie McMurray did the same thing in 2004. Advanced metrics via NASCARNomics.com predicted that Earnhardt should have won at least two races in 2013. But he didn't. He was driving better, but not getting to Victory Lane. At the 2013 Hendrick Motorsports season-ending banquet, a video of the team's four drivers' seasons showed Jimmie Johnson, Jeff Gordon, and Kasey Kahne celebrating their wins—once for Gordon, twice for Kahne, *six times* for Johnson. The only clip of Junior featured him walking through the garage.

Walking through the garage? It was the kind of thing that could crush a man, or cement his determination to win at the next opportunity: the 2014 Daytona 500.

CHAPTER 25

@DALEJR

ON A GATED-OFF street dubbed Bullet Lane, alongside a fork of Withrow Creek just north of Mooresville, Junior lives on 140 acres that feature a sprawling mansion, a pool, three separate go-kart racetracks, and a six-hole par-3-level golf course. Junior spent two years creating "Dirty Mo' Acres," his private Xanadu, in the mid-2000s, seeking a place where he could wear the T-shirts he wanted to wear, cuss, and kick back away from the tabloids' prying eyes.

It's not tough to find Dirty Mo' Acres in the era of Google Maps, and fans occasionally park themselves at his front gate. "They think they're going to just drive up here and get a meeting with somebody," he has complained. "I've gotten woke up a couple times in the middle of the night by people who've jumped the fence."

People go the distance to visit their heroes. Bruce Springsteen once jumped the fence at Graceland trying to meet Elvis. But Graceland is a lot closer to the street than Earnhardt's mansion. "The fact that the driveway's a mile and a half long and they'll walk it at three a.m.," Earnhardt said, "that's probably more shocking than anything."

These days, "Dirty Mo' Acres" is more of an honorary title than an expectation. Club E used to host legendary parties for hundreds of guests. Life is more sedate now. The grandfather clock Junior won at Martinsville in 2014 has replaced the fish tank once featured on *Cribs*. The most prominent relic of Junior's wealthy-playboy days remains Whisky River, the complete down-to-the-tumbleweeds Old West town he had built back in his wilder days.

Whisky River started as a joke between friends, a sketch on a bar napkin. Junior had been watching a profile of Willie Nelson on *60 Minutes* in which Nelson showed off his own western town—a movie set he'd converted into usable buildings. Heedless of the fact that Nelson was constantly in tax trouble as a result of projects such as this, Junior gathered a few buddies and began the design work. Buildings included the Silverado Saloon, featuring a full bar, pinball machines, and a pool table for the Dirty Mo' Posse; a sheriff's office complete with jail cells; a hotel with beds for crashing after a long night at the saloon; plus a church, post office, pharmacy, bank, barbershop, and general store. These weren't just facades; the pharmacy was stocked with period medicine bottles, and locks adorned the cell doors.

Junior regularly retreated to his estate during his long losing streak to dodge fan sniping and the public glare. "I just get nervous about showing off material things that are expensive," Junior once told Gluck while on a tour of Whisky River. "When you build something like this, people might [say], 'Man, that's cool' and some people might say, 'That's just a guy with a lot of money making dumb decisions.' And I didn't want to have to listen to that."

By 2013, on the cusp of forty, Junior had grown more comfortable with himself and his stature—and he was beginning to outgrow some of his toys. Junior and his friends rarely make it down to Whisky River these days, sometimes going months between visits.

Out past the three different racetracks (go-kart, dirt, and Martinsville-style oval), a visitor wandering the grounds might come upon a curious relic: a completely demolished car from NASCAR days of yore. Beyond that wreck sits another, and another, stretching deep into the Carolina woods.

Junior happens to be the curator of one of the most distinctive automotive collections in the nation. He has dozens of demolished race vehicles on his property, scattered among the trees. The collection is so vast that he doesn't know its true scope, estimating that there are "fifty to sixty" pieces of racing history slowly rusting under the canopy of the forest. Here's the car Juan Pablo Montoya drove into a jet dryer at the 2012 Daytona 500, causing a wreck that burned the track and delayed the race for hours. Over there are the wrecks driven by Jimmie Johnson, Brad Keselowski, Jamie McMurray, and others. A Will Power Indy car is lodged in the branches of a tree.

When he spots a wreck he likes, "we get a forklift, or a tractor with a forklift or front-end loader, and just carry it into the woods and just set it there somewhere," Junior said. There's an odd beauty to these cars, their bright blue or blazing orange paint schemes jarring against the greens of the North Carolina forest. It's a reminder of both the perils of speed and the inexorable advance of time.

If you spend any time talking with Junior—within the confines of a press conference or outside the track—it's clear that he is, as Gluck puts it, "a normal person trapped in a superstar's life." He plays online racing games, shops on eBay, seeks out the newest iPhones, and goofs around on Twitter. No matter how badly he's finished in a race, he's always available for a question or two.

"The old man could be abrasive enough to alienate people," Dick Berggren says. "I don't think Junior ever alienates people. It's just his way to be more welcoming. You never felt as if Dale Earnhardt Sr. was really welcoming."

His father treated the press like broccoli, an annoying necessity. Junior's press conferences are often remarkable—part therapy session and part stand-up routine. His openness and accessibility are rare in his profession and make him markedly different from his father.

"The guy cares if he's perceived well," Gluck says. "He never leaves the track in a huff. He's so classy. It's mind-blowing that a person in that position would think like that."

THE 2014 SEASON began with auspicious Earnhardt news: after thirteen years, the No. 3 would return to NASCAR's Sprint Cup series. Austin Dillon, a promising young racer and the twenty-three-year-old grandson of Richard Childress, would drive the No. 3, starting at the same track where it had last run 13 years before.

Dillon, an Xfinity Series champion, held up well under the weight of a situation that could have been crushing. Bringing in a relative unknown like Dillon created some distance between past and present. He bathed in the media coverage during the first days of Speedweeks 2014, then ended up with the pole at Daytona. Nobody was particularly shocked.

"Just as long as they don't make it look like the No. 3," Martha Earnhardt said. "If they painted it a different color, I can sort of deal with it, but I don't want to see the black No. 3 just like Dale's."

The infields at NASCAR tracks are secular spaces for the worship of drivers, and the infield at Daytona is sanctified ground for the Church of Earnhardt. There's a "Club 3" there—a neon-lit tent city devoted to the worship of all things Dale. But the number of 3s across NASCAR's fan base has begun to dwindle. Look around a NASCAR infield now, and you'll see as many 88s for Junior, 24s for Gordon, 48s for Johnson, and 14s for Stewart.

FOR MOST OF the week leading up to the 2014 Daytona 500, Junior wasn't particularly happy. While Kelley and her husband L. W. Miller were out enjoying the Daytona nightlife—they hit an

Outback Steakhouse the night before the race and mingled with fans—Junior stayed in his motor home, cooking himself fish and tossing a salad. The days when he could show up at Daytona with a bunch of pals and drink beer all week were long behind him.

The race suffered a six-hour rain delay, and what should have been an afternoon finish stretched late into the evening. The race finally restarted with about fifty laps remaining, with Earnhardt at the front of the pack. Behind him were a dozen of NASCAR's hungriest dogs. With Brad Keselowski and Denny Hamlin charging hard, Earnhardt had to make his car three lanes wide—a move that would have warmed his father's heart. Kelley, sitting in the pit box, couldn't watch. She could hear the screams of the crowd, though, and that was enough.

"White flag," Junior's spotter T. J. Majors said. "Watch that 2 [Keselowski] . . . both lanes have help . . . 11 [Hamlin] is closer . . . 11 is not clear . . . help on the bottom . . . you're clear . . . you're going to win."

"What a day!" Junior shouted over the radio when the deed was done. "We won! I can't believe it! I cannot believe it!"

Victory Lane is a stage set at most tracks—a ten-foot-high wall with nothing behind it. The production looks good on television, but in person it's anticlimactic. At Daytona, however, Victory Lane fronts the five-story-high 500 Club, a black-glass monolith that reflects the light of the popping flashes and spotlights. It had been years since Daytona's Victory Lane saw a celebration like February 23, 2014.

Kelley stood off to the side as the confetti flew, a wistful look on her face as she talked to a handful of reporters. "I see him maturing," Kelley said. "His relationship with Steve really is the foundation of that. As a crew chief, he's a constant believer and constant cheerleader. Steve doesn't get negative, and that's helped [Junior] mature as a driver."

Over in the media center, writers from around the world pecked away at their stories, writing in the shadow of the gargantuan Harley J. Earl trophy. Newspapers no longer had the budget to send reporters to most NASCAR tracks, but Daytona remained special. Photographs of the greatest finishes and finishers—Dale Sr. among them—lined the walls, permanent reminders of what the sport had been.

The side door opened, and the newest piece of history stomped right in with a loud "Wooooooooo!!!!!" There's no cheering in the press box, but when Junior shouted, there were more than a few smiles.

"I bet nobody's yelled like that in here in thirty years," Earnhardt said as he sat down, still wet with champagne and grinning through his red beard. "People used to yell like that all the time when they won."

He understood the role he played in NASCAR's transition from its past to its future. His father, who'd won one Daytona 500, had taken the sport as far as it could go with the baby boomers. Junior and his contemporaries now had to take the sport to the millennials.

Proof of that came the very next morning after the traditional champions' breakfast, when Junior stood beside the statue of his father outside Daytona International Speedway, pulled out his cell phone, and took a selfie, which he posted as his very first tweet on Twitter under the name @DaleJr.

"Way back when America Online started out, when you had that modem that went into the phone line, I would do online racing," Junior said. "I'd run up these huge phone bills, and my dad would always wonder why I was on the computer. He had no use for it. Unless it had four tires and a motor on it, he didn't want to fool with it."

Dale Sr. would have understood social media's power to extend a brand. And few have taken advantage of Twitter the way Junior has—posting classic family pictures, telling jokes, offering behind-the-scenes looks at races, even giving romantic advice. (For the dumped: "1. Focus on the 1 thing about them that annoyed u the most. 2. Party with friends.") He's connected with his fans in a way that his father never could. He's become a more human hero to the masses, winning NASCAR's Most Popular Driver for a decade-plus and running.

THE 2014 DAYTONA 500 launched one new phase of the Earnhardt legacy and marked the end of another. For the first time since 1996, no team bearing the Earnhardt name would be running in the Cup series. Over the years since Junior's departure, the onetime Dale Earnhardt Inc. had gone through multiple mergers and name reworkings, finally arriving at the unwieldy hybrid name "Earnhardt Ganassi Racing with Felix Sabates." Team owner Chip Ganassi had worked out the merger to improve his standing in NASCAR, gaining access to Chevrolet cars and Earnhardt Childress Racing engines. But Ganassi formally dropped the Earnhardt name early in 2014 as the contract between Ganassi's team and Teresa Earnhardt came to a close.

Ganassi officials said all the right things in announcing the change, thanking Teresa Earnhardt and praising her contributions to the NASCAR community at large and to Earnhardt Ganassi Racing in particular. It was clear to all that Teresa had no impact on the day-to-day operations of the team, and that the name change was more a matter of altering business cards than corporate fundamentals. It was also a matter of recognizing the reality of Ganassi's relationship with Teresa.

"I wish I could explain it, but I can't explain it," Ganassi said early in 2014. "I don't have a good answer for you. We had a relationship and I don't know what happened. We can't get her on the phone; it's hard to try to communicate with somebody. She obviously has some other things on her plate, I guess, and that's her prerogative. . . . She just wasn't there anymore."

At the same time, Earnhardt-Childress Racing Technology quietly changed its name to simply ECR. "The E no longer stands for anything," a source told NBC Sports. "It doesn't stand for Earnhardt. It's just ECR now."

NASCAR FANS LOVE a good conspiracy theory, as evidenced by the suspicion that greeted many of Junior's high-profile wins. But if NASCAR had been trying to rig its championship system to favor Junior—the surest way to bolster the sport's popularity—it hadn't been doing a very good job. As he reached his fortieth year, Junior still lacked even one championship.

The 2014 season saw the introduction of a new format for the Chase for the Cup. NASCAR grafted an NCAA basketball–style bracket onto the existing Chase arrangement in the hope of achieving a so-called Game 7 moment. If that sounds like too much stick-and-ball influence on wheels-and-engines, that was exactly the complaint of longtime fans.

The new system worked like this: sixteen drivers would make the ten-race Chase based on their performance in the regular season. A win in any of the year's first twenty-six races would guarantee entry into the Chase. After every three races, the four lowest-ranked drivers would be "eliminated" from Chase competition—they'd still drive because there are sponsors to consider, but they'd be ineligible to win the Cup.

Winning the Daytona 500 gave Junior a free pass into the 2014 Chase on the season's very first day. It was an enviable position to be in, and Junior's relaxed mood influenced the rest of the team. Earnhardt swept both Pocono races and spent the entire regular season at or near the top of the standings.

"Having that comfort of knowing we were locked in made the rest of the season so enjoyable. It took a lot of pressure off, and really allowed us to just go race and have fun," Earnhardt told Yahoo Sports in Richmond before the regular season's final race. "We haven't been riding around with a backpack full of pressure and the tension like you typically do in the old format."

Still, there were troubling signs. After the second Pocono win, Earnhardt had difficulty cracking the top ten, finishing that high only once in the last five regular-season races. Earnhardt was in an unfamiliar situation—racing from ahead rather than behind.

Every playoff team faces the question of whether it's better to enter the postseason with momentum or rest. Junior had an entire season's worth of the latter. For the first time in a decade, he was racing with house money.

NASCAR expected fireworks from its new framework, and the drivers didn't disappoint. The first round of cuts took out drivers with respectable but relatively small fan bases. Disaster struck on a number of fronts in Charlotte, the Chase's fifth race. Both Johnson and Earnhardt got caught up in wrecks, putting their hopes for advancement in real jeopardy. Former Cup champions Brad Keselowski and Matt Kenseth traded paint and words, culminating in a postrace wrestling match.

Junior entered the Chase's sixth race in mid-October with his once-promising season hanging in the balance. His only hope to remain eligible for the championship was a victory in that race, which happened to be at NASCAR's most treacherous track: Talladega. It had been a decade since Junior's last visit to Victory Lane there, but he'd already taken Daytona, the circuit's other superspeedway. With the backing of tens of thousands of fans in the stands, it was almost a home game for Junior. Plus, Earnhardts had a way of coming through big at Talladega.

The task was daunting; he'd not only have to win at a track

notorious for its field-shattering wrecks, but he'd have to outrun two insanely talented drivers needing the same thing—Johnson and Keselowski, who had each won at Talladega more recently than Junior.

The change in Junior's demeanor was dramatic as Talladega's race weekend began. Gone was the exuberant, smiling, own-the-world Earnhardt. The slump-shouldered defeatist—absent since 2011—had returned. At a press conference the day before the Talladega race, Junior appeared resigned, almost fatalistic. He knew the odds were long against him, and his body language suggested he was preparing for the inevitable.

He didn't intend do anything special to prepare for the most critical race he'd run in the last decade, saying, "I've been racing here a long time. Just have to get my suit on and get in the car. There isn't much to do it. You get in there and do it. I just don't need to eat any bad fish or junk food. Physically, it's very simple to race here. When you end the race, you don't feel any physical drain or anything like that. Mentally, it's very tough."

Earnhardt managed to avoid the wrecks that snuffed out the championship hopes of some of his fellow drivers, including an absolutely livid Kyle Busch. He even spent some time at the front of the field, bringing the entire mile-long grandstand to a full-throated roar.

But it wasn't his day. Keselowski and Johnson kept getting better runs, and Earnhardt kept sliding back in the field. When Keselowski won the race, there was nothing for Earnhardt to do but wheel the neon-green 88 over to pit road. At a time when he might have wanted to sink into the pavement and disappear, he had to answer the inevitable questions.

"There's probably been worse things in my career," he said quietly, and everyone knew what he meant. "I'm not retiring or anything. We'll try next season. We have a lot to look forward to. I'm not too tore up about it." On paper, the words sounded breezy, almost detached. In person, though, he was gutted.

The irony of the Chase flameout is that Junior's rebirth would come sooner than anyone possibly could have imagined. He'd always joked that he wanted to win a grandfather clock—the trophy that Martinsville gives to its race winners. He went out and did just that the very next week. Earnhardt outdueled Gordon to notch his first win at Martinsville on the tenth anniversary of the plane crash that took the lives of ten Hendrick Motorsports employees and family members. It was emotional, it was spectacular, and it was one race too late.

"I don't believe in fairytales," Earnhardt said after the race. "It's only destiny in hindsight, you know. This wasn't our year. It's only magical after the fact when you see it happen."

It was impossible to see Earnhardt and Hendrick celebrate together in Martinsville's Victory Lane and not feel a twinge of sympathy—a sense that some loops had closed, some wounds were a little closer to healing. A son who'd lost his father. A father who'd lost his son. Both finding strength in the other. Both, amid the confetti and beer spray, finding some kind of peace.

CHAPTER 26

TIME ROLLS ON

WHERE WOULD NASCAR be if Dale Earnhardt had not died in 2001? It's the great counterfactual—the what-if that's hard to resist.

Earnhardt likely would have raced two or three more seasons, then retired from full-time driving for Childress. He may have run occasional races—Daytona likely would have remained too tempting. He would have transitioned into an owner role at DEI—Dale Earnhardt Incorporated, that is, not Earnhardt Ganassi or any other hybrid. Junior likely would have remained with DEI, taking the 8 to ever-higher levels, perhaps even winning a championship or two under his father's tutelage.

"DEI with Senior at the helm would be right there with [championship teams like] Hendrick, Gibbs, Stewart-Haas and Childress," Texas Motor Speedway's Eddie Gossage said. "Dale would not have accepted anything less."

Earnhardt would have been an icon in winter. If Fox Sports had carried through on its plans to make him a cross-platform presence, he'd be charming the hell out of NFL and baseball audiences as well as NASCAR ones. Maybe he'd have run for public office; more likely, he'd have kept on driving his tractor out behind the Garage Mahal—a man content to have achieved all he ever wanted, and inspired more than he could have ever believed.

That's one way of looking at it.

It's also possible that without the death of Earnhardt as an impetus, NASCAR would not have moved forward as quickly as it could have on safety improvements. Other drivers who now walk away from catastrophic wrecks might not have been so lucky. Junior might have chafed under the leadership of his father, and struck out on his own regardless. DEI might not have survived the economic downturn that hit NASCAR; once-strong teams like Richard Petty Motorsports, Michael Waltrip Racing, and Roush Fenway are hanging on by their fingernails. Earnhardt would have had enough money and fans to keep DEI afloat from a merchandising standpoint, but running a race team is exponentially more expensive than selling souvenirs.

TIME ROLLS ON. There's always another turn ahead, another race next weekend. In 2015, Jeff Gordon, the Intimidator's longtime rival, announced his retirement, having done all he could do behind the wheel of a car. He was feeling the pain of both a back injury and lost family time. "I want to be with my kids," Gordon said in announcing his retirement. "I'm seeing them grow up before my eyes and I'm never here." Family or racing, pick one. No one could escape that pitiless math.

With Gordon's retirement, only five drivers who ever competed against Dale Earnhardt are still racing regularly for top-flight teams: Junior, Matt Kenseth, Kurt Busch, Ryan Newman, and Tony Stewart. The wide-eyed rookies who drew the Intimidator's wrath and respect are now the sport's elders. Earnhardt's name comes up as often as ever, but it's in the spirit of a Michael Jordan—an impossible mountaintop, always visible, never conquerable.

Today's drivers only possess, at most, one facet of Earnhardt's personality: Jimmie Johnson channels his championship hunger, while Carl Edwards possesses Earnhardt's branding genius. And then there's Brad Keselowski, the 2012 champion whose not-here-to-make-friends style has enraged the rest of the garage. Late in the 2014 season Keselowski fought with Gordon, Kenseth, Harvick, and others, all the while winning more races than anyone in the sport.

Richard Childress paid Keselowski the highest praise: "I like Brad. He's a hard racer," Childress said. "I had a racer like that with me once and people gave us a little heat back in the day. You just take it and go on and race to win."

Childress remains active in the sport—in 2014 his driver Ryan Newman came as close as anyone at Childress to winning a championship since the Intimidator, finishing second to ex-Childress driver Kevin Harvick. His grandson Austin Dillon continues to drive the No. 3, and the protests about the number's return to the track have vanished.

Harvick long ago outran the shadow of the Intimidator. As Harvick became his own man, his relationship with Childress and RCR deteriorated. In 2012, the news leaked that Harvick would be leaving Childress after the 2013 season, and that led to eighteen months of awkwardness. "They knew I didn't want to be there," Harvick said, "and they didn't want me there anymore because they knew I didn't want to be there." The situation culminated in an ugly war of words in October 2013.

In a truck race in Martinsville, Harvick collided with another of Childress's grandsons, Ty Dillon, and exploded. "That's exactly the reason I'm leaving RCR is because you've got those punk-ass kids coming up," he told *Sporting News*. "They've got no respect for what they do in this sport and they've had everything fed to them with a spoon. . . . It's a shame you've got to get taken out by some rich kid like that."

Childress seethed, comparing his grandsons' progress up the ranks with the rise of Earnhardt, the Wood brothers, the Pettys, and other great NASCAR families. Harvick would apologize the next day for the comments, but the damage had been done.

As for Junior? After long stretches where racing was more a grind than a love affair, he's rediscovered his passion for the sport. Retirement? Forget it. He's only three years younger than Gordon, but he doesn't face the same issues. "Jeff made his decision based on factors in his life, whether it be his health or his kids," Junior said before the start of the 2015 season. "I don't have any back issues and I don't have any kids on the way. I don't have any factors."

He can't junk it up on pizza and beer the way he used to—not if he wants to fit into the same fire suit—but he's found happiness in a way that would warm his father's heart.

"I didn't even know I could have this much fun," he said of the 2014 season. "I felt like a kid. I had the same feeling I had when I would drive down to Myrtle Beach with my late model. We were just on top of the world having so much fun. That freedom came back in the last couple years to just enjoy it and just release the pressure. So that's made me really think I can do this a lot longer."

He also found love. After a succession of "girlfriends" in the early 2000s, he kept his personal life private in the latter half of the decade. He's since gone public with his relationship with interior designer Amy Reimann. Every observer, from his sister to his competitors, acknowledges Reimann's steadying presence in Junior's life as a reason for his increased success.

"Being single was fun, but life's a whole lot more fun when you've got someone to share it with, and talk to, and go through ups and downs," Junior told Dan Patrick in August 2014. While on a June 2015 trip to Germany to delve into the history of Johannes Ehrenhart, Junior and Amy announced their engagement via Twitter. Tens of thousands of Earnhardt fans celebrated the couple's happy news with likes and retweets.

Junior's mother, Brenda—his first fan— remains a devoted fan of NASCAR, watching every lap her son runs. "I try to text after every race," she said, "and say 'good job.'"

Sometimes she adds a more personal spin; after a ninth-place finish at Indianapolis in 2014, Brenda texted, "U remind me of ur dad, take shit car & do something with it, congrads."

"Thanks momma," Junior texted back. "That's the best thing I think you've ever told me." He added, possibly with an eye toward public consumption, "And for the record my cars are always good."

Early in 2015, Junior revealed on Twitter that he'd claimed an important relic of his family's history: the sign that once stood above Metrolina Speedway, the sign that had been present when Ralph and Dale ran their first races. Junior is having the sign re-furbished and placed above one of the tracks on his property. It's one of the last youthful indulgences he plans to allow himself, and it's a good one.

THE EARNHARDT BRAND remains vibrant. Earnhardt-themed souvenir trailers continued to do brisk business at NASCAR tracks until the trailers were replaced by merchandise tents in the summer of 2015. Intimidator roller coasters thrill visitors at two amusement parks. The Kannapolis Intimidators, a Class Low-A affiliate of the Chicago White Sox—a team in which Earnhardt invested just months before his death—play just a few miles north of Earnhardt's childhood home. The Intimidators retired Earnhardt's No. 3 and emblazoned it on the outfield wall of CMC-North Stadium, where his legacy is hard to avoid. There's a replica No. 3 car out front and a range of Earnhardt-branded souvenirs for sale in the gift shop.

KERRY RETIRED FROM racing in 2007 and now operates several businesses, including home building and outdoor products

sales under the Earnhardt name. Both of Kerry's sons have joined the main family business. Jeffrey has run in the Xfinity Series since 2009, finally achieving full-time status in 2014. In September 2015, Jeffrey Earnhardt joined Junior in the lineup for the Federated Auto Parts 400 in Richmond, making the first time two Earnhardts had run in a Cup-level race since Junior and Kerry did in October 2005 at Talladega. In the 2016 season, Jeffrey competed for Rookie of the Year at the Cup level, the same award his grandfather won nearly four decades before.

Bobby—who goes by the name Bobby Dale Earnhardt—won the ARCA Truck Series rookie of the year in 2012, but has not yet cracked any of NASCAR's top three national series. Both fourth-generation Earnhardts have learned that the family name is a double-edged sword. You don't escape the name Earnhardt; it defines you, for better or worse.

AS FOR TAYLOR Earnhardt Putnam, she has a standing joke: the rest of her family earned a living using 800 horsepower, but she needs only one. Taylor is now a professional rodeo barrel racer of renown. She's come a long way from that little girl who wept in her mother's arms during the 1990 Daytona 500, when a flat tire cost Dale the win and handed it to Derrike Cope.

Taylor enjoyed a very different relationship with her father than her three older half-siblings. Earnhardt introduced her to horses from a young age and kept her outdoors, enjoying the world outside. She began competing as a child, and in 2002 won North Carolina's National Barrel Horse Association championship. The next year, she won the Southern Rodeo Association's championship. The farther Taylor advanced in the world of horse racing, the more success she found. She won the World Champion All-Around title in 2008. In 2009 she traveled to London to participate in a prestigious Ross Nye Stables equestrian training program. She and her husband, Brandon, travel the country to dozens of rodeo events each year.

Taylor now manages a stable of two dozen horses at her forty-acre Davidson, North Carolina, farm. Her barrel-riding course involves riding around three 55-gallon barrels set 60 to 105 feet apart in a cloverleaf pattern. She rides her horses two hours a day with the intention of making the horse an extension of herself. Sound familiar?

"It helps immensely if you bond with the horse and learn every bend and lean," Taylor said in a 2014 newspaper profile. "Nine times out of ten, it's the rider's fault if you fail."

Taylor shares one of her father's defining attributes—the ability to enjoy a track until it's time to start racing. "He was always carefree and playful with people," she said. "I'm always happy and messing with people until it's time to compete. Then I have tunnel vision, and I don't hear what anyone is saying to me or hear anyone screaming in the bleachers. I'm totally focused."

Taylor's focus broadened a bit in 2016. She and Brandon welcomed their first child, daughter Sage Nicole Putnam, to the world on July 12, 2016. The Earnhardt lines rolls on.

TERESA EARNHARDT REMAINS a mystery. She has made

no public appearances since Earnhardt's 2010 Hall of Fame induction. Her reclusiveness is understandable given the resentment many old-line fans bear for the way she's handled Earnhardt's affairs in the years since his death. Perhaps she continues to believe that she's doing the same job she had when her husband was alive—protecting his name and his honor—but it's not a widely held view.

"Do I think she did things the way Dale would have wanted

them done? No," Larry McReynolds said. "DEI is a museum with a bunch of empty buildings. That's not what Dale would have wanted."

It's possible, with the passage of time, to take a more charitable view of Teresa Earnhardt, even though she herself has made that task exceedingly difficult. This is a woman who is quiet by nature. She had a certain way of doing things, yes, but her life was inextricably bound to a man inextricably bound to racing. How much must it have hurt her to go to tracks and see his number, his name, his face, everywhere? It wounded Junior at every turn during those dark days in 2001. Teresa, too, had to face the sudden, irrevocable loss followed by perpetual reminders. Fans continued to leave flowers and tributes at DEI's front gates for years. It's not easy to heal when strangers keep opening the wound for you every morning.

Without meaning to, Junior made it more difficult for Teresa to win any public sympathy. He put on a strong face and went racing, returned to Daytona, answered the questions, signed the autographs. She decided on silence as the better—maybe the only—course of action, and many Earnhardt fans couldn't accept that.

Teresa appears to have withdrawn completely, not just from the racetrack but from many manifestations of Earnhardt's life. As of late 2016, the website for the outdoors-focused Dale Earnhardt Foundation had been updated once in three years. The page for "the official fan club of Dale Earnhardt," dubbed "Club E" (the name Junior once used for his party basement), now reads "Temporarily closed for restructuring. But it will be back!" Buildings and rooms on the Earnhardt estate and in the Garage Mahal are now rented out for private functions. DEI's Twitter and Facebook pages have seen only sporadic updates, mostly documenting Taylor's riding exploits.

NASCAR has publicly said that Teresa is always welcome. "It's natural for the NASCAR community to stay in touch," Helton said in 2015. "Anything we can do for her, we would. It's more on a personal level. When you're talking about bringing back DEI as a team . . . that would be much more complicated."

Junior and Kelley, the most vocal of the Earnhardts, remain polite on the subject of Teresa, but the tension is evident. When asked on her podcast what relics of her father she has today, Kelley's answer was telling: "We didn't get a lot handed down to us. Maybe one day we will, who knows."

That day doesn't appear to be close. By 2016, the NASCAR world had moved on from Dale Earnhardt Inc., the sadness and rage at Teresa's actions, and inaction, in the wake of Earnhardt's death largely passing into live-and-let-live memory. And then Teresa Earnhardt came roaring back into the sport's consciousness in the form of a court filing that reminded so many fans of exactly why they'd been so infuriated with her all those years ago.

Since 2012, Teresa had quietly sought to prevent Kerry from using the name "Earnhardt" in his business ventures, specifically the line of homes he and his wife were marketing under the "Earnhardt Collection" name. Early in 2016, the U.S. Patent and Trademark Office's Trademark Trial Appeal Board denied Teresa's legal challenge of Kerry's company name. Teresa re-filed the case in the U.S. Court of Appeals in April, and that's when the news broke wide.

Reaction against the idea that Teresa Earnhardt would attempt to deny Kerry Earnhardt the use of his own name was swift, decisive, and as universal as NASCAR opinion ever gets. Kelley broke her own long public silence on her stepmother by tweeting, "Hate that my brother & family have to deal w/ this nonsense for over 4 yrs. It's our name too! We were born w/ it!"

Kerry's testimony in the early stages of the case left no doubt as to the state of his relationship with Teresa. "Just me and my wife trying to build a brand for our family and everything," he testified, "and then for her to come and oppose it—I don't think if you had a relationship that any family member would do that."

Teresa still owns the trademark to the name "Dale Earnhardt," but not "Earnhardt." She did not testify during the case's initial phases, and did not make a public statement in connection with the appeals court filing, leaving that role to her attorneys. "The naming of any project called 'Earnhardt Collection' causes confusion as being associated with Dale Earnhardt, as the Dale Earnhardt brands and marks are so diverse across multiple industries and philanthropic causes," Teresa's law firm, Alston & Bird, said in a statement. Using "Earnhardt Collection" in a business venture unrelated to Dale Earnhardt Sr. "could be used to exclude Dale Earnhardt Inc., the designated steward of Dale's legacy, from the same use."

However, Kelley had testified during the case that no one has confused the Earnhardt Collection with being associated with Dale Earnhardt Jr., who by 2016 was far more visible in the public eye than images of his father.

Junior, for his part, remained quiet for several weeks before speaking out. "Obviously, I'm in support of my brother," he told the *Charlotte Observer* shortly before the Coca-Cola 600. "This is a business venture that he's put a lot of effort and heart and soul in that I think he deserves. So in this particular case, I side with my brother and his belief to be able to use the name as is—without any alterations or changes."

The Earnhardt-versus-Earnhardt case began its long journey through the federal appeals process in the summer of 2016, a sad reminder that—once again, as has happened so many times in NASCAR history—money tramples family.

A FEW YEARS back Jimmy Elledge, Kelley Earnhardt's then-husband, took their eight-year-old daughter, Karsyn, to a midweek go-kart race at Millbridge—fast, dirt-in-the-face racing, an adrenaline rush even for spectators. Karsyn noticed a black cart with pink numbering, and asked her father if that was a girl. When she was told that the driver was, the wheels began spinning in Karsyn's head, the way they did for three generations before her.

In June 2013, a twelve-year-old Karsyn stood in Victory Lane at Sonoma Raceway and announced her racing intent by unveiling her own sprint car—a Nickelodeon-themed beauty festooned with a drawing of the SpongeBob SquarePants character Sandy Cheeks and No. 3 painted on its gigantic stabilizer wing. Karsyn herself wore a bright pink fire suit, exactly what you'd expect of a twelve-year-old Earnhardt daughter. Of all the ways in which the No. 3 has been displayed—T-shirts, tattoos, bumper stickers, even shaved into someone's back hair—surely this was the most idiosyncratic: a bright pink sprint car.

Maybe Karsyn will go on to a career behind the wheel, or maybe she'll be behind a desk. NASCAR has come a long, long way. "I wasn't allowed in the shop as a kid," Kelley said, adding that the message was, "'Don't come in here. This is boys' territory and they're saying nasty things. And you'll get dirty in there.'" If women aren't in the garage today, it's probably because they're up top running the show.

TALLADEGA, MAY 2015. The drivers inside the cars change. The fans get a little older, a little grayer. But the numbers on the cars don't change, and neither does the love for the Earnhardt name. It's as relentless as the Alabama sun, as pervasive as the campfire smoke that hangs above the entire valley around the track.

Junior entered this race running well but not spectacularly; he and new crew chief Greg Ives had yet to lock into the groove Junior had with Letarte. Meanwhile, Jimmie Johnson was charging hard at a seventh championship, which would tie Dale Earnhardt and Richard Petty. Kevin Harvick was running off a string of first- and second-place finishes that demonstrated he'd capitalized on every bit of the potential Earnhardt and Childress saw in him back in the 1990s.

But this is Talladega, and this is Earnhardt, and every so often magical things happen when the two come together. Junior hadn't won here since 2004—back when a stray "shit" in Victory Lane fluttered the hearts of a tender-eared nation. Coming into the 2015 Geico 500 he'd made thirty Talladega starts, he'd led 832 laps, and on each one, an avalanche of sound rolled from the mile-long grandstands.

Junior led sixty-seven laps, the most he'd led in a Talladega race since that 2004 victory. He finished the day by leading the only lap that mattered—the final one—reaching the checkered flag just ahead of Johnson.

Every race is a metaphor, and for Junior, this meant the culmination of years of work—digging himself out of holes created by circumstance and deepened by his own hand. He'd returned to Victory Lane, he had a stable home life, and he still had the adoration of millions.

"Everything is just so good for me right now in my personal life and my racing," Junior said, blinking back tears as the confetti flew. "I don't feel like I deserve this."

Later, in a moment of striking honesty, he conceded that he knew he still had a job at Hendrick Motorsports during the lean years of 2009 and 2010 only because of his name. That shame burned him, even as he tried hard to live up to that same name.

As he circled the track, waving to the thousands of fans pressed against the retaining fences, Junior held three fingers out the window. "I've known him for twenty years, and I've known him real well for ten," ESPN's Marty Smith said. "I've never seen him hang three fingers out the window. That was a moment of expression unlike any he's ever had."

"I love when we go to Victory Lane here, because I just feel like I add to his legacy," Junior said after the race, his voice wavering. "All I ever wanted to do was make him proud, and I feel like when we win at those tracks where he was successful like Talladega, that's exactly what we're doing."

"The greatest tragedy of it all when [Earnhardt] died is that Junior had just gotten to that point where he was a peer for his father," Smith said. "He felt that respect over the last two to three years before Dale died."

"His father would be more proud of him today than he even was in that first victory ceremony," Helton said. "He has handled the challenges he's been dealt in such a mature fashion. He has an appetite to be not just a successful driver but a successful person."

An Earnhardt had won again at Talladega, and for one brief spring afternoon, all was right with the world.

THE COLLISION DIDN'T look like much, a little wall-scrape at the June 2016 FireKeepers Casino 400 in Michigan. Rookie Chris Buescher hooked Junior in the left rear quarter panel and sent the No. 88 into the wall and, from there, into the garage. Three weeks later in Daytona, Jamie McMurray and Jimmie Johnson collided, setting off a twenty-two-car wreck that again damaged Earnhardt's car. Individually, they were two more terrible finishes in Junior's winless, increasingly disappointing 2016 season. Together, they combined for something far more ominous.

After the Daytona wreck and an unremarkable Kentucky race, Junior began experiencing disturbingly familiar symptoms, problems with balance and gaze stabilization—that is, the ability to focus on an object while moving the head. Both abilities are, of course, essential for a driver . . . and both, Junior knew, had been affected the last time he'd had a concussion, after a vicious wreck at Talladega in 2012.

That wreck had sidelined him for two races. This set of symptoms, which doctors traced to the Michigan incident, would keep him out of the car for much more. Concussion symptoms worsen with every repeated trauma, and Earnhardt had now suffered at least three in his career.

"I've struggled with my balance over the last four or five days, and I definitely wouldn't have been able to drive a race car this weekend," Junior said on his podcast in mid-July, announcing that he would step out of the 88 for the short term. "I made the decision I had to make." From there, he pursued a range of balance, vision-adjustment, and anxiety-management therapies designed to help manage the symptoms, therapies that Junior often filmed and posted on social media for his fans.

It was a fascinating turnabout, the son of a man who raced with maladies of every stripe, who once tightened seatbelts down on a cracked sternum, opting to take a more prudent, measured approach to healing. Junior had already announced earlier in the year on Twitter that he would be donating his brain to science to aid in the study of concussion-related trauma ("What use is it to you at that point?" he reasoned) and this was another sign that the era of Quit Your Crying and Go Race was over. The awareness of concussion severity, driven in large part by several high-profile NFL players' suicides and mental health concerns, had improved since the days of the Intimidator, and Junior's own openness positioned him at the front of concussion awareness across all sports.

Even more fascinating, for NASCAR fans, was the man who would replace Junior in the 88 for several races: none other than recently-retired legend Jeff Gordon. If you'd told an Earnhardt fan back in, say, the summer of 1995 that Gordon would one day step in to help out the Intimidator's son, that fan probably would have knocked you out cold. But here was Gordon, graying but still game, stepping into a car that still carried Earnhardt Jr.'s name across its windshield, driving in support of the son of his oldest, greatest rival.

Junior revealed a vulnerability uncommon in any athlete at a striking news conference at Watkins Glen in August 2016, his first public appearance since stepping out of the car. "This situation, my doctor tells me, is good therapy: go somewhere that makes you feel worse," he said. "'Go in there and get exposure and then get out and go somewhere where you can kind of get calmed back down and then repeat the process.' And so, I've been going and eating and having lunch with my family. I go to Kelley's house and get in the living room with her kids. Boy, that drives up the symptoms pretty good."

The concussion-like symptoms cast a pall over Earnhardt's entire 2016 season. And although no one really wanted to mention the r-word—"retirement"—Earnhardt and everyone around him understood that this was indeed a sign that the ending of his career was much closer than the beginning.

"As soon as I can get healthy and get confident in how I feel and feel like I can drive a car and be great driving it, then I want to drive," he said. "I want to race. I miss the competition. I miss being here. I miss the people and, as Rick (Hendrick) likes to say, 'We've got unfinished business.' I'm not ready to stop racing. I'm not ready to quit."

IN THE EARLY 1980s, as Dale Earnhardt was winning his first championships, the Cannon Mills—where he and his father likely would have lived out their lives without racing—were nearing their end. A hostile takeover of Cannon in 1982 resulted in the sale of company housing; soon afterward, many mill employees lost their jobs to automation. Within two decades, the entire Kannapolis textile operation would be gone, and the mills were torn down in 2005 and 2006.

Martha Earnhardt, now in her mid-eighties, still lives in Kannapolis near the site of the old mills, still makes occasional public appearances talking of old days. She's known the heights of maternal pride and joy as well as the depths of tragedy, having lost her husband young and her oldest son before his time. She loves racing, and she knows what she'd like her family's legacy to be. "I would hope," she told Kelley not long ago, "that there would be an Earnhardt still racing as long as I live."

She still lives in that same house on Coach and Sedan. Only a small "3" sign by the front steps would indicate to a stranger that this is the birthplace of racing's greatest dynasty. Every month since February 2001, a flower has arrived on her doorstep, courtesy of Richard Childress.

The famous garage—the place where it all began—still stands behind the house. It's immaculate—just how Ralph would have liked it.

IT'S A CHEERY afternoon at JR Motorsports, and why not? The Boss Man is enjoying his best seasons in a decade, if not his entire career. The Xfinity teams are winning, including a Chase Elliott championship in 2014. There's sponsor money rolling in—maybe not the tall 1990s dollars, but cash is cash.

JR Motorsports sits in a cul-de-sac at the end of a long series of industrial roads in Mooresville dotted with other race team shops and ancillary businesses, like parts warehouses and crew member training academies. This is racing central, and JR Motorsports is an integral part of the entire picture. Junior's two-story image looms over the entrance to JRM's headquarters like some grinning, red-bearded god.

You walk into the gift shop—there's always a gift shop—and you're struck with the array of T-shirts, die-cast cars, prints, and other souvenirs available, each price ending in .88. There are some curious touches, like the creepily lifelike mannequin of Junior in one corner. (Signs nearby encourage pictures, but No Touching.) Farther inside the gift shop is a large window onto the JRM garage, and there's activity in every corner. Close to the window for easy photographing sits the Wrangler No. 3 Junior took to Victory Lane in Daytona back in 2010. Farther back, the garage is humming in anticipation of the next race.

The Dirty Mo' Radio "studio," stocked with sleek new microphones and old chairs from Junior's house, sits adjacent to the garage window. The "studio" isn't much more than a glassed-in walk-in closet, but it's the place where JR Motorsports is connecting with its fan base in an entirely new, more personal way. Various DMR podcasts tape daily, and on the occasions when Junior pops in for a visit, the gift shop fills up with fans who want a look through glass at their hero.

You can see souvenirs dedicated to Junior's name and business ventures, including the Whisky River Bar and the rather ill-defined Dirty Mo' Posse. And if you spend $88, you get your very own authentic race-used tire.

This is Junior Nation. Not only is it still very much alive, it's growing.

FROM JR MOTORSPORTS, you drive east toward Kannapolis, right through downtown Mooresville—you'll pass Junior-approved restaurants like Pie in the Sky Pizza and Whataburger—until you come to State Route 3. New subdivisions are popping up on previously empty property here, gaining a foothold on the relentless crawl of kudzu. The road opens up after a few miles, and you're in a land of lakes and horse farms, punctuated by the occasional historical marker commemorating a Civil War battle.

You know you're at your destination when you can see stark white buildings and high fences amid the expanses of farmland. Then it's there in front of you—the Garage Mahal. Once the white-hot center of racing—the home of the sport's greatest driver—it now houses little more than his legacy.

The museum and gift shop are open three days a week, three hours a day, a schedule that seems less symbolic and more expedient. On this Saturday afternoon, you're the only visitor here. You walk into the Garage Mahal, and in the two-story entranceway you see one of Earnhardt's classic Goodwrench No. 3s, flanked by backlit portraits of the man. The stuffed heads of bucks he brought back from hunting expeditions sit high on the surrounding walls.

The entire place is—*tomblike* isn't the right word, because tombs have dust. It's sterile, that's it, the floors and marble walls buffed to a high shine. A small television in one corner emits the hum of race cars and the excited chatter of announcers—old race telecasts playing in a loop.

The north wing of the museum hosts several of Earnhardt's winning cars. Six Goodyear trophies, replicas of Earnhardt's championship cars, each worth tens of thousands of dollars, sit stacked atop one another. In a gargantuan case, you can see all seven of his Winston Cup championship trophies, each one accompanied by a picture of Earnhardt—young, arrogant, still looking like he'd knock you on your ass.

The image that the DEI museum presents is a carefully honed and curated one. This isn't the Dale who learned at his father's side or the Dale who struggled throughout the 1970s, his family life a shambles as his racing career lurched forward. No, the Dale Earnhardt presented here is a fully formed champion, as remote and unapproachable as a god.

This image of him is commodified in the gift shop, marketed as a character as far removed from reality as Iron Man or Mickey Mouse. Dale Earnhardt Jr. only exists to the extent that he was under DEI's copyright control. There's a small display of Budweiser 8 merchandise here, but no other indication that Junior even exists— or, for that matter, any other NASCAR driver outside of a few DEI stalwarts.

Nothing resembling a race team operates out of here any longer. DEI still provides technical assistance to race teams and hosts the occasional automotive technology seminar. But the absence of the man who built this empty majesty looms over it all.

In a gargantuan, pristine garage you can see many of DEI's most famous recent cars on display. The splashy colors and the seven trophies right around the corner are a sharp contrast to the relatively paltry achievements of these particular cars. It's been a long, long time since a checkered flag flew at the Garage Mahal.

The arrangement of cars in the showroom gets changed once a year or so. With no new winners to display, it's a rearrangement of antiquities. Every year on April 29, Earnhardt's birthday, fans gather on the grounds of the Garage Mahal for a DEI-sponsored cookout and memories of times gone by.

The rest of the property is surrounded by high fences and ornate wrought-iron gates like something out of eighteenth-century Europe—all of it enclosing the Earnhardt estate, acres upon acres of meadows and ponds. The Clydesdale he once received from Budweiser may still be back there, along with old cars and relics of a world that started in 1979 and stopped two decades later.

He's buried back there behind the walls that line his farm, his tomb far from the road and the prying eyes of his fans. High fences and shrubs surround the crypt, which sits in the center of a field. You can see it on satellite photos, but to get any closer than that, you'd have to follow Dale Jr.'s lead. He used to fly right over the mausoleum when he'd helicopter from his home to Charlotte Motor Speedway, checking from above to make sure the shrubs were trimmed and the place looked as sharp as his father deserved.

When asked if there's ever been any talk of opening Earnhardt's grave to the public, a clerk at the Garage Mahal's souvenir shop says "No" in a way that does not invite further inquiry.

For now, this is how it ends for Earnhardt—his cars gleaming in a museum in a way they never did in reality, his trophies sealed behind glass. His fire suits are framed along one wall: a white one from the Rod Osterlund days in 1980, a blue-and-yellow Wrangler model from 1985, a black-and-white Goodwrench suit with sleeves showing damage from a Talladega wreck. They hang there, empty, like suits of armor from half-remembered wars.

You take a last look around and leave, your footsteps echoing in the empty museum. You exit—through the gift shop, of course—and wheel your car out onto the empty lanes of State Route 3.

With the open road stretching wide before you, you do what's only right.

You grip the steering wheel.

You grin.

You floor it.

RALPH EARNHARDT DIDN'T give young Dale a whole lot of sage racing advice, preferring to let his engine do the teaching. But once, after Dale had gotten spun out going into a corner, Ralph offered up this bit of wisdom:

"Anytime a man's trying to wreck you or mess with you, or if you're running with a man in the corners, save a little gas," he said. "When he does hit you, you got some power to play with, to work the car with." The following people were my extra throttle as I drove into the corners and rode the high banks with this book, and I'm grateful for them all.

First and foremost, thanks go to my parents, Howard and Mary, who have encouraged me as a writer every step of the way, and my kids, Riley and Logan, who have both inspired and tolerated me. (Yes, kids, the book is *finally* done.)

Eternal gratitude to my agent, Byrd Leavell, for firing me up with one ass-kicking phrase: "It's time to add a book to your résumé." So many thanks to David Hirshey at HarperCollins, who saw the potential in this book, then made it even stronger.

Radiating outward from there . . . my extended family was extraordinarily supportive in every way. Thanks to the Busbees: Stephen, Valynnda, Vendela, Cadence, Whitt, Andrew, Ann, David, James, Brian, Shannon, Cohen, and Hadley; and the Summerfields: Toby, Stacey, H. G., and Watson. If you see any of them—and there's a good chance you're within arm's reach of one right now—make sure to thank them for me. Deep thanks also to Annarita McGovern, my kids' mom, for being there at the start and through my long, lean years of writing about landfills.

So many friends at so many parties put up with so many stories about so much racing. My thanks to the Madisons, Barbers, Hollands, Kellys, Martins, Molands, Roberts, Shirmeyers, Welches, Wyners, and many more.

Tip of the Talladega ball cap to the people who took time to read sections of the book prior to publication, including Jordan Bianchi, Nick Bromberg, Howard Busbee, Jay Hart, Pat McCall, Geoffrey Miller, and Beth Wyner. Thanks also to Hawkeye, my beagle, who listened patiently as I read passage after passage out loud. Good dog.

The behind-the-scenes folks were essential as well. Juliana Wojcik at Waxman Leavell, plus Sydney Pierce and Kate Lyons at HarperCollins, made the terrifying process of publishing a book slightly less terrifying. Deep thanks to Richard Rosen and Will Bennett for their thoughtful edits, Miranda Ottewell for a delicate literary scalpel, and Chris Goff for his legal eye. Don Smyle of Smyle Media, Nigel Kinrade, and Dustin Bixby at Atlanta Motor Speedway were instrumental in helping me with photo selection. Speaking of photos, Jen Wunderlich made me look better than I have any right to in my author photo.

My patient colleagues at Yahoo Sports deserve high praise, not just for the support they've given me but the work they do every day. Kevin Kaduk, Jay Hart, Nick Bromberg, Frank Schwab, Dan Wetzel, Al Toby, Eric Edholm, Johnny Ludden, Eric Adelson, Ryan Ballengee, Greg Wyshynski, and Bob Condor are the best of the best, and you should totally use Yahoo Sports for all your sports information needs.

Friends in the industry who offered advice, introductions, and/or a beer to drown sorrows are invaluable. Thanks to Jamie Mottram, Mark Pesavento, Shane Bacon, Geoffrey Miller, Drew Magary, Will Leitch, Jeff Pearlman, Dan Levy, Shane Ryan, Brad

Meltzer, Maggie Hendricks, the Marbleheads, Eric Von Haessler, Mike Buteau, Jonah Keri, and Wil S. Hylton. Thanks also to the Augusta Suicide Mansion crew, including Rustin Dodd, Spencer Hall, Steve Politi, Brendan Prunty, and Wright Thompson.

Is the music playing yet? No? Cool, let's roll through some more. Hundreds of people spoke with me for this project, either on the record or in an advisory capacity. There's not enough space to thank all of them to the degree they deserve, but a few warrant special mention. Ryan McGee of ESPN has been a friend, mentor, and confidant from the first day I walked, wide-eyed, into a NASCAR media center. He's probably the nicest guy in sports, even if he still thinks the Avengers are better than the X-Men. Jeff Gluck at *USA Today* has been a good friend at tracks all over the circuit, and his description of Dale Earnhardt Jr. encapsulated the second half of the book in a single sentence. I'm thankful for earlier generations of NASCAR reporters, guys like Tom Higgins, Ed Hinton, Steve Waid, and Monte Dutton, who continue to write of this confounding, exhilarating sport with grace, honesty, and a keen eye.

Megan Englehart at Fox Sports worked tirelessly to set me up with some of the best interviews of the entire book. Brett Jewkes, Matt Humphrey, and David Higdon at NASCAR were instrumental as well. Track execs like Russell Branham at Talladega, Ed Clark at Atlanta, and Eddie Gossage at Texas gave me some of the finest stories in this book. Ryan Dayvault of the Kannapolis City Council, as well as the Kannapolis Museum, the Concord and Kannapolis libraries, and the Cabarrus County Visitors Bureau, provided invaluable historical insight. And sitting in RVs or on pit roads and talking racing with so many past NASCAR winners and champions is something I won't soon forget, and I'm grateful to so many drivers for their time.

Several people passed away during the course of this project, and I'm deeply grateful for their contributions and the time I got to spend with them. Condolences to the families of Buddy Baker, Rudy Branham, Steve Byrnes, Denny Darnell, and Marcy Scott.

Thanks to you—yes, you, holding/scrolling through/listening to this book—for giving me a slice of your time. I appreciate you more than you can imagine, whether you're reading me here or on Yahoo, Twitter, Facebook, or wherever. Feel free to write your name in right here: _____.

Finally, I'm grateful to the Earnhardt family for their contribution to American sports and culture. The Intimidator was one of the most important cultural figures in the twentieth century, and Dale Earnhardt Jr. remains one of the most thoughtful and insightful athletes (yes, athletes) in sports. The name, and its place in history, is secure.

Thanks so much for reading, everyone. See you next race.

JAY BUSBEE
August 2015

MATERIAL FOR THIS project was compiled from an array of sources, including author interviews; contemporaneous news reports; academic research; print, audio, and video collections; and documentary films. Conversations and descriptions of events were reconstructed according to the recollections of participants.

ARTICLES

Adelson, Eric. "The Day Dale Earnhardt Died." *The PostGame*, Feb. 13, 2011.

Anderson, Lars. "Daddy Would Be Proud." *Sports Illustrated*, Feb. 23, 2004.

———. "In the Name of the Father." *Sports Illustrated*, May 26, 2004.

"Baby Girl on the Way for Taylor Earnhardt Putnam." *People* magazine, May 19, 2016.

Ballard, Steve. "NASCAR Releases Earnhardt Findings." *USA Today*, Aug. 21, 2001.

Bechtel, Mark. "The Son Rises." *Sports Illustrated*, Dec. 3, 2001.

Bernstein, Viv. "Another Earnhardt (Jeffrey) Slides Behind the Wheel." *New York Times*, July 30, 2008.

———. "Bidding War Expected for Earnhardt Jr.'s Services." *New York Times*, May 11, 2007.

Bezjak, Lou. "Mike Dillon Recalls Taking Over the 3 for Late Dale Earnhardt." *South Carolina Morning News*, April 12, 2014.

Bianchi, Jordan. "Dale Earnhardt Jr. Appreciates History of Indianapolis, NASCAR Brickyard Race." *SB Nation*, July 29, 2012.

Blount, Terry. "Dale Jr. Doesn't Think No. 8 Gone for Long." ESPN.com, April 18, 2009.

———. "Dale Jr.: Teresa Made 'Ridiculous' Requests for No. 8." ESPN.com, Aug. 18, 2007.

Bonkowski, Jerry. "Chip Ganassi Explains Why 'Earnhardt' Is No Longer Part of Team Name." *NBC Motorsports Talk*, Feb. 21, 2014.

Borden, Brett. "Motegi: Earnhardt Jr. on Track with Father for the First Time." NASCAR.com, Nov. 21, 1998.

Busbee, Jay. "Return of the 3: Fans Ready to Accept Iconic Number with New Driver." Yahoo Sports, Feb. 22, 2014.

———. "Talladega Delivers Another Vicious Wreck, Pitting Driver Safety vs. Fan Wants." Yahoo Sports, Oct. 7, 2012.

Cain, Holly. "Earnhardt's Daughter to Race as No. 3." NASCAR.com, June 22, 2013.

———. "Inside Daytona Hospital, Tony Stewart Was a Witness." *AOL Fanhouse*, Feb. 10, 2011.

———. "Sharing Final Moments and a Driver's Seat With Dale." *AOL Fanhouse*, Feb. 10, 2011.

Caldwell, Dave. "Drivers Stand By Earnhardt's Victory." *New York Times*, July 11, 2001.

Caraviello, David. "Dale Jr.'s Daytona 500 Triumph Still Resonates." NASCAR.com, Feb. 22, 2014.

———"Dislocated Sternum Couldn't Slow Earnhardt in '96." NASCAR.com, March 1, 2013.

Cherry, Kevin. "Cannon Mills." NCPedia.org, 2006.

Clarke, Liz. "So Much for Santa Claus." *Charlotte Observer*, Feb. 15, 1993.

Colton, Andrew. "Thousands Gather for Earnhardt Memorial Service." *ABC News*, Feb. 22, 2001.

Cook, Kevin. "Playboy Interview: Dale Earnhardt Jr." *Playboy*, September 2001.

Crossman, Matt. "Long and Winding Road." *Sports on Earth*, Feb. 12, 2014.

Diaz, George. "Earnhardt's Ride Goes to Harvick." *Orlando Sentinel*, Feb. 23, 2001.

———. "Lives Changed Dramatically for 3 EMTs at Earnhardt Accident Scene." *Orlando Sentinel*, Feb. 14, 2011.

———. "Martha Earnhardt: A Lifetime of Racing, Happiness, and Heartbreak." *Orlando Sentinel*, Feb. 15, 2011.

Foster, Jim. "Race Solutions Offered at AIR." *Spartanburg Herald-Journal*, Mar. 26, 1961.

Fowler, Scott. "Dale Earnhardt Jr. takes a side in family feud about usage of Earnhardt name." *Charlotte Observer*, May 27, 2016.

Frederick, Henry. "Driver's Widow Determined to Fight Media Attempts." *Daytona Beach News-Journal*, June 13, 2001.

Friend, Tom. "Heir Force." *ESPN: The Magazine*, Feb. 18, 2002.

Fofaria, Rupen. "One Year after Earnhardt's Death." ESPN.com, Feb. 13, 2002.

Fryer, Brit. "Hamlin Knew Earnhardt Had Some Strange Agenda." *Red Bull Magazine*, Feb. 18, 2011.

Fryer, Jenna. "Earnhardt Buried in Private Service." Associated Press, Feb. 22, 2001.

———. "Eury Out as Crew Chief for Slumping Earnhardt Jr." *Associated Press*, May 28, 2009.

Gladden, Rebecca. "Dale Earnhardt's 'Lucky Penny Girl' Honored in Exhibit at U.S. Mint in Philadelphia." *Inside Racing News*, June 29, 2012.

———. "David Poole's Pet Project, Wessa Miller, Still Inspires Others." *Inside Racing News*, January 28, 2011.

Gluck, Jeff. "Dale Earnhardt Jr. Having Too Much Fun to Think about Retiring." *USA Today*, Jan. 29, 2015.

———. "Dale Earnhardt Jr. Talks Privacy, Danica Dating." *USA Today*, Jan. 30, 2013.

Gross, Ken, and Meg Grand. "Racer Tim Richmond Set Records Aplenty, but His Lovers Now Fear That AIDS Will Be His Real Legacy." *People*, Jan. 8, 1990.

Habina, Joe. "Earnhardt Mentor Back in Racing." *Modesto Bee*, Aug. 19, 2007.

Hart, Jay. " 'Mad' About the Good Ol' Days." *Allentown Morning Call*, Feb. 22, 2006.

———. "How Jeff Gordon Became the Face of NASCAR." Yahoo Sports, Feb. 21, 2015.

"Harvick Takes Page from Earnhardt." Associated Press, March 12, 2001.

Hembree, Mike. "Suitcase Jake Elder Dead at 73." SpeedTV.com, Feb. 25, 2010.

Henson, Steve. "Loss Is a Test of Strength for Teresa Earnhardt." *Los Angeles Times*, April 29, 2001.

Higgins, Tom. "Another Title, Please." *Charlotte Observer*, Nov. 19, 1990.

———. "Earnhardt's 'Going to Be a Star.' " *Charlotte Observer*, May 29, 1976.

———. "A Few Screws, and Good as New." *Charlotte Observer*, Aug. 4, 1982.

———. "Good Win, Terrible Day." *Charlotte Observer*, Nov. 12, 1984.

———. "History Lives on Sedan Avenue." *Charlotte Observer*, May 23, 1981.

———. "Jim . . . I'm Going to Quit." *Charlotte Observer*, August 4, 1981.

———. "Lucky in Vegas." *Charlotte Observer*, Nov. 17, 1980.

———. "Martin's Lesson from 1990." ThatsRacin.com, Nov. 13, 2009.

———. "Osterlund Issues Earnhardt a Five-Year Ticket to Ride." *Charlotte Observer*, Jan. 25, 1980.

———. "Pass the Torch? I Don't Think So." *Charlotte Observer*, Nov. 14, 1995.

———. "Verbal Sparks Fly." *Charlotte Observer*, Oct. 4, 1986.

Hinton, Ed. "Attitude for Sale." *Sports Illustrated*, Feb. 6, 1995.

———. "Dale Jr., Not Stepmom, Has All the Support." *Orlando Sentinel*, January 26, 2007.

———. "Earnhardt's Death a Watershed Moment." ESPN.com, Feb. 14, 2011.

———. "Finally, a Breakthrough Victory for Dale Jr.?" ESPN.com, July 3, 2010.

———. "Forgotten 'E': That's Kerry Earnhardt." *Orlando Sentinel*, July 18, 2003.

———. "The Great Race." *Sports Illustrated*, May 12, 2004.

———. "Hard Work Made the 3." ESPN.com, Feb. 22, 2013.

———. "The Human Side of the Hall of Famers." ESPN.com, May 20, 2010.

———. "More Than Tim Richmond Died in 1989." ESPN.com, Aug. 17, 2009.

———. "Richard Childress: Tragedy and Triumph." ESPN.com, Aug. 20, 2010.

———. "Their Finest Moments." *Sports Illustrated*, May 26, 2004.

———. "There Wasn't a Nicer Guy Than Neil Bonnett." ESPN.com, Feb. 11, 2009.

Houston, Rick. "Earnhardt, Labonte Dueled in Two of Bristol's Most Famous Night Races." NASCAR.com, Aug. 23, 2011.

Jenkins, Chris. "Childress Denies Claims of Improper Belt Installation." *USA Today*, Aug. 24, 2001.

Jensen, Tom. "Feb. 18, 2001: Dale Earnhardt and NASCAR's Darkest Day." *Fox Sports*, Feb. 18, 2014.

———. "Richard Childress Says Keselowski and Earnhardt Are Two of a Kind." *Fox Sports*, Jan. 29, 2015.

———. "#TBT: Earnhardts Share Magical Moment at 2001 Rolex 24." *Fox Sports*, Jan. 22, 2015.

———. "What Might Have Been: Tim Richmond vs. Dale Earnhardt." *Fox Sports*, Aug. 12, 2014.

Jordan, Pat. "Dale Earnhardt, Jr.: The Son Also Races." *Men's Journal*, June 2003.

———. "In the Name of the Father." *New York Times Magazine*, Aug. 5, 2010.

Knight, Buck. "Pit Stop." *Fredericksburg (Va.) Free-Lance Star*, Aug. 25, 1967.

Livingstone, Seth. "*USA Today* Interview: At Home with Jr." *USA Today*, Jan. 11, 2007.

Long, Dustin. "Earnhardt Responds to Comment Pole Was Rigged." *Hampton Roads Virginian-Pilot*, Feb. 16, 2011.

Lyons, Andrew. "Earnhardt Family Seeks to Halt Release of Autopsy Photos." *Daytona Beach News-Journal*, Feb. 24, 2001.

Lyons, Andrew, and Henry Frederick. "Earnhardt Autopsy Photos to Remain Sealed, for Now." *Daytona Beach News-Journal*, June 12, 2001.

Macur, Juliet. "Skinner Again Wins Exhibition in Japan." *Orlando Sentinel*, Nov. 23, 1998.

McCullough, Andy. "Royals Manager Ned Yost Goes Way Back with the Earnhardts." *Kansas City Star*, Feb. 24, 2014.

McGee, Ryan. "Post-9/11 Healing Began at Dover." ESPN.com, Sept. 21, 2011.

———. "The Night Terry, Dale, and Rusty Dueled." ESPN. com, Aug. 19, 2015.

———. "The Real Rick Hendrick Can Be Found." ESPN.com, May 16, 2012.

———. "Tim Richmond Took It to the Limit." ESPN.com, Oct. 19, 2010.

McKee, Sandra. "Death of Best Friend Bonnett Is Hardest Loss Yet for Earnhardt." *Baltimore Sun*, Feb. 20, 1994.

Moses, Sam. "All Hail Dale." *Sports Illustrated*, Nov. 26, 1990.

———. "Dale Turns 'Em Pale." *Sports Illustrated*, Sept. 7, 1987.

"Motegi Post-Race Notes." NASCAR.com, Nov. 23, 1998.

Myers, Chocolate. "Myers Recalls Brickyard Memories." NASCAR.com, July 3, 2013.

Myslenski, Skip. "Earnhardt Still Fuming over Fix Allegations." *Chicago Tribune*, July 13, 2001.

Newton, David. "Harvick Says Teresa Earnhardt Should Show Up." ESPN.com, Jan. 24, 2007.

———. "Junior Took a Back Seat to Big Sis Kelley." ESPN.com, Jan. 26, 2010.

———. "Kerry Earnhardt Taking On New Job at DEI." ESPN.com, Jan. 11, 2007.

———. "Martin Wouldn't Change His Tough Days." ESPN.com, Oct. 20, 2009.

Nidetz, Stephen. "Earnhardt Has Disc Surgery." *Chicago Tribune*, Dec. 18, 1999.

"1987 'Pass in the Grass' a Defining Moment." CharlotteMotorSpeedway.com, April 24, 2007.

Owens, Jeff. "Ned Yost Carries Memories of Friend Dale Earnhardt into World Series." *Sporting News*, Oct. 21, 2014.

"Parks Wins Dura Lube 400." Associated Press, Feb. 27, 2001.

Pearce, Al. "Danger Always Close at Hand for Pit Crews." *Newport News Daily Press*, Nov. 20, 1990.

———. "Earnhardt Inherited Drive from His Father." *Newport News Daily Press*, Oct. 26, 1994.

"Pepsi 400 to Field Three Earnhardts." Associated Press, Aug. 18, 2000.

Petchesky, Barry. "When I Get a Clear Shot . . ." *Deadspin*, Aug. 21, 2012.

Phillips, Benny. "A Crew Chief's Memories of Dale Earnhardt." *Stock Car Racing*, March 1, 2002.

Pockrass, Bob. "Dale Earnhardt's Death Still an Unforgettable Day." *Sporting News*, Feb. 18, 2014.

———. "Kerry Earnhardt in battle with Teresa Earnhardt over name." ESPN.com, May 6, 2016.

———. "Richard Childress Defends Grandsons, Furious with Kevin Harvick." *Sporting News*, Oct. 27, 2013.

Poole, David. "Dale Earnhardt and His Lucky Penny (and One Lucky Girl)." *Charlotte Observer*, June 14, 2008.

Reaves, Tim. "Earnhardts Remember Ralph: He Raced Hungry." *Kannapolis Independent Tribune*, Feb. 4, 2015.

Rippel, Amy C. "Attorney Questions NASCAR's Influence." *Orlando Sentinel*, April 4, 2001.

Rodman, Dave. "2000 Winston 500: Earnhardt's Talladega Surprise." *Motor Racing Network*, April 13, 2011.

Ryan, Nate. "Dale Jr., Sister Share Earnhardt Stories on Podcast." *USA Today*, Aug. 6, 2014.

———. "Kelley Earnhardt Reflects on a Career That Might Have Been." *USA Today*, Dec. 15, 2009.

"A Schism Could Cost Dale Earnhardt Inc. an Earnhardt." Associated Press, February 9, 2007.

Shontz, Lori. "Dura-Lube 400 Opening-Lap Crash by Earnhardt Jr. Mars Rain-Delayed Race." *Pittsburgh Post-Gazette*, Feb. 26, 2001.

Smathers, Jason. "Ralph Dale Earnhardt Sr. FOIA: FBI Files." *Muckrock*, Feb. 15, 2011.

Smith, Marty. "Dale Jr. Ready to Stop Driving No. 3." ESPN.com, June 27, 2010.

———. "Earnhardt Jr. Earns First Win since 2008." ESPN.com, July 3, 2010.

———. "Earnhardt Jr. Has Opportunities, But . . ." ESPN.com, March 29, 2013.

————. "Hendrick Stronger 10 Years Later." ESPN.com, October 25, 2014.

————. "Petty, Dale Jr. Greatness Times Two." ESPN.com, Feb. 11, 2013.

Spencer, Lee. "Teresa Earnhardt Remains Mysterious Figure." *Fox Sports*, June 6, 2014.

"Taylor Earnhardt-Putnam, Daughter of Dale Earnhardt Sr., Competes in Virginia Stampede Rodeo at Colonial Downs on Friday Evening." *Hampton Roads Daily Press*, Aug. 1, 2014.

"Taylor Earnhardt Takes Dad's No. 3 for a Spin at Goodwood." ThatsRacin.com, July 3, 2009.

Thompson, Wright. "The Son Also Rises." ESPN.com, 2006.

Touré. "Inherit the Wind." *Rolling Stone*, July 11, 2001.

————. "Kurt Is My Co-Pilot." *Rolling Stone*, May 11, 2000.

Tresniowski, Alan, Michaele Ballard, and Don Sider. "Life after Dale." *People*, Feb. 10, 2003.

Turner, Jared. "A Family Tradition." *Roanoke Times*, Jan. 25, 2007.

Vega, Mike. "Rusty Wallace Fondly Recalls Inaugural Loudon Win." *Boston Globe*, July 10, 2013.

Waid, Steve. "Rain Created a Most Unusual Start Time for the 1995 Brickyard 400." *Popular Speed*, July 25, 2014.

Wetzel, Dan. "On the Anniversary of His Father's Death, Dale Earnhardt Jr. Smiles." Yahoo Sports, Feb. 18, 2015.

BOOKS

Arthur-Cornett, Helen. *Remembering Kannapolis: Tales from Towel City*. History Press, 2006.

Bartlett, Jeff, et al. *Dale Earnhardt: Always a Champion*. Chicago: Triumph, 2001.

Bechtel, Mark. *He Crashed Me So I Crashed Him Back*. New York: Back Bay, 2011.

Branham, Herb. *Big Bill: The Life and Times of NASCAR Founder Bill France Sr.* New York: Fenn/McClelland & Stewart, 2015.

Caldwell, Dave. *Speed Show: How NASCAR Won the Heart of America*. Boston: Kingfisher, 2006.

Chapin, Kim. *Fast as White Lightning: The Story of Stock Car Racing*. New York: Crown, 1998.

Dale Earnhardt: The Legend Lives. New York: ESPN Books, 2010.

Dale Earnhardt: Rear View Mirror. Champaign: Sports Publishing, 2001.

Earnhardt, Dale, Jr., with Jade Gurss. *Driver #8*. New York: Warner, 2002.

Earnhart, Clarence. "The Earnhart Family Lineage." 4th ed. Courtesy Cabarrus County Public Library, Concord, NC.

Edelstein, Robert. *NASCAR Legends: Memorable Men, Moments, and Machines in Racing History*. New York: Peter Mayer, 2011.

Ernsberger, Richard, Jr., *God, Pepsi, and Groovin' on the High Side: Tales from the NASCAR Circuit*. New York: Evans, 2003.

Fresina, Michael. *Dale Earnhardt: Defining Moments of a NASCAR Legend*. Chicago: Triumph, 2011.

Giangola, Andrew. *The Weekend Starts on Wednesday: True Stories of Remarkable NASCAR Fans*. Osceola, WI: Motorbooks, 2010.

Gillispie, Tom. *Angel in Black*. Naperville, IL: Cumberland House, 2008.

Golenbock, Peter. *The Last Lap: The Life and Times of NASCAR's Legendary Heroes*. New York: Macmillan, 1998.

Gurss, Jade. *Into the Red: The 2001 Season with Dale Earnhardt Jr.* Austin, TX: Octane, 2012.

Hagstrom, Robert G. *The NASCAR Way: The Business That Drives the Sport*. New York: Wiley & Sons, 1998.

Hembree, Mike. *Dale Earnhardt Jr.: Out of the Shadow of Greatness*. New York: Sports Publishing, 2003.

Hemphill, Paul. *Wheels: A Season on NASCAR's Winston Cup Circuit*. New York: Simon & Schuster, 1997.

Ingram, Jonathan. *Dale Earnhardt: The Life Story of a NASCAR Legend*. London: Carlton, 2001.

Lucido, Jerome. *Racing with the Hawk: The Man behind Dale Earnhardt*. Grand Rapids, MI: Baker Book House, 1998.

MacGregor, Jeff. *Sunday Money: Speed! Lust! Madness! Death! A Hot Lap Around America with NASCAR*. New York: Harper-Collins, 2005.

McGee, Ryan. *Ultimate NASCAR: 100 Defining Moments in Stock Car Racing History*. New York: ESPN Books, 2007.

Montville, Leigh. *At the Altar of Speed: The Fast Life and Tragic Death of Dale Earnhardt*. New York: Doubleday, 2001.

Moriarty, Frank. *Dale Earnhardt, 1951–2001*. New York: Metro, 2001.

Thompson, Neal. *Driving with the Devil: Southern Moonshine, Detroit Wheels, and the Birth of NASCAR*. New York: Random House, 2006.

3: The Dale Earnhardt Story. Introduction by Kenny Mayne. New York: ESPN Books, 2004.

Thunder and Glory: The 25 Most Memorable Races in NASCAR Winston Cup History. Chicago: Triumph, 2004.

Vehorn, Frank. *The Intimidator*. Asheboro, NC: Down Home, 1991.

Waltrip, Darrell, and Jade Gurss. *DW: A Life Spent Going Around in Circles*. New York: Putnam, 2004.

Waltrip, Darrell, and Nate Larkin. *Sundays Will Never Be the Same*. New York: Simon & Schuster, 2012.

Waltrip, Michael, and Ellis Henican. *In the Blink of an Eye: Dale,*

Daytona and the Day That Changed Everything. New York: Hyperion, 2011.

Watson, Stephanie. *The Earnhardt NASCAR Dynasty.* New York: Rosen, 2010.

Wheeler, Humpy, and Peter Golenbock. *Growing Up NASCAR: Racing's Most Outrageous Promoter Tells All.* Osceola, WI: Motorbooks, 2010.

Wolfe, Rich. *Remembering Dale Earnhardt.* Overland Park, KS: Lone Wolf Press, 2001.

MOVIES/TELEVISION SHOWS/DVDS

3: The Dale Earnhardt Story. ESPN Productions, 2002.

Back in the Day. Hammerhead Entertainment, 2006.

Dale: The Movie. CMT Films, 2005.

The Day: Remembering Dale Earnhardt. Speed Channel, 2011.

The History of Kannapolis and Cannon Mills. Historic Cabarrus, n.d.

I Am Dale Earnhardt. NASCAR Productions, 2015.

In Depth with Graham Bensinger: Kevin Harvick. Yahoo Sports, 2015.

To the Limit: The Tim Richmond Story. ESPN 30 for 30, 2010.

PODCASTS

Bromberg, Nick, Geoff Miller, and Jay Busbee. *The Chrome Horn.* Yahoo Sports, 2009–15.

Goldberg, Bill. *Who's Next.* Podcast One, 2014.

Miller, Kelley Earnhardt. *Fast Lane Family.* JR Motorsports, 2014–15.

Patrick, Dan. *The Dan Patrick Show.* NBC Sports, 2014.
Smith, Marty, and Ryan McGee. *Marty & McGee.* ESPN, 2014–15.

WEBSITES

The author is grateful for the online archives of Racing Reference, Yahoo Sports, ESPN, Fox Sports, CBS Sports, NBC Sports, YouTube, ThatsRacin.com, and NASCAR.com.